THE VISIBLE GOD

Staging the History of Money

Rafaël Newman

University Press of America,® Inc.
Lanham • New York • Oxford

Copyright © 1999 by
Rafaël Newman

University Press of America,® Inc.
4720 Boston Way
Lanham, Maryland 20706

12 Hid's Copse Rd.
Cumnor Hill, Oxford OX2 9JJ

Library of Congress Cataloging-in-Publication Data

Newman, Rafaël Francis David Amadeus.
The visible God : staging the history of money / Rafaël Newman.
p.   cm..
Includes bibliographical references and index.
1. Drama—History and criticism. 2. Money in literature.   I. Title.
PN1650.M65N48 1998   809.2'9355—dc21   98-38403 CIP

ISBN 0-7618-1252-0 (cloth: alk. ppr.)

To the memory of my grandparents:
Annie Dubin, Franz Kornpointner, Leon
Newman, and Eva Strassner

Contents

Acknowledgments

Walter Benjamin's short essay "Erfahrung und Armut" opens with a parable: a father on his deathbed instructs his children to dig in the garden, where there is said to be a treasure buried. They dig and dig, and find nothing; come the following spring, however, green shoots appear where they have been laboring. "Da merken sie, der Vater gab ihnen eine Erfahrung mit: Nicht im Golde steckt der Segen sondern im Fleiß." The people I wish to acknowledge here have passed on a similar wisdom: it is in the work of digging that the unexpected will come to light out of the earth, to be stored away against periods of fallowness and loss.

In the course of excavating the garden below, which went on to have its first season as a Ph.D. dissertation at Princeton University, I have had the advice, support, and kindness of many. Froma I. Zeitlin is a constant source of creative instruction and thoughtful criticism, of professional example and unwavering engagement, in four countries, over the ether, and at the eleventh hour; this book is a testament to a precious friendship. Richard P. Martin was a thoughtful and precise reader under pressure, as ready with praise as with dissent; and Alessandro Schiesaro shared with me freely his erudition and civility. At an early stage my work benefited from the attention of Stanley Corngold and Robert Lamberton, diligent and feeling editors both; and during a year spent at the Seminar für Altphilologie of the Freie Universität Berlin, where my ideas germinated, I was received most hospitably into the office and home of Bernd Seidensticker.

I want to acknowledge as well the extraordinary support of the Mellon Fellowships in the Humanities, of the Deutscher Akademischer Austauschdienst, of the Social Science and Humanities Research Council of Canada, and of Dr. Frances Newman of the Toronto Institute for Contemporary Psychoanalysis, without all of whose generous assistance I would long since have been scavenging for roots.

Agricultural metaphors notwithstanding, libraries have been the site of this work's actual means of production. I would like to acknowledge therefore my gratitude to the staffs of the Firestone Library at Princeton University, of the Staatsbibliothek in Berlin, and of the library at the École normale supérieure in Paris, where I was also most charmingly assisted by Eric Guichard.

It is an odd duty to credit personal friends in this sober context, but I am in truth indebted to the people whose names follow just as I am to more conventional academic guides. Sarah Hardy, Ulf Heinsohn, John Knechtel, and Daniel Mendelsohn have all been as true and as loving as one could wish, never hesitating to lend their considerable and various talents to my enterprise. I owe a special thanks to Carol Szymanski, an unparalleled friend and adviser across the years and above the call; and to Cass Garner I am grateful for unfailingly cheerful support. Carol Wiedmer-Homan and I did battle together with the Cerberus of a three-computer household, and I have never enjoyed editing as much as with her. At a very late stage in my work I was aided invaluably by the companionable technical expertise and good humor of José Rodriguez and Marion Blake. Thanks to the Meier Hüsli, too, for timely shelter.

My family has been a constant and hundred-handed ally. Thanks go especially to my mother Frances, my father Jerry, my stepfather Fred, and my many dear siblings and nifties, and love to them all. A three-way correspondence with Adam and Zoë sustained me particularly throughout the thorniest periods. I have dedicated this book to our late grandparents, variously exemplary for their mistrust of power and superstition and for their nourishing irony, and I trust that whatever piety, awe, and solidarity is manifest in that gesture will be shared by all who knew and loved them.

Thanks are not enough, finally, for a brave and faithful fellow traveler. Caroline Wiedmer and I have been engaged in writing now for some years and will be for many more. In the work that follows she is a numinous presence, watching over it in its life as in its gestation, countering wrath and fear with effortless love and wisdom. May the strength of our opinions be matched only by the readiness of our compromises. Hella is the dearest proof that this is possible, and that it surely brings the best to bear.

Author's Note

I have transliterated most Greek names faithfully ("Ploutos," "Karion") but have rendered Latinate spellings as they appear in the commentators I cite, or where they have become familiar in that form.

Translations of Greek, Latin, French, and German sources are mine unless otherwise noted. I have endeavored always to provide both the original text and my translation, wherever possible on the same page.

I have not used quotation marks to set off Greek citations, as I find them cluttered-looking in that context and feel that the difference of alphabets is sufficient to mark them as citations.

Introduction

The Birth of an Allegory

Prior to the modern age, which began with the expropriation of the poor and then proceeded to emancipate the new propertyless classes, all civilizations have rested upon the sacredness of private property. Wealth, on the contrary, whether privately owned or publicly distributed, had never been sacred before.

Hannah Arendt

Money is a historic reality: that is to say, it belongs to human history, and it has a history of its own. Money is shaped by events and circumstances ranging from natural disaster, through human biological exigencies, to cultural constructs; it has also, at least in the case of the latter two sets of phenomena, exerted a correspondingly transformative force. Caught up as fundamentally and at times as violently as it is in the processes of present-day human society's development, money's own coming into being has occasioned much confusion, speculation, and indeed mistrust. Its nature is the subject, in earliest texts, of ambivalent representation: the boons it brings with it, such as increased ease in barter-transactions, are offset by its disadvantages and even dangers, such as indebtedness, interest, and parasitism. Arisen from land- and crop-wealth, among other means of ostensibly natural extraction of riches from the earth, money seems on occasion to turn against these origins, through its propensity to displace and denature the ostensibly organic relations of dweller to earth. Although it is manifestly the bringer of luxury, prestige, and security, money is itself frequently reviled as cowardly, shabby, blind, ethically indifferent, untrustworthy, and nowhere at home. Money is a crucial switch-point of social relations, a concatenation of grotesque opposites, and as such a natural topic for comic critiques of society.

It is the aim of my study to examine the changing representations of money in the Western or European tradition through a connected series of readings of examples of four different sorts of critique, the first three drawn from ancient comic texts, the last from an early modern tragic variant, all chosen to demonstrate and question the comic tradition of money's representation. Money has of course not been a self-identical entity throughout its history, and its representations have changed accordingly; the relative persistence of a certain frame for representing wealth and poverty, however, into which can be slotted the monetary realities appropriate to the age of a given text's composition, will be seen to act as a sort of barometer of socio-economic change. From the burlesque, deified presence of the blind god Ploutos in Aristophanes' comedy of the same name, through the uncannily irreal figure of Luxuria and her counterpart the Sycophant in Plautus' *Trinummus*, to the cantankerous realist pastiche of the Ploutos in Lucian's *Timon,* and his withering-away altogether into an allegorized materialism in Shakespeare's unfinished tragedy on the same theme, one possible parabola of money's development and representation can be drawn. In the process, it should become clear that at the center of the problems faced by the dramatic-allegorical representation of money is the fact that money is already itself a species of symbolic system, another way of speaking about the relations of property and power it expresses, even as it is also in and of itself an objective form of wealth. It is surely this hybrid quality that has rendered money both good to represent, and at the same time somehow shameful, a presence to be repressed or elided.

In what exactly might money's scandalous hybrid quality consist?[1] The first appearance of the divinized form of wealth, literally the birth of the allegory that will come to be known as Ploutos, in Hesiod's *Theogony*, seems entirely positive; and yet the seeds of division are already to be discerned. The passage is well-known: "Demeter, bright among goddesses, mingling in pleasant love with the hero Iasion in the thrice-ploughed fallow land, in the rich country of Crete, gave birth to good Ploutos, who ranges over the whole earth and the wide back of the sea; and whomever he meets, and falls into his hands, he makes him rich, and furnishes him with much happiness."[2] Iasion's lot, as we know from the *Odyssey*, is not particularly happy: he is to be struck down by Zeus's thunderbolt.[3] Demeter, of course, is the goddess of the earth (or of the grain) seasonally in mourning for her kidnapped daughter Persephone.[4] Ploutos' lot, however, seems to be one-dimensionally benevolent and untroubled, without major incident or intrigue. And this apparent banality is fitting, perhaps, for what is after all simply the allegorization of agricultural plenty: "When mythology tells that Plutos, Wealth, is Demeter's son, sired on a thrice-ploughed corn field, the wealth is the store of corn, just as the treasury, *thesauros*, is the granary."[5]

And yet this very Ploutos is to become the subject, already in the archaic and certainly in the classical period, of a series of most disobliging thumb-nail sketches. These portraits in verse and prose may be briefly sampled here, before the connection between Hesiod's allegory and the classical Greek economic view of money is adduced. Fragments of Hipponax and Timocreon attest to sixth- and early fifth-century conceptions of Ploutos' blindness and cowardice. Hipponax is cited in a scholion to Aristophanes' *Plutus* as having written, "But Ploutos never came to me -- for he is very blind -- into my house and said, 'Hipponax, I give you thirty silver minae and much else.' For he is cowardly-spirited."[6] Timocreon, quoted in yet another scholion to Aristophanes, to the *Acharnians*, is the author of the drinking-verse, "Oh blind Ploutos, you ought to be seen neither on earth nor on the sea nor on land, but you should dwell in Tartaros and Acheron; for it is on account of you that humans have so many troubles."[7] Theognis, straddling the centuries,[8] for all his patrician esteem of wealth (see vv. 523-526 and 885-886), invokes the ambiguous power of the god: "Ploutos, most beautiful and most desirable of all the gods, with you even a bad man becomes noble."[9] Later in the fifth century, in his *Phoenissae*, Euripides has Polyneikes reply to his brother Eteokles' threats with the taunt, "Yes I see [Eteokles' hands, threatening to kill], but Ploutos is cowardly, vile, and fearful for his life."[10] Aristophanes, besides being responsible for the *Plutus*, the *locus classicus* of wealth's scurrilous representation, elsewhere contributes less directly to the fund of images: in the *Frogs* and in the *Ecclesiazusae*, mention is made of the habit of the wealthy to pretend to be poor, in order to avoid having to make financial contributions to Athens. The vision given in those passages of Wealth dressed in rags is vivid, and surely related to the eventual Aristophanic representation of Ploutos himself as shabby and dissembling.[11] A final, early fourth-century example, taken from Plato's late dialogue the *Laws*, holds out a certain hope for the ethical reconstruction of wealth: a hope, however, for which the traditional warts-and-all portrait is implicit, and indeed constitutive. The Athenian interlocutor is naming the minor virtues; last on the list, after health, beauty, and speed, comes wealth: "Fourth is Ploutos, not blind but sharp-sighted, *as long as he follows prudence*."[12]

The fourth-century economic reflections of Aristotle in his *Politics* suggest the reason for this pervasive mistrust of monetary wealth.[13] Aristotle is concerned, in Book 1, to distinguish between the οἰκονομική and the χρηματιστική, or the utilization and acquisition, respectively, of goods (1256 a 10 ff.).[14] To this end he draws a distinction between property (κτῆσις) and wealth (πλοῦτος), commenting that the two are indeed separate, despite the fact that they are both multiform (πολλὰ περιείληφε μέρη); he then goes on to give examples of different types of societies -- the nomadic, the hunter, and the agricultural -- distinguished according to their relations to various forms of "natural" property (1256 a 15-40). For it transpires, following Aristotle, that there are natural (φύσει) and unnatural (oὐ φύσει) means of acquiring property; that the former have their best exemplars in war and hunting; and that the latter, the unnatural or "technical" means (ἐμπειρίας τινὸς καὶ τέχνης), have theirs in exchange-value (1256 b). Money, according to Aristotle, arose out of these latter means, out of trade, which is the practice of the theory of exchange-value; money, therefore, was meant to make barter more convenient (1257 a). The oἰκονομική and the χρηματιστική, then, correspond roughly to use-value and exchange-value, to the utilization and disposition of goods with an eye to their use as ends in themselves, and to their deployment as means in the secondary aim of acquiring other goods.

Aristotle sums up this distinction, finally, in a passage that both demonstrates the contemporary scandal of money, and suggests an explanation for the ambivalence of its representation in classical Greece. "The acquisition of things is double in nature," he explains, "as we have said: the commercial and the economic. The latter is necessary and praiseworthy, while barter is justly criticized, for it does not act in accordance with nature but only mediates; usury is with very good reason hated, since it aims at acquisition through the coin, and not at the purpose for which it arose. For it came into being for the sake of trade; but interest causes it to increase, from which 'interest' [τόκος, child or interest] has taken its name. For the begotten are like their begetters, and interest is the coin of the coin. Thus this is the most unnatural of the forms of money-making."[15]   Aristotle's reasoning is remarkable: it is exactly in its mimicry of procreation and birth, to the point of borrowing the name "child" (τόκος) for interest, its by-product and end, that usury, the extremest form of exchange-value, is most unnatural.[16] The parasite of a parasite (it grew up, after all, to serve the ends of financial transactions in trade, themselves already a mere convenience), usury, with its constitutive corollary, interest, behaves nevertheless like something organic, like something submitted to and furthering of the processes of birth and begetting: a scandal.[17]   Ploutos, who was born of the union of an agricultural goddess and her mortal lover in a fertile field, and who originally symbolized wealth in grain, has made manifest his dangerous ability to take over and pervert, to his own denatured ends, the very means by which he came into being.[18]

The most natural means of acquisition is war and hunting; most peoples live, however, from agricultural yield; trade is an unnatural or "technical" means of acquisition; money came into being to facilitate trade; and usury, developed for the sake of trade and its financial exigencies, reproduces itself in a monstrous imitation of the "natural" process of birth. So might Aristotle's economic anthropology be summed up. What began as the metaphor of a natural relation to the earth and to its organic products -- Ploutos as "wealth in corn"[19] -- has ended in a grotesque aping of those same products. The Ploutos of trade, of money, of usury, and of interest is the blind, cowardly, morally corrupt and corrupting vagabond-god of old comedy; the only quality he has preserved from the Hesiodic portrait is his tendency to wander. His is a doubly-determined involvement in birth and burgeoning, in view of his coming-into-being in the union of a grain-goddess and her crop-sacrificial mortal lover on a fertile field as the expression of the earth's potential yield;[20] now this natural origin has been inverted into the unnatural reproduction of himself as an end, rather than to the simple and organic furthering of agricultural life.

This agricultural life as an ideal is well described, and prescribed, in the *Economics*, attributed to Aristotle but in fact a congeries of fourth-century and later Xenophontic and Aristotelian imitation. Three books, featuring respectively almanac-like advice on estate house-keeping, anecdotal forays into economic history and anthropology, and designs for conjugal concord, suggest a Hellenistic vision of rural subsistence infused with nostalgia for the small independent farm of the era of the city-state, coupled with an awareness of the increasing economic inter-dependence of political entities in an age of expanding empires.

The first book of the *Economics*[21] establishes as self-evident the inter-relatedness of man and property, a formulation tending almost to the robotic: "The human being (ἄνθρωπος) and the property (κτῆσις) are parts of the household (οἰκία)."[22] In this household, of course, only one particular ἄνθρωπος, the male, as it happens, is master, since the οἰκία is, in contrast to the city-state, a kind of monarchy. Citing Hesiod *Works and Days* v. 405, the author of the first book of the *Economics* advises that a wife (γυναῖκα) be acquired along with an ox and a plough to outfit the household;[23] in fact, in the adapted formulation, woman's place comes only after the stores (τροφή) and the free laborers (οἱ ἐλεύθεροι) who work the estate (1343 a). The primacy of these stores, this "nourishment" or τροφή, however, is expressed in predictably feminine terms: "For it is natural for all to get their nourishment from their mother, so that it is the same too [in the case of] humans [getting their stores] from the earth."[24] In this suspension between indebtedness and mastery, the man's conduct toward his wife acquires great importance: having acquired her still virginal, so that she may learn "wise ways," he is in fact to treat her as if she were a suppliant in his house, with clemency and fidelity.[25]

These prescriptions for marital conduct, as well as the association of woman and earth, are continued and amplified in the third book of the

Economics, extant only in a medieval Latin translation.[26] There it is taught that the woman is to be treated with more care than a mere slave would receive;[27] that children are the guardians of one's old age, and that therefore their mother must be educated in order to bring up the best children possible, just as the soil to which the farmer commits his seed must be carefully tended;[28] and that this same practitioner of husbandry is not to sow his seed just anywhere, so as not to deprive his wife of her honor and create a scandal for his legitimate sons.[29] Woman is likened explicitly to the arable field, and the Hesiodic references that stud the first book make her symbolic association with the household also clear.[30]

Between these two books of pastoral-patriarchal folklore (Penelope and Alcestis, for example, are held up at *Economics* III 142 as wives who owe their renown exclusively to their husband's misadventures), there is inserted a book of anecdotal accounts of various forms of political organization and fundraising. Amid the epic timelessness of the first and third books, the second can hardly fail to impress with its dogged realism, even if, as has been remarked in regard to the book's theoretical preamble, "what is noteworthy about these half a dozen paragraphs is not only their crashing banality but also their isolation in the whole of surviving ancient writing."[31] From general remarks on the four different types of οἰκονομίαι, that is, the monarchic (βασιλική), the satrapic (σατραπική), the city-state (πολιτική), and the private (ἰδιωτική), the second book of the *Economics* passes to detailed considerations of individual examples of these four types, and of their characteristic methods of raising revenues. The Byzantines, for instance, short of funds, were obliged to sell public land to various concerns, including traveling merchants, on whom they then also levied a tax (1346 b); Dionysios of Syracuse, in similar straits, struck a coin of tin and urged his subjects to use it, whereupon the assembly voted to consider it as equivalent to a silver coin (1349 a). The principal revenues of the satrapic economy are listed: land, precious metals, trade, internal commerce, cattle-levies, and income tax. The message is clear: all wealth does not arise from the rustic interrelationship of farmer-patriarch and earth-mother/wife.

The concept of wealth as immanent in land to which one has natural autochthonous rights, then, rights that are mirrored in male (re)productive hegemony, co-exists in this document with a lively sense that title to land can and on occasion must be converted into liquid assets. And indeed, such had already been the actual state of affairs in the polis since its coming into existence, despite the Athenian need, in particular, to claim and require a mythic inalienability of land. Moses Finley explains, with regard to the period of archaic history leading up to the blossoming of the Greek city-state in the fifth century, how this tendency was already evident in earliest times: "With the interlocked development of urbanism and the *polis*, profound structural changes followed, in the land regime as in other respects. Urbanization created new uses for land and wealth, introduced chattel slavery, made possible the existence of classes (and even of considerable wealth) not tied to land, and eventually fostered a considerable monetization of the economy."[32]   Land, agricultural wealth, and rural real estate may have been hold-overs from the "pre-urban, pre-*polis*, pre-monetary society," in which "alienation of land would have been extremely rare,"[33] and landed and inherited property may have been central to the ideology of autochthony or native ownership crucial to the coherence of the city-state; these institutions, however, seem also to have called forth out of themselves a system of monetary or mobile wealth not always in accordance with their own ideals.   In his consideration of "visible" (φανερά) and "invisible" (ἀφανής) property, Vincent Gabrielsen maintains that the distinction had in classical Athens properly to do with declared and undeclared assets, but concedes nevertheless that "realty came to be considered as φανερὰ οὐσία *par excellence* simply because this form of wealth, more than anything else, was likely to exist as visible, while, for exactly the opposite reasons, movables and especially cash could in common parlance go under the name ἀφανὴς οὐσία."[34]   Whether considered as having been developed to simplify trade, or as derived from agricultural property but somehow lacking its self-evident nature, money's representation in classical texts inevitably stresses its secondary character, its corruption or untrustworthiness, its status as a negligeable supplement to wealth in inherited land.

Recent theoretical work on the history of money by the economic historians Gunnar Heinsohn and Otto Steiger, however, has proposed the interdependent and simultaneous appearance of money and private ownership of land, in such a way as to suggest that the ambivalence surrounding the representation of money in ancient texts is a token of the repressed fact of the essential fragility (or constructedness) of the very system whereby land is privately and patriarchally owned.   In Heinsohn and Steiger's estimation, repression of money's centrality and primacy arose from the fear that, were the link between private ownership and the money economy to become evident, the tendentiousness of the claims made on privately owned land would be similarly "unmasked."   The theoretical basis for this claim is laid principally in Heinsohn's *Privateigentum, Patriarchat, Geldwirtschaft: Eine sozialtheoretische Rekonstruktion zur Antike.*[35]   In a critique of the classical conception of money's having grown out of barter as a means of making trade easier (as may be read in Aristotle), and thereby helping to further the ends of the allegedly hardwired human impulse to exchange (as may be read in Adam Smith), Heinsohn marshals the

testimony of various classical sources, notably Hesiod, Vergil, and
Apuleius, as well as that of the Gilgamesh-epic and other near eastern
texts, to produce a theory of the inextricability of the monetary
economy and private property. Heinsohn's debt to the work on money
and private property of John Maynard Keynes is clear, and
acknowledged, although he is careful to indicate his divergences: the
importance of the Keynesians, he maintains, is to have shifted the
focus away from money as a facilitator of exchange, and onto its
having grown up parallel to the uncertainties of a private property
economy. The only problem, as far as Heinsohn and Steiger are
concerned, is that these same Keynesians have things the wrong way
around when they assign money the task of expressing wealth, instead
of seeing in wealth the operations of money as the crystallization of
private property relations.[36]

Heinsohn's own reconstruction of the development of private
property, patriarchy, and the monetary economy stresses the birth of
the polis in a revolt by renegades from matrilineal tribes against the
conditions of feudal command economy obtaining in the pre-historic
world.[37] Drawing on a fund of myths and sagas concerning fatherless
heroes who are forced out of their mothers' homes, and who then turn
against those homes by establishing their own anti-communal
settlements with vindictively severe restrictions on the comportment
of, and the traffic in, women, Heinsohn postulates the origins of
interest, and therefore money, in the necessity, newly-arisen for these
first private owners of land, to borrow from each other in times of
need, without the guarantees of either tribal loyalty or primitive
communal welfare should their personal enterprises fail. At the origins
of this revolution, maintains Heinsohn (in distinction to the
Darwinian-materialist school of economic history, which posits
"primitive accumulation," presumably driven by a postulated biological
need or drive to barter, as the key to the "survival of the fittest"-birth of
early capitalism), stood desperate poverty and scarcity of resources,
necessitating an entirely new social organization in which individual
men would at once be masters of their own fates (and the fates of the
women and children now claimed as comprising their property),
although also delivered over to the mercy of each other in the event of
disaster. "Uncertainty about existence and poverty," Heinsohn writes,
"stand at the beginning of the new private property relations, whose
greater wealth-producing ability was also in no way -- as functionalists
are forced to suggest -- known in advance, and thereafter put
intentionally into play."[38] It was therefore also not because these first
private property owners, newly emerged from their tribal or feudal
communities, were particularly solicitous of the father-son relation,
that they established a complex system of male inheritance laws and
statutes providing for the legal and economic disenfranchisement of

women, but for the simple fact that these same women, whom the patriarchal private property society required to take care of the household and therefore of the sole means of support, represented the constant threat of a return to the matrilineal-communal organizations of pre-history.[39] Private property demands both control over production and reproduction, and the availability from other private property owners of loans of resources, the interest on which necessitates the development of money; money's uncanny ability to reproduce itself through usury and speculation, seemingly without the intervention of material transactions, is then only logically represented in terms of sexual uncontrollability and lack of fidelity.

These themes have of course been treated, in specific relation to the mythic history of money and property in ancient Greece, by Louis Gernet, in his essay "La Notion mythique de la valeur en Grèce."[40] Gernet describes the ambivalent power attached to objects of value, or ἀγάλματα, in Greek myth, their ability to bring prestige or woe upon their possessors; and he maintains the survival of this pre-monetary magic down into the historical economies of classical Greece, for "a mythical way of thinking endured right to the very moment at which the invention of coinage became possible. By which I mean to say that there is, in 'value' and so in the very token that represents it, a core which cannot be reduced to what they call rational thought."[41] This "core," in Gernet's reckoning, consists in a complex of mythemes having to do with the maleficence of valued objects, the importance of livestock and precious metals to the agricultural well-being of the mythic collectivity, and the role of women in the storing up and manipulation of wealth.[42] In this last regard he connects the mythic places where wealth is hoarded and those where women are kept: "The chamber in which the ancient hoards of princes were kept was called a *thalamos* (the same word, interestingly enough, was used for the wife's or the daughter's apartments)."[43] The legend of the Golden Fleece provides a glimpse at the ideas of agricultural prosperity and livestock wealth in the very process of being transformed, indeed sublated, into the abstractions of value made fully possible only later by the economic circulation of metal coins: "The manner in which the fleece is presented in myth is evolving into an image of an *agalma* even while it preserves, as it were, its material substance."[44]

Jean-Pierre Vernant refers to this same process, whereby material prosperity, sexual relations, and the growth of a monetary economy are intertwined in ancient Greek epistemology, with the terms "thésaurisation" and "capitalisation," which he in turn links intimately with the double cult of Hestia, goddess of the hearth, and Hermes, god of mobility and transition.[45] In Vernant's symbolic reconstruction, based in large measure on Homer and the tragedians, the feminine, internal, enclosed space of the house, the province of Hestia, is the

place of wealth calculated in fixed stores of material goods; the open
fields, meanwhile, the province of Hermes, are the place of mobile
wealth, or cattle: "D'une part les biens qui se prêtent à thésaurisation et
qui peuvent être emmagasinés dans le palais. . . . L'autre aspect . . .
est constitué par les troupeaux. Trésor et troupeaux font contraste, sur
le plan des valeurs économiques, comme le dedans et le dehors, le fixe
et le mobile, l'enclos domestique et l'espace ouvert de l'ἀγρός."[46] The
increase of cattle, watched over by Hermes, eventually lends itself
allegorically, as we have seen in the passage from Aristotle's *Politics*
cited above, to the rhetoric of money, of interest (τόκος); these are
figured in reproductive terms when the treasures of house, field, and
inheritance are represented not merely as property but as the spawn of
their master.   The regulation of inner and outer wealth, of those
resources which are stable and those which are mobile, "la richesse qui
'gît' dans la maison et celle qui 'court' la campagne,"[47] is thus
inevitably bound up with reproductive propriety even as it tends toward
the abstractions of commerce in a money economy.   The pairing of
Hestia and Hermes, finally, maintains the gendered polarity of the
spaces involved even as it insists on their interconnection, the
importance of the circulation of activities and goods around the
immobile Hestia and the crucial fixity of the center for the unstable
Hermes.[48]   Money, land, property, and reproduction are thus
inextricably linked in the ancient as in the classical Greek economic
symbologies.[49]
     Hence the insistent presence of ordinances governing the proper
conduct of husband and wife in texts, like the Aristotelian and pseudo-
Aristotelian examined above, that purport to concern land-tenure and
revenue collection; hence, as suggested below, the shadow of domestic
and sexual relations to be discerned to a greater or lesser degree behind
the ostensible allegory of money in the various dramatic works here
studied.   What seems clear is that cultures based on repression and
mastery are in need of propaganda -- otherwise known as education or
socializing -- in order to sustain themselves, and that this propaganda
may take different forms: from organized state religion, with ritual and
credo; through public cultural display, at dramatic festivals and in
monuments; to private social institutions, in domestic routine and
symposiastic recitation. Theater is a particularly apt communicator of
ideologies and epistemological systems, capable as it is of literally
staging scenes of private conflict as public spectacle, and thus putting
into play the paradoxes and contradictions of the prevailing social
organization, the better to render them ostensibly natural and viable.[50]
Ancient tragedy has received much scholarly attention for its speculated
origins in just such a context;[51] the present study proposes to focus on
the contribution of comedy to the propagation of certain patriarchal

notions of social power, particularly as made (problematically) visible in the form of allegorized wealth.[52]

Comedy lends itself to scrutiny of this kind both because of its relatively uninterrupted production throughout several centuries of classical antiquity,[53] which makes it a good gauge of changing mores and continuing frames of reference, and because of its generic tendency to subvert order in the aim of maintaining it, which renders it a distorting glass in which can be glimpsed the sutures of ideology. This last characteristic, here assigned to classical (old, middle, and new) comedy, has been developed most fully by contemporary critics of mass culture, who have emphasized such techniques of the work of popular art as its ability to put into play apparently natural yet significantly polysemous situations and characters, in order to consolidate a given ideology, to subvert it, and finally to recontain the threatening revolutionary pressures exerted by that same initial subversion.[54] Ancient comedy, with its links to carnival and the ritual reversal of institutionalized relations (with an eye to their eventual re-establishment), is a natural candidate for an investigation along such critical-methodological lines.[55]

The works I have chosen for study here are all concerned in an explicit way with money and/or private property, and they all, as I shall argue, exhibit the above-mentioned tendency to the subversion of a dominant ideology, and to the subsequent recontainment of that same subversive energy. They are not all, however, comedies: they are not even all theatrical works, strictly speaking. The two works of Aristophanes and the two of Plautus studied in Chapters 1 and 2 are classic examples of their genres, old (perhaps middle) Greek comedy and Roman new comedy respectively; the satiric dialogue of Lucian explored in Chapter 3 has strong links with classical comedy, and was probably meant for performance of some kind, although on a limited, more personal scale; and the Shakespearean tragedy with which Lucian's dialogue is contrasted in Chapter 4, an unfinished play never performed during its author's lifetime, I have selected as an example of what the neo-tragic form can make of the classical themes treated in the earlier works. I have thus allowed thematic and generic considerations to influence each other in my selection of texts, in a heuristic and very partial reconstruction of the vicissitudes of a certain allegory through various modes of western or European literature; an addendum to the last chapter, however, attempts briefly to restore the original comic paradigm by speculating about the possible presence in a Shakespearean comedy of echoes of the same economic allegory followed in the earlier chapters.

The vicissitudes of this allegory may be reconstructed as follows: out of the classic Athenian democratic city-state, built on the establishment of patrilinear land-division and a restricted political economy as a safeguard against tribalism and feudalism, there arose a full, personified allegory of Wealth, the guarantee of native agricultural plenty who was nevertheless dressed in outlandish rags and had therefore to be recuperated from this degradation. From the early Roman republic, tending toward world domination and the concentration of riches in a new class of men, there grew a new formulation of this same figure, only now displaying an uncanny autonomy or automatism, and introducing the danger of a doubling or a split between Wealth and his possessor. Amid the ultimate fading of the Greek city-states at the apogee of Roman imperial power there emerged the figure of Wealth as fragmented, hypocritical, and bizarrely polymorph, barely concealing any longer the power relations that engendered and that maintain it. Finally, on the Elizabethan stage, during the rise of nascent capitalism and the disintegration of the medieval feudal order following private property revolutions much like the ones posited by Heinsohn and Steiger as the cause of the archaic feudal system's downfall,[56] the personified allegory of Wealth disappeared altogether, and was assimilated instead into a series of purely verbal tropes. On the Elizabethan comic stage, meanwhile, I have discerned an entirely new personification of Ploutos, whose human features allow the new-found respectability of commerce and money to displace its repressed self onto an easily identifiable, demonized anti-hero, and thus effectively to permit the recuperation of Aristotle's χρηματιστική for the purposes of the ruling οίκονομική.[57]

The readings offered below are necessarily speculative to some degree, based as they are on a dialectic of literary representation as testimony and sometime furtherer of historical change. Accordingly, a certain tension of theoretical approaches may also be sensed. Building on Heinsohn's model of private property relations as crystallized in money and Vernant's male-female polarity in the construction of relations of economic prosperity, and discovering these relations to be both revealed and concealed by money's representation on the comic stage, I move from a predominantly Marxist reading of the Aristophanic texts, to an attempt, in the chapter on Plautus, to correct the sometimes rigid economic materialism of that approach by lending it a psychic dimension, with an experimental use of the psychoanalytically-oriented work on ideology and culture of the cultural critic Slavoj Zizek to interpret the place of allegories of wealth within a new comic "economy" now thoroughly inhabited by family romance and ethico-sexual dynamics. In the latter chapters the texts of Lucian and Shakespeare take centerstage: their pre-modern and early modern self-consciousness -- in the first case that of an aesthete and a purveyor of a culture in decline, in the second that of a bourgeois member of a drastically changing society -- allows them to perform fruitfully deconstructive readings of themselves.

Indeed, the ultimate revelations of Shakespeare's *Timon of Athens*: that money is in and of itself already an allegory, without the trappings of classical personification; that what it represents, however, is the sheerly aleatory nature of the monetary economy, based as it is on loveless domination, and on borrowing and lending on the strength of uneasily held property; and that that property is itself utterly without affective or autochthonous connection to its possessor: all of these may have contributed to the play's sinking under the weight of its own destabilizing message. For the melancholy suggestion of the societies reflected in all of the works I have selected for study is twofold: that the monetary economy is deeply harmful and inorganic; and that it is virtually inextricable from the network of human culture. Money functions as a sign and as an object, as a word and as a thing; however dreadful an infrastructure of repression and exploitation it may condense within its protean form, it has woven itself round with the quotidian so effectively that it can no longer be called a stranger.

Notes

[1] I borrow the notion of the scandalousness of early Greek representations of money from the study of Dominique Arnould, "Ploutos et Pénia dans la poésie lyrique, élégiaque et iambique archaïque," in *L'univers épique,* ed. Michel Woronoff (Paris: Les Belles Lettres, 1992), 157-170; the relevant passage can be found on p. 158: "Certes, on le savait déjà avec Homère qui notait que Zeus donne l'*olbos* aux bons comme aux méchants (*Od.* VI, 188), mais l'idée revient sans cesse, au VIe siècle, comme un scandale moral mais aussi politique et social." Arnould's focus, as her title indicates, is the lyric manifestations of the pair Ploutos-Penia, or Wealth and Poverty; she is very thorough and helpful on the archaic literary background of the conceit's later appearance in drama. Crucial to the present study is also Gerhard Hertel, *Die Allegorie von Reichtum und Armut: Ein aristophanisches Motiv und seine Abwandlungen in der abendländischen Literatur* (Nürnberg: Hans Carl, 1969). Hertel's philological precision and language-philosophical essays on three of the six principal works discussed below have been of inestimable help.

[2] Δημήτηρ μὲν Πλοῦτον ἐγείνατο, δῖα θεάων, / Ἰασίων' ἥρωι μιγεῖσ' ἐρατῇ φιλότητι / νειῷ ἐνὶ τριπόλῳ, Κρήτης ἐν πίονι δήμῳ / ἐσθλόν, ὅς εἶσ' ἐπὶ γῆν τε καὶ εὐρέα νῶτα θαλάσσης / πᾶσαν· τῷ δὲ τυχόντι καὶ οὔ κ' ἐς χεῖρας ἵκηται, / τὸν δ'ἀφνειὸν ἔθηκε, πολὺν δέ οἱ ὤπασεν ὄλβον, vv. 969-974.

[3] *Odyssey* 5. 125 ff. See Walter Burkert, *Greek Religion,* trans. John Raffan (Cambridge: Harvard Univ. Press, 1985), 108-109: "The fact that in mythology Iasion is struck by a thunderbolt indicates that a sacred marriage of this kind stands closer to sacrifice than sensual pleasure." Much more

could be said, of course, on the issue of Ploutos' birth in these circumstances: that the child born to Demeter is male and said to be benevolent, at least initially, though his mortal father dies in the act and his mother will go on to become associated mythically much more closely with her daughter than with her son, all this points both to the crucial implication of mortals in the work of ploughing, and to their inevitable dispensability in the larger natural process of burgeoning and growth. This ambivalence in the first appearance of the god will be carried on throughout his later career, in which he will be continually associated with mortal boons and with mortal woes (note especially his association with the underworld, adumbrated here in his γηγενής or chthonic origins). I am grateful to Froma Zeitlin for these last important observations.

[4] See Burkert (1985) 159 for a discussion of the various possible meanings of Demeter's name: he rules out both Earth Mother and Corn Mother as etymologically unsatisfactory, but notes that, however her name may have been derived, "corn is unquestionably at the centre of her power and favour."

[5] Burkert (1985) 159.

[6] ἐμοὶ δὲ Πλοῦτος - ἔστι γὰρ λίην τυφλός - / ἐς τὦικί᾽ ἐλθὼν οὐδάμ᾽ εἶπεν "Ἱππῶναξ. / δίδωμί τοι μνέας ἀργύρου τριήκοντα / καὶ πόλλ᾽ ἔτ᾽ ἄλλα· δείλαιος γὰρ τὰς φρένας. Hipponax fr. 36 West, Iambi et Elegi Graeci, vol. 1 (Oxford: Oxford Univ. Press, 1971).

[7] ὤφελεν σ᾽ ὦ τυφλὲ Πλοῦτε / μήτε γῆι μήτ᾽ ἐν θαλάσσηι / μήτ᾽ ἐν ἠπείρωι φανῆμεν. / ἀλλὰ Τάρταρόν τε ναίειν / κ᾽Ἀχέροντα· διὰ σὲ γὰρ πάντ᾽ / αἰὲν ἀνθρώποις κακά. Timocreon fr. 731 Page, Poetae Melici Graeci (Oxford: Oxford Univ. Press, 1962).

[8] For dating see Arnould in Woronoff (1992) 159, and Jean Carrière, Théognis: Poèmes élégiaques (Paris: Les Belles Lettres, 1975) 7-8.

[9] Πλοῦτε. θεῶν κάλλιστε καὶ ἱμεροέστατε πάντων. / σὺν σοὶ καὶ κακὸς ὢν γίνεται ἐσθλὸς ἀνήρ. Theognis vv. 1117-1118. On this passage as reflective of the dangers of wealth, see Walter Donlan, "Pistos Philos Hetairos," in Theognis of Megara: Poetry and the Polis, ed. Thomas J. Figueira and Gregory Nagy (Baltimore: Johns Hopkins Univ. Press, 1985), 223-244: "But the causes and results of civic stasis are much more complex, for they relate not only to interactions between men but to the dynamics of a social order in flux.. . . . This state of affairs is blamed in part on the notion that the kakoi have gained wealth (149-150, 321-322, 865-867, 1117-1118)," p. 239. Wealth does not transform the κακός, in other words, so much as disguise him. Against this genetic interpretation of Theognis' use of words like ἐσθλός and κακός, however, see Nagy, "Theognis and Megara: A Poet's Vision of His City," pp. 22-81 in the same collection.

[10] The exchange between the brothers is as follows: Πολυνείκης· . . . τίς ὧδ᾽ ἄτρωτος. ὅστις εἰς ἡμᾶς ξίφος / φόνιον ἐμβαλὼν τὸν αὐτὸν οὐκ ἀποίσεται μόρον: / Ἐτεόκλης· Ἐγγύς. οὐ πρόσω βέβηκας· ἐς χέρας λεύσσεις ἐμάς: / Πολυνείκης· Εἰσορῶ δειλὸν δ᾽ ὁ Πλοῦτος καὶ φιλόψυχον κακόν. vv. 594-597. Earlier in the play Polyneikes has himself apparently praised money (τὰ χρήματ᾽ ἀνθρώποισι τιμιώτατα. v. 439,

"Money is the most valuable to humans"), and delivered himself of a Theognidean reflection on the nobility of wealth (πένης γὰρ οὐδὲν εὐγενὴς ἀνήρ, v. 442, "No well-born man is poor"); but the passage is suspected of being interpolated, and in any case the insults exchanged in stichomythic flyting need not necessarily proceed from an integral character-psychology. The insult may also be understood in the context of improper marital relations, so typical of the Theban symbolic economy. See Froma I. Zeitlin, "Thebes: Theater of Self and Society in Athenian Drama," in *Nothing to Do with Dionysus? Athenian Drama in Its Social Context*, ed. John J. Winkler and Froma I. Zeitlin (Princeton: Princeton Univ. Press, 1990), 130-167: "The most conspicuous symptom of this maladaptive system is the problem of marriage in this city, the institution that normally regulates relations between non-kin and circulates women as signs to be exchanged between men. When it is not refused altogether (as by Antigone in her play or Eteokles in his), marriage brings danger from two different directions, either as excessive endogamy in the form of incest or as its contrary, when Polyneikes' search for a bride *outside* -- too far from home -- instigates the expedition of the Argive Seven against his native city;" Polyneikes' claim to inclusion in the land of his birth, then, is posed in terms of his opposition to Eteokles' management of the native "economy" -- Eteokles is "intent on not letting the women *inside* come outside," p. 148.

[11] Αἴσχυλος· Οὐκοῦν ἐθέλει γε τριηράρχειν πλοῦτον διὰ ταῦτα. / ἀλλὰ ῥακίοις περιειλάμενος κλαεῖ καὶ φῆσι πενέσθαι. *Frogs* vv. 1065-1066; Βλέπυρος· Πῶς οὖν ὅστις μὴ κέκτηται γῆν ἡμῶν, ἀργύριον δὲ καὶ Δαρείκους. ἀφανῆ πλοῦτον: *Ecclesiazusae* vv. 601-602. Vincent Gabrielsen, in a discussion of "visible" and "invisible" wealth, sees these two Aristophanic allusions as evidence that the distinction was current already in the fifth century: see Gabrielsen, "Φανερά and ἀφανὴς οὐσία in Classical Athens," *Classica et Mediaevalia* 37 (1986): 99-114, esp. pp. 104-105.

[12] Τέταρτον δὲ δὴ πλοῦτος οὐ τυφλὸς ἀλλ' ὀξὺ βλέπων. ἄνπερ ἅμ' ἕπηται φρονήσει. *Laws* 631 c. Emphasis supplied.

[13] Aristotle wrote, of course, no extended treatise on economics: the *Oikonomikos* attributed to him is in fact a pastiche of fourth- and third-century tracts, written by one or more disciples of the Lyceum and inspired by Xenophon and the Peripatetics; there is even some suggestion that the third book, which survives only in a medieval Latin translation, may have been composed by a Stoic of the Roman imperial epoch. See for dating B. A. van Groningen and André Wartelle, *Aristote: Économique* (Paris: Les Belles Lettres, 1968), xxii-xx.

[14] The word οἰκονομία appears for the first time only in 380 B.C.E., in the *Economics* of Xenophon, and refers to the maintenance and disposition of agricultural property. "Par οἰκονομία le Grec entendait donc en premier lieu l'administration d'une fortune privée. Les biens fonciers en constituaient toujours la partie essentielle. Ainsi, quand l'économie domestique s'intéresse à l'οἶκος, c'est le domaine rural qu'elle a en vue; entendons: un domaine rural d'une certaine importance, puisque l'exploitation d'un petit

lopin de terre ne présente guère de problèmes théoriques," van Groningen and Wartelle (1968) vii. See Moses I. Finley, *The Ancient Economy* (Berkeley and Los Angeles: Univ. of California Press, 1973), 20-21 for remarks on the second book of the pseudo-Aristotelian *Economics* as the single classical attempt to extend the term οἰκονομία to the management of public revenues.

[15] Διπλῆς δ' οὔσης αὐτῆς, ὥσπερ εἴπομεν, καὶ τῆς μὲν καπηλικῆς τῆς δ' οἰκονομικῆς, καὶ ταύτης μὲν ἀναγκαίας καὶ ἐπαινουμένης, τῆς δὲ μεταβλητικῆς ψεγομένης δικαίως (οὐ γὰρ κατὰ φύσιν ἀλλ᾽ ἀπ᾽ ἀλλήλων ἐστίν), εὐλογώτατα μισεῖται ἡ ὀβολοστατικὴ διὰ τὸ ἀπ᾽ αὐτοῦ τοῦ νομίσματος εἶναι τὴν κτῆσιν καὶ οὐκ ἐφ᾽ ὅπερ ἐπορίσθη. Μεταβολῆς γὰρ ἐγένετο χάριν, ὁ δὲ τόκος αὐτὸ ποιεῖ πλέον· ὅθεν καὶ τοὔνομα τοῦτ᾽ εἴληφεν· ὅμοια γὰρ τὰ τικτόμενα τοῖς γεννῶσιν αὐτά ἐστιν, ὁ δὲ τόκος γίνεται νόμισμα νομίσματος· ὥστε καὶ μάλιστα παρὰ φύσιν οὗτος τῶν χρηματισμῶν ἐστιν. Aristotle *Politics* 1258 a 38-1258 b 8.

[16] A consideration of Aristotle's use of the word φύσις, or "nature," and its adverbial phrases κατὰ φύσιν and παρὰ φύσιν, is obviously beyond the scope of the present inquiry. It may suffice to point out the appearance of the term in passages immediately preceding that under discussion here, in order to demonstrate the context in which φύσις suggests the very biology here being claimed for money's extremest form, yet somehow also constitutive of its "unnaturalness." At 1253 a 2-3, the famous formulation ἄνθρωπος φύσει πολιτικὸν ζῷον ("the human being is by nature a political [or *polis*-dwelling] animal") uses the word φύσις to endorse a supposedly self-evident existential observation; at 1253 a 18 ff., καὶ πρότερον δὴ τῇ φύσει πόλις ἢ οἰκία καὶ ἕκαστος ἡμῶν ἐστιν· τὸ γὰρ ὅλον πρότερον ἀναγκαῖον εἶναι τοῦ μέρους ("And indeed the *polis* is prior to the family and to each of us, for the whole is necessarily prior to the part"), φύσις is again the guarantee of organic, logically provable reality.

[17] This is on a continuum with the scandal identified by Dominique Arnould above: that is, the possibility of the wrong or morally inferior person becoming wealthy. Here meanwhile money's uncanny ability to proliferate in a way that resembles nature introduces the possibility of an uncontrolled (re)production of wealth. There is also the complementary problem (the reverse of the Theognidean phenomenon of wealth that ennobles the vile, as at Theognis vv. 1117-1118) that an otherwise good person will become vile through trading in money and its paraphernalia: see the introduction to van Groningen and Wartelle (1968) x. Commenting on the family and domestic economy as the basis of political life in Aristotle's (and pseudo-Aristotle's) conception, van Groningen gives this exegesis of the present passage of the *Politics*: "Cette économie est, avant tout, de nouveau, celle du domaine rural, dont le propriétaire doit administrer les diverses parties (c'est l'οἰκονομία au sens propre du mot) et s'efforcer d'augmenter les revenus (c'est la κτητική). Moins naturelle, et par conséquence moins recommandable, est la χρηματιστική qui cherche le profit matériel par l'échange de produits ou d'argent, occupation parasitaire *qui tend à abaisser le niveau moral de celui qui s'y adonne*." Emphasis supplied.

[18] This notion of wealth as somehow involved with denatured or illicit forms of begetting is of course already present at Theognis 184 ff., where the power of Ploutos to mix up classes and produce debased offspring is explored: see the discussion of this passage in Nagy, "A Poet's Vision of His City", in Figueira and Nagy (1985) 54-55.

[19] Burkert (1985) 108.

[20] "Here [in the sacred marriage of Demeter and Iasion], perhaps from ancient Neolithic tradition, we find the association between ploughing/sowing and procreation, and between harvest and birth. Since Mannhardt, this has been connected with popular customs of couples rolling on the cornfield, the *Brautlager auf dem Ackerfeld*," Burkert (1985) 108. In light of Aristotle's remarks on the primacy of war, hunting, and agriculture as means of acquiring goods it is interesting to note that in classical Greece marriage formed a feminine social practice parallel to warfare: thus the sacred union of Demeter and Iasion is situated, appropriately, on the same "primitive" or "natural" level as war, one of Aristotle's *masculine* pre-monetary activities. See on marriage and warfare in the classical symbology Jean-Pierre Vernant, "Oedipus Without the Complex," in J.-P. Vernant and P. Vidal-Naquet, *Myth and Tragedy in Ancient Greece*, trans. Janet Lloyd (New York: Zone Books, 1990), 99.

[21] Composed between 325 and 275 B.C.E. and certainly influenced by Xenophon: see van Groningen and Wartelle (1968) xii.

[22] Μέρη δὲ οἰκίας ἄνθρωπός τε καὶ κτῆσίς ἐστιν. *Economics I* 1343 a.

[23] Οἶκον μὲν πρώτιστα γυναῖκά τε βοῦν τ' ἀροτῆρα. v. 405.

[24] Φύσει γὰρ ἀπὸ τῆς μητρὸς ἡ τροφὴ πᾶσίν ἐστιν. ὥστε καὶ τοῖς ἀνθρώποις ἀπὸ τῆς γῆς. *Economics I* 1343 a-b.

[25] *Economics I* 1344 a; the teaching of "wise ways" is drawn from another Hesiodic citation: "Marry a virgin, so you may teach her wise ways" (παρθενικήν δε γαμεῖν. ἵνα ἤθεα κέδνα διδάξεις), *Works and Days* v. 699.

[26] Van Groningen (1968) xix-xx speculates that the author was either a Peripatetic of the generation immediately following Aristotle's death or a Stoic of the second or third century C.E.

[27] *Economics III* 141.

[28] *Economics III* 143.

[29] "Nihil quoque majus nec propius est uxori ad virum quam societas honorabilis et fidelis. Propter quae non decet hominem sanae mentis ut ubicumque contingit ponere semen suum, nec ad qualecumque accesserit, proprium immittere semen, ut non degeneribus et iniquis similia liberis legitimis fiant, et quidem uxor honore suo privetur, filiis vero opprobrium adiungatur," *Economics III* 144.

[30] This association is stressed by means of an insistence on the intactness or integrity of the household as of the virgin, a theme already implicit in Hesiod. See Nicole Loraux on *Works and Days* vv. 504-535 in her preface to Giulia Sissa, *Le corps virginal: La virginité féminine en Grèce ancienne* (Paris: Librairie philosophique J. Vrin, 1982), 7-16: "Précieuse *parthénos*, que la clôture très symbolique de la maison protège doublement -- du *dia* (à travers), à quoi le souffle hivernal de Borée soumet hommes et bêtes, et des 'travaux' de l'amour dans l'attente desquels toutefois elle baigne et oint son

corps délicat -- telle apparaît la jeune fille dans l'un des textes fondateurs de la tradition grecque," pp. 7-8.

[31] Finley (1973) 20-21.

[32] Finley, *The Use and Abuse of History* (London: Chatto & Windus, 1975), 159.

[33] Finley (1975) 158.

[34] Gabrielsen (1986) 110.

[35] Gunnar Heinsohn, *Privateigentum, Patriarchat, Geldwirtschaft: Eine sozialtheoretische Rekonstruktion zur Antike* (Frankfurt: Suhrkamp, 1984). See also Gunnar Heinsohn and Otto Steiger, "Private Ownership and the Foundations of Monetary Theory," *Économies et Sociétés* 9 (1987): 229-243; Heinsohn and Steiger, "The Veil of Barter: The Solution to 'The Task of Obtaining Representations of an Economy in which Money is Essential'," in *Inflation and Income Distribution in Capitalist Crisis: Essays in Memory of Sidney Weintraub,* ed. J. A. Kregel (London: Macmillan, 1988), 175-201; and Heinsohn and Steiger, "A Private Property Theory of Credit, Interest and Money," *Économies et Sociétés* 26 (1994): 9-24.

[36] Heinsohn and Steiger (1987) 229-243.

[37] See Heinsohn (1984) passim.

[38] "Existenzunsicherheit und Armut stehen am Beginn der neuen Privateigentumsverhältnisse, deren höhere reichtumschaffende Potenz von ihren Begründern auch keineswegs -- wie etwa Funktionalisten nahelegen müssen -- vorab gewusst und daraufhin planvoll ins Werk gesetzt werden konnte," Heinsohn (1984) 95.

[39] Heinsohn (1984) 75-85 and 94-5.

[40] Translated by R. L. Gordon as "'Value' in Greek Myth" in *Myth, Religion and Society,* ed. R. L. Gordon (Cambridge: Cambridge Univ. Press, 1981), 111-146.

[41] Gernet in Gordon (1981) 146.

[42] Gernet in Gordon (1981) 120, 121, and 144, respectively.

[43] Gernet in Gordon (1981) 140.

[44] Gernet in Gordon (1981) 137.

[45] "Hestia-Hermès: Sur l'expression religieuse de l'espace et du mouvement chez les Grecs," in Vernant, *Mythe et pensée chez les Grecs: Études de psychologie historique* (Paris: François Maspero, 1965), 97-143.

[46] Vernant (1965) 129-130.

[47] Vernant (1965) 130.

[48] Vernant adduces of course the vital exception of marriage (along with its limit case, the epiclerate), in which the gendering of inside and outside is reversed: Vernant (1965) 105-106, 117-121. It will be seen that the comedies of Aristophanes studied below play on just such polarities, as the female figure of Peace is brought outside to the fields, and the male figure of Wealth is brought inside (in a scene reminiscent of both marriage and slavery). Nicole Loraux, in "Aristophane, les femmes d'Athènes et le théâtre," in *Aristophane,* ed. Reverdin and Grange (Geneva: Fondation Hardt, 1993), 203-244, makes illuminating comment on the use of this dynamics in the *Peace* in particular.

[49] The sexual implications of a female representation of agricultural land in Attic comedy and elsewhere are of course notorious, and have been explored variously by Page DuBois, *Sowing the Body: Psychoanalysis and Ancient Representations of Women* (Chicago: Univ. of Chicago Press, 1988); Carol Dougherty, *The Poetics of Colonization: From City to Text in Archaic Greece* (Oxford: Oxford Univ. Press, 1993), and by Nicole Loraux in Reverdin and Grange (1993), among others.

[50] New historical studies of Shakespeare, in particular, have stressed these qualities of theater: "We could argue further that one of the ideological functions of the theater was precisely to create in its audience the sense that what seemed spontaneous or accidental was in fact fully plotted ahead of time by a playwright carefully calculating his effects, that behind experienced uncertainty there was design, whether the design of the human patriarchs -- the fathers and rulers who unceasingly watched over the errant courses of their subjects -- or the overarching design of the divine patriarch," Stephen Greenblatt, *Shakespearean Negotiations* (Berkeley & Los Angeles: Univ. of California Press, 1988), 17.

[51] The literature is extensive: see among many others Vernant and Vidal-Naquet (1990) and Winkler and Zeitlin (1990). For the sake of an example relevant to the present discussion, see the discussion of male socialization through tragedy in Froma I. Zeitlin, "Playing the Other: Theater, Theatricality, and the Feminine in Greek Drama," in Winkler and Zeitlin (1990) 63-96. Zeitlin discusses the problem of woman's necessary but perilous control over the household, the "inside," at pp. 76 ff.; her ability to deceive men radically by bringing forth children who may not be his, in association with the myth of Pandora and the notion of woman as "the mimetic creature par excellence," is examined at p. 85. For valuable work on the issues of mimesis and the feminine in ancient comedy, see also Zeitlin, "Travesties of Gender and Genre in Aristophanes' *Thesmophoriazousae*," *Critical Inquiry* (winter 1981): 301-27.

[52] "[P]arce qu'elle mime la quotidienneté, la comédie passe pour le laboratoire autorisé des représentations partagées de la vie en cité. Que chez Aristophane le corps virginal devienne matière pour le rire, la chose donc n'est pas sans importance," Loraux in Sissa (1982) 15. The same claim could certainly be made for money's importance in Aristophanes; it is only later in the comic tradition, as we shall see, that these two important social themes begin to be merged, and the interdependence of sexual and financial control rendered at once more explicit, as well as better rhetorically encoded.

[53] As compared to classical tragedy, which barely survived the fifth century: see Vernant and Vidal-Naquet (1990) 29.

[54] On consolidation, subversion, and containment, see Jonathan Dollimore, "Introduction: Shakespeare, Cultural Materialism and the New Historicism," in *Political Shakespeare: New Essays in Cultural Materialism*, ed. Dollimore and Sinfield (Manchester: Manchester Univ. Press, 1985), 2-17; on the polysemy of the apparently natural in works of popular art, see Fredric Jameson, "Reification and Utopia in Mass Culture," *Social Text* 1/1 (1979): 130-148. "Suture," in the sense of "a synonym for

ideological closure, for the gesture by which a given ideological field encloses itself, effaces the traces of the material process which generated it" while leaving in fact a discernible rhetorical scar, is a somewhat controversial term, shared as it is between Lacanian cultural criticism and deconstructionist film theory. The definition I have cited here is from Slavoj Zizek, *For They Know Not What They Do: Enjoyment as a Political Factor* (London: Verso, 1991), 19, in a passage decidedly partisan of the Lacanian cultural-critical school.

[55] See, on ancient comedy and carnival in general, J. C. Carrière, *Le Carnaval et la politique: Une introduction à la comédie grecque -- suivie d'un choix de fragments* (Paris: Les Belles Lettres, 1979); for a classicist's reflections on the use of contemporary sociological and literary theory to interpret ancient texts, see Wolfgang Rösler, "Michail Bachtin und die Karnevalskultur im antiken Griechenland," *Quaderni Urbinati di Cultura Classica* NS 23/2 (1986): 25-44.

[56] For the peasant rebellions of late medieval England and their role in bringing about early modern capitalism, see Heinsohn (1984) 11-12, 20, and especially 158: "Eine neuerliche, aus existentieller Unsicherheit von Privateigentümern geborene Geldwirtschaft mit faktisch freier Verkaufbarkeit von Boden und Arbeitskraft entsteht in Europa (und damit auf der Erde) erst wieder im 14. Jahrhundert u. Z. in England, wo nach der Rebellion der Lollarden unter Wat Tylor . . . Grundherren ihre leibeigenen Bauern -- die Lollarden -- verlieren."

[57] The reference is of course to *The Merchant of Venice*, and to its use of a racial stereotype in the form of the character of Shylock onto which to project the uncanny and dangerous elements of the money-allegory, so as to leave the representative member of the dominant culture, Antonio, ethically free to pursue his course, a course that just happens to be the once-reviled business of trade or commerce. Significantly, in a note on Aristotle's *Politics* 1258 a 38-b 8 (the passage cited above in which trade and usury are condemned as unnatural), the nineteenth-century French commentator Barthélemy-St.-Hilaire makes the following remarks: "Depuis Aristote, cet anathême contre le commerce a été mille fois répété. . . . Il me semble assez remarquable que Rousseau n'ait jamais attaqué le commerce. Dans toute l'antiquité, le commerce fut une profession peu honorable; il ne commença à être estimé qu'à l'époque des républiques italiennes *et de la grande prospérité de Venise*," J. Barthélemy-St.-Hilaire, *Politique d'Aristote* vol. 1 (Paris: L'imprimerie royale, 1837), 60. Emphasis supplied.

Chapter 1

Allegory, Recontainment, Possibility: Aristophanes' *Peace* and *Plutus*

What chance has Vulcan against Roberts & Co., Jupiter against the lightning-conductor, and Hermes against the *crédit mobilier* ?

Karl Marx

Prologue

The issue of Aristophanes' politics is notoriously vexed.[1] Efforts have been made to connect his work developmentally with changes in Athenian society over the 40 years of his artistic flourishing;[2] whether Aristophanes be associated with conservative democrats or oligarchic insurgency, however, it seems clear that by virtue of his function as comedian there is an inherently reactionary and/or subversive tendency to the ideas, if not to the ideology, expressed in his comedies. One commentator has stressed the double function of ancient comedy, both critical and conformist because of its origins in what he calls "'démocratie' paysanne," or rural 'democracy': "parcequ'elle est prête à critiquer à la fois l'ordre existant et les nouveautés 'excessives' par rapport à cet ordre, elle semble prédisposée à fonctionner comme une sorte de régulateur social et politique."[3] It will be the aim of this chapter to evince from a reading of two of Aristophanes' comedies a sense of the subversive possibilities of the comic poet's use of these categories in the construction of an entertainment that simultaneously criticizes and upholds its immediate social milieu, as well as to infer from the two plays discussed the rudiments of a sort of vocabulary for the discourse surrounding money in the classical satiric tradition.

Both the *Peace* and the *Plutus* of Aristophanes are overwhelmingly concerned with material prosperity. Unlike the *Acharnians* and its fantasy of economic self-determination, the political hallucinations of the *Knights*, the *Birds*, *Lysistrata*, and the *Ecclesiazusae*, the social satire of the *Clouds*, the *Wasps*, and ,the *Thesmophoriazusae*, and the *Frogs'* longing for an indeterminate moral salvation (σωτηρία), the *Peace* and the *Plutus* seem simply to stage a generalized desire for the good life, whether that entails the boons of pastoral or of urban abundance. Both of these last-mentioned plays, of course, demonstrate a well-developed socio-political interest, especially the *Peace*, with its inventive use of the truce in the Peloponnesian War of 421 B.C.E.; what is at issue in the following discussion is the imagistic means by which each play's particular utopia is represented, and the extent to which that utopia is implicated in civic or rural institutions.

The *Peace* concerns the desperate peace-mission to Olympus of the farmer Trygaeus,[4] who has commandeered a special flying dung-beetle for the rescuing of the goddess Peace. Once at the home of the gods he finds only Hermes in attendance. Hermes informs him that the goddess Eirene, or Peace, has been left by the other divinities to the devices of the cruel Polemos, or War, who is planning to pound the cities of Greece into a powder. With the help of his fellow Attic farmers, and despite the significant recalcitrance of certain Greek factions, Trygaeus rescues the Goddess and returns to Earth with her and her two attendants, Opora, or Harvest, and Theoria, or Festival; amid epithalamial ribaldry he weds the former and consigns the latter to the Athenian Council, having tormented the now unemployed (and quite disgruntled) Greek arms-manufacturers with the promise of a returned Golden Age of peace.

The *Plutus* has for its theme the plight of the peasant Chremylus, who is uncertain as to whether he should destine his son to a country existence of upright poverty, or instead counsel a city life of lawless gain. On the advice of the oracle, Chremylus has attached himself to the first passerby, an unprepossessing old man who turns out to be the blind god of Wealth. With the help of his slave Karion, Chremylus cures the god's blindness and thus insures that prosperity will henceforth be the lot of the virtuous rather than of the scoundrels. A debate with the scorned goddess of Poverty follows, as well as a series of encounters with figures exemplary of the old and new dispensations. The god Hermes is given a marginal place in the utopian order, having suffered a demotion from his previous authority but not being overturned entirely, as is Zeus.[5]

The *Peace*, of course, is set in contemporary Peloponnesian war-time, during the short-lived Peace of Nicias which it celebrates, and has a manifestly redemptive action not unreminiscent of the *Frogs*; but its insistence on winning the material form of the allegorical figure of Eirene sets it apart from the *Frogs'* more conventionally dramatic contest between the tragedians Aeschylus and Euripides. Like the

Plutus, the *Peace* figures its fantasy's wish-fulfilment absolutely, not as a means,[6] but as an end, as the very prosperity that would eventually be brought about by the more fantastical methods proposed in the rest of the corpus, but whose attainment is left otherwise largely to chance. In Aristophanes' other nine plays most of the protagonists' effort is expended in the jerry-rigging of schemes designed to help bring about a change in fortune; in the *Peace* and the *Plutus*, effort is funnelled into acquiring the very stuff of fortune itself.[7]   In both plays, in other words, there is a curious foreshadowing of the "commodity fetishization" described by Marx in *Capital*; indeed, in the *Plutus* there is a hint of a fetishization of money, not as instrumental in the attainment of goals, but as a commodity in itself, as that which confers value simply by symbolizing it, a magical presence whose properties are equivalent to its characteristics -- an older, more traditional view, drawn from the relative security of the Hesiodic Ploutos-allegory.[8]   At the same time there is manifest in these two plays the by now equally traditional ambivalence with regard to money as such, evidenced by the attention paid the squalor and ethical confusion of the figure of Wealth in the *Plutus*. But it is of course just this ambivalence that will lead in the comedy to the healing of Ploutos, and to his re-insertion into a money economy now provisionally cleansed of its links with an older, more bucolic system of exchange, spoofed by Aristophanes' protagonists as embarassingly out of date.   The contrast of the rural goddess of Peace, enmired yet resplendent damsel in distress, with the urban god of Wealth, blind and shabby until medically treated, even as it plays on a utopian desire for an economy of pure wealth by means of either rural or urban labor relations, indicates something of the disrepute of monetary instruments, as against the respectable solidity of land, contemporary to the play's milieu.

Money and Land

This distinction, of course, was not always rigorously drawn in the ancient world, but depended on social circumstance and period. M. I. Finley goes so far as to suggest that "the ancient world was very unambiguous about wealth.   Wealth was a good thing, a necessary condition for the good life, and that was all there was to it," despite the aristocratic protests of a Theognis, for example, against wealth construed either as πλοῦτος or as χρήματα.[9] Finley is concerned primarily to establish the radical difference of the ancient economic world from that of its modern students, and points out that, so far from possessing the same instruments of commerce as the moderns, the ancient world had a very different notion of political economy as well: the discipline of "economics," he argues, only came into existence in its present-day form as the "science of the wealth of nations" in the late eighteenth century, having previously meant rather more what is denoted today by the term politics, and having furthermore received no systematic study by Aristotle, whose pan-epistemic claims might otherwise have led one to expect such a work.[10]   Nevertheless, there was of course money in the ancient world, as distinct from landed property and hoarded resources, and its function bore more than a simple family resemblance to that of modern currency.[11]   But as Austin and Vidal-Naquet observe, even in the fourth century, a period in which banking, loans and financial transactions were thriving, a certain archaizing conception of money and land persisted:

> The world of land remained dissociated from that of money. Although land did indeed change hands frequently in the fourth century, it did not for all that become a genuine marketable commodity exploited for its economic possibilities. A whole system of archaic values remained linked to it, values of a non-economic kind, far removed from the spirit of Aristotle's *chrematistike*.[12]

Louis Gernet locates the origins of this distinction in heroic prehistory:

> The objects given as prizes [to legendary ἀθληταί] belong to a category both extensive and definite. . . . As a class of goods, they are the medium of aristocratic intercourse. . . . [T]hey constitute a special form of property -- private property in the narrow sense, which, in the case of the warrior caste we are shown in the epics, is defined both in terms of the behaviour and customary rules which regulate it and by contrast with other property held on a juridical or quasi-juridical basis (such as ownership of land or livestock). . . .   And finally, it is precisely this notion of private possession which is stressed in the vocabulary: the term *ktemata* is normally used to refer to objects of this kind, emphasizing the idea of acquisition -- acquisition in war, through the games, by gift; but never, in principle, by mercantile trade.[13]

It may be instructive to note as well Peter W. Rose's recent discussion of the ancient conception of "unfree labor," as he finds it reflected in Marx's humanist utopianism:

> It is often assumed that Marx's emphasis on human labor is entirely incompatible with the perspective of ancient Greece, where, we are repeatedly told, labor was disparaged. What was disparaged was in fact unfree labor -- as in Marx. For an ancient Greek, as for Marx, unfree labor included both slavery and paid labor under the command of another."[14]

Particularly scorned were the so-called banausic trades, the commercial and the manufacturing.[15]

The point here is not to equate money with wage-labor as equally distasteful categories but simply to show that money and the unfree laboring classes were typically associated in ancient Greece. It will be seen below that there was indeed ample respect and desire for money amongst the fifth- and fourth-century Athenians, but that these positive feelings were mingled with a certain class-based contempt. As Jacob Hemelrijk explains, in his influential work on the concepts of wealth and poverty in classical Greece, this had largely to do with the phenomenon of established wealth coming into contact with newly-amassed riches, and with that of hereditary nobility becoming impoverished, and vice versa: "Πλοῦτος ohne Adel ist ein schlechter Hausgenosse. Diese Auffassung behauptet sich in der Literatur, mit der Änderung, daß Adel ein ethischer Begriff wird."[16] The nobility were of course proud to be wealthy, or πλούσιοι (if indeed they were) for the prestige afforded them by their being able to afford public service, or λειτουργία; but not all πλούσιοι were noble, and some of those who supported the state with money, entitling them to the name πλούσιοι, might have had to work for that money, and were thus technically paupers or πένητες.[17] As Hemelrijk says, "die Grenze zwischen diesen [= those who supported the state with money but who could not subsist without working] und den πένητες ist nicht immer dieselbe."[18] The critical distinction was more typically that between the πένητες (connected etymologically with the word πόνος meaning labor or toil), or those who had to work for a living, and the πτωχοί, or beggars.[19] (A contemporary gloss on the doublet might be "working poor" and "homeless.") "The absolute pauper," writes Victor Ehrenberg, "the wholly destitute, was called a 'beggar', and he was treated not with pity and charity, but with contempt."[20] This contempt, however, was not reserved entirely for the indigent and the laborer: the *nouveaux riches* came in for abuse and suspicion as well, on account of their alleged contempt for their origins, their vulgarity, their cowardice, and their affinity for tyrants,[21] though they might try to disguise themselves:

> As far as fortunes in land are concerned, it is noteworthy that the *nouveaux riches* in Athens in the fourth century tended to take over the aristocratic values of the social élite once they had reached the top. Pasion, after making his fortune and becoming a citizen, eagerly acquired estates which conferred on him the social respectability reserved to landowners.[22]

Money occupied, then, in late fifth- and early fourth-century Athens, an ambiguous position. Furthermore, the destruction of the country-side wreaked by years of battle had had a direct effect on Attic farmers, driving them to abandon their traditional lives and to swell the ranks of an already over-burdened and maligned urban poor. In his monograph on the late Aristophanes and his social milieu, E. David describes the period thus:

> The agrarian sector of the economy had the most ruinous damage inflicted on it, although other sectors too, especially mining, were, for a time, seriously affected. However, those who suffered most, economically, were the farmers, owners of small or moderate estates, who constituted a kind of agrarian middle class. These social elements, which had previously formed one of the cornerstones of economic stability in Attika and elsewhere, were now faced with difficulties with which, in many cases, they could not cope. Many of them lost all hope of improving the situation in their fields. Some were compelled to sell their estates; others could not even do that, since their land was in such poor condition as a result of the devastation caused by the war: as a result they decided to abandon it. Those who had tried, in spite of everything, to rehabilitate themselves by means of loans were often hopelessly burdened with debt and, sooner or later, became paupers. After having abandoned, sold or lost their land, these agrarian elements were to join the ranks of the agricultural or urban proletariat. Some of them were compelled to work for low salaries, others were unemployed, since the cheap labour force of the slaves was often preferred to that of freemen.[23]

Hence the moral ambivalence of Aristophanes' representation of the squalid, wandering, urban[24] god of Wealth, distributing his largesse to those least deserving of it, because he has been blinded by Zeus for his offensive boasting (vv. 87-92); by contrast, the goddess of Peace is represented as beautiful, immobile, and agrarian, incapable of even the corrupted beneficial agency of Wealth in her thrall to the jealous god of War, but certainly invested with a pristine if earthy allure unavailable to her pecuniary counterpart.[25] This distinction has not been lost on commentators. Thus van Leeuwen likens the entrance of the goddess Peace, at v. 523, to that of the great epic heroines,[26] while the god of Wealth is likened by Victor Ehrenberg to "not only a beggar, but a sort of money machine."[27] Gustav Droysen is, like van Leeuwen, ingratiating in his description of the monumental goddess Peace and her attendants ("Mit der Göttin Eirene kehren wieder die Opora und Theoria, diese beiden sind wirkliche Frauenzimmerchen, während die Göttin Frieden ein Colossalbild ist . . .),[28] while his note on the appearance of Wealth tends to the anti-Semitic in its overly vivid exegesis ("Ein Gelehrter meint, schon damals seien die Juden in die Welt zerstreut gewesen, und der Reichtum sei gewiß ein alter reicher Jude"), thus continuing and updating the tradition of an ambivalent literary representation of wealth.[29]

In this representational difference we may read a difference in status between landed and moneyed wealth, and indeed between property as constituted by land, and property as constituted by money. Victor Ehrenberg calls this last "invisible wealth," after the phrase ἀφανής πλοῦτος at *Ecclesiazusae* 603, "a general contrast to 'visible' property such as fields and houses."[30] "The popular opinion," he writes,

> was that people with 'invisible wealth', that is capital on loan, had gained their money by perjury. . . . Wealth had always been an indispensable attribute of the aristocracy, but that was wealth inherited, not earned, and for a long time it had consisted of fields and houses rather than money. . . . The social changes which began, as Theognis shows, as early as the sixth century, and which still dominated the age of Old Comedy, also changed the general views about property and income.[31]

Mobile credit and monetary wealth may have been associated with dissembling, hiding, and invisibility, but on the fifth- to fourth-century Athenian comic stage the figure of Ploutos was to be made visible in such a way as to highlight this distinction, and to play on its role in the ongoing transformation of a traditional society.

Hermes and Method

This social transformation, from the power of landed wealth to that of newly acquired wealth, is interestingly reflected in the two plays under discussion by their differing representations of the divine order, whose theatrical treatment is always a good index of socio-political position in Aristophanes.[32] In particular, attention in the *Peace* and the *Plutus* is drawn to the god Hermes, a figure central to ancient constructions of social space, interaction, mobility, and exchange, symbolic as well as actual.[33] Hermes appears in both plays, alone among traditional pantheon-gods:[34] centrally in the *Peace* (vv. 180-235 and 361-728) and in an extended coda to the action of the *Plutus* (vv. 1099-1170); apart from these places, his appearance in the Aristophanic corpus is limited to a disputed walk-on at the very end of the *Clouds* and miscellaneous invocations in four other plays.[35] The presence in the two plays under discussion of Hermes, god of exchange and manipulation, points to the involvement of these two texts in the contemporary drama of social upheaval, for Hermes is himself, as remarked, a consummate figure of change: "Présent au milieu des hommes, Hermès est en même temps insaisissable, ubiquitaire. Jamais là où il est, il apparaît soudainement pour disparaître."[36] The god's counter-revolutionary loyalty to Zeus's tyrannical order is enshrined in the *Prometheus Bound*, where he taunts the rebellious Titan and counsels accomodation to his father's regime (vv. 944-end);[37] but the possibility of the mythological figure's own adaptation to social change, human or divine, is summed up well by Laurence Kahn in her study of Homer's *Hymn to Hermes*, in a reflection on the *Hymn*'s depiction of Hermes having himself to win his prestige from his father Zeus:

> Ce mythe, outre qu'il évoque la possibilité ténue de transgresser ce qui semble séparé à jamais, en l'occurrence pour Hermès de franchir la limite infranchissable qui distingue le monde des dieux du monde des hommes, fixe l'accidentel et le fugace dans le champ des forces qui organise la quotidienneté des activités et des affects, pour les définir, leur faire clairement place, leur affecter un signe: Hermès.[38]

Hermes, then, is a complex and pivotal figure in the economics of Greek mythology, subsuming under his cult-personae as he does so many diverse aspects of classical social organisation, including the relatively diverse provinces of commercial exchange and guidance of the dead.[39] He is also, of course, involved in elementary land-property demarcation: he is associated with (or perhaps indeed derived from) the cairn-like boundary-markers known as "herms" ('Ερμαῖ), introduced at Athens by Pisistratus in the late sixth century "to mark the midway points between the various Attic villages and the Athenian agora."[40]

Hermes' changing mythological status in these two plays, particularly in the *Plutus*, reflects some of the material change being wrought in Greek society of the late fifth and early fourth centuries B.C.E. by the pressures of war and population. An examination of Hermes' role will then lead into a consideration of the plays' central allegorical figures, Peace and her attendants, and Wealth, figures who play an important role in the mythological mediation of social conditions carried out by their respective, eponymous comedies. The figure of Hermes may be read as a positive critique of the existing Athenian regime, while Peace and Wealth, reifications of popular discontent and hopes for change, are rather to be seen as negative in their implicit insertion into a political strategy of containment, designed to preempt and defuse that discontent; a careful reading may reveal the hope for social change nevertheless still latent in those figures. In the case of the two plays by Aristophanes under discussion here, it will be argued that the turn from the Hermes represented in the *Peace* to that in the *Plutus* represents an evolution in the positive critique of existing social inequities; the reification of peace and prosperity, while seeming at first glance to effect a salvational overturning of hierarchies and the establishment of a new order, actually works, especially in the *Plutus*, as a negative support for the status quo, as a regressive strategy of containment.

The terms "positive" and "negative" critiques, and "strategy of containment," used in the remarks above, are borrowed from Fredric

Jameson's notion of a "double hermeneutic," as specifically applied to classical texts by Peter W. Rose in *Sons of the Gods, Children of Earth*.[41] Rose's thinking arises from a committed engagement with the historical theories of Marx and his intellectual heirs, but it is a fundamental discomfort with the apparently rigid Marxist formulation of the one-way materialist cause for social ideology that leads Rose to adapt Jameson's rethinkings of Marx to his project. "Jameson's more openly dialectical conception of the process of ideological struggle offers the most meaningful way out of the depressing either/or designation of particular classical authors as 'good guys' or 'bad guys' which has . . . characterized much of previous Marxist or even loosely political readings of the classics," writes Rose.[42] Drawing on the hermeneutic method associated with the Frankfurt School thinkers and elaborated by Jameson in his *Marxism and Form* (Princeton: Princeton U. P., 1971),[43] Rose outlines his ideas for the investigation of a classical text's relation to the power structure of its time, its implicit challenges to that power, and the strategies it may employ to contain those challenges. What follows here is an attempt to introduce Marx into the problematics of my discussion, with a consideration of the way Rose's Jamesonian views can be used to understand the workings of Aristophanes' social criticism.[44]

In the passage from which the epigram to this chapter is drawn, from the introduction to his *Grundrisse* of 1857-8, Marx is in the process of analyzing the relation of the means of production available at a given historical period with the forms of art produced by that period. The passage runs in full:

> It is well known that Greek mythology is not only the arsenal of Greek art but also its foundation. Is the view of nature and of social relations on which the Greek imagination and hence Greek [mythology] is based possible with self-acting mule spindles and railways and locomotives and electrical telegraphs? What chance has Vulcan against Roberts & Co., Jupiter against the lightning-rod and Hermes against the *crédit mobilier*? All mythology overcomes and dominates and shapes the forces of nature in the imagination and by the imagination; it therefore vanishes with the advent of real mastery over them.[45]

Setting aside the obvious persistence of mythologies of one kind or another in an age of the aggressive mastery of nature, Marx's observation seems in line with the tenets of the mythologist: first, that there is a clear interdependence between Greek mythology and Greek art; and second, that mythology is informed by geographic, economic, and social realia, all of which, being themselves subject to change, bring about an eventual mutation of the mythology they have helped to shape. Here is a certain formulation of the historical-materialist doctrine of base-and-superstructure, whereby the totality of economic relations of production in a given society is held to give rise in turn to that society's political and intellectual life process. Terry Eagleton, in *The Ideology of the Aesthetic*, describes the doctrine evocatively:

> The story Marxism has to tell is a classically hubristic tale of how the human body, through those extensions of itself we call society and technology, comes to overreach itself and bring itself to nothing, abstracting its own sensuous wealth to a cypher in the act of converting the world into its own bodily organ. That this tragedy should occur is not, of course, a mere question of technological overweening but of the social conditions within which such technological development takes place. Since these are conditions of struggle, in which the fruits of labour are fiercely contested, there is need for a range of social institutions which will have, among other functions, the task of regulating and stabilizing these otherwise destructive conflicts. The mechanisms by which this can be accomplished -- repression, sublimation, idealization, disavowal -- are as familiar to psychoanalytical as to political discourse. Yet the strife over the appropriation and control of the body's powers is not so easily quelled, and will inscribe itself within the very institutions which seek to repress it. Indeed this struggle is so urgent and unremitting that it ballasts the whole of that institutional history, warping it out of true and skewing it out of shape. This process, whereby a contention over the body's powers comes to trace our intellectual and institutional life to its roots, is known to Marxism as the doctrine of base and superstructure. Like the neurotic symptom, a superstructure is that place where the repressed body succeeds in manifesting itself, for those who can read the signs.[46]

According to this psycho-pathological interpretation, then, the superstructure is merely the record of the always-prior struggles of human economic history, but a record that will tend to claim for itself, for a variety of ideological reasons, a causal priority to that history. In the passage cited above from the *Grundrisse*, actual technology -- the whole production-relationally conditioned chain of invention leading up to, and beyond, Roberts & Co., the lightning-conductor, and the *crédit mobilier* -- represents this "base" of economic history, while the place of the "superstructure" is taken by Vulcan, Jupiter, and Hermes -- by mythology.

The Hermes of the *Peace* is an ambiguous character, invested at once with the lowly position of caretaker of the gods' property, and of sole representative of the divine order that has cynically turned over management of human affairs to War and Battle-Din.[47] His authoritative explanation of the situation to Trygaeus follows the comic bathos of his own diminished function:

TP. Πῶς οὖν σὺ δῆτ' ἐνταῦθα κατελείφθης μόνος;

ΕΡ. Τὰ λοιπὰ τηρῶ σκευάρια τὰ τῶν θεῶν.
χυτρίδια καὶ σανίδια κἀμφορείδια.

TRYG: However did you come to be left here alone?
HERM: I'm guarding the rest of the gods' utensils,
Their potlets, little plates and little amphorae. (vv. 200-203)

The laughable nature of these details is recalled later on in the play, when Trygaeus is making ready to install the statue of the goddess Peace with a ritual sacrifice. In an exchange with one of his slaves, he suggests making the sacrifice with common pots as offertory objects; when the servant protests, scandalized, that such an offering would be worthy rather of Hermes than of Peace, the quotidian diminutive has made its way from the utensils to the god's name:

ΟΙ. Ἄγε δή, τί νῷν ἐντευθενὶ ποητέον;
ΤΡ. Τί δ' ἄλλο γ' ἢ ταύτην χύτραις ἱδρυτέον;
ΟΙ. Χύτραισιν, ὥσπερ μεμφόμενον Ἑρμῄδιον;

SLAVE: Well then, what should we do now?
TRYG: What else but install the goddess with offerings of pots?
SLAVE: With pots, like for that blamed little Hermes? (vv.922-4)

The diminutive here employed, Ἑρμῄδιον, is a near-*hapax* in the Aristophanic corpus, the only other use being at v. 382 of the present play;[48] significantly, the appellation is there used not contemptuously but in obsequious beseechment, as Trygaeus begs Hermes not to expose his seditious arrival on Olympus to the rest of the gods:

ΕΡ. Ἀλλ', ὦ μέλ', ὑπὸ τοῦ Διὸς ἀμαλδυνθήσομαι,
εἰ μὴ τετορήσω ταῦτα καὶ λακήσομαι.
ΤΡ. Μή νυν λακήσῃς, λίσσομαί σ', Ὡρμῄδιον.

HERM: But, my good man, I'll be crushed by Zeus
If I do not proclaim in ringing tones these events.
TRYG: Please don't proclaim, I pray, oh little Hermes. (vv.380-2)[49]

Between these two diminutives lies much of the comedy's main action. This consists principally in the unearthing and re-establishment of Peace, Harvest, and Festival, an action in which Hermes plays a central role, initially as would-be inhibitor of Trygaeus' Great Idea,[50] and then as alternating straight-man and buffoon as he and Trygaeus expound in call-and-response a comic history of the events leading to the disappearance of the goddess Peace (vv. 603-648). Thus the multiplicity of Hermes' functions is highlighted and exploited by the plot of the *Peace*, as he is presented both in his aspect of sinister harbinger of death to overweening mortals at the punishing hands of Zeus, and of enlightened sponsor of human ingenuity.[51]

For all that Hermes is present in the *Peace* under more than one aspect, however, the element of his cultic personality not notably exploited there is his patronage of market exchange and commercial transactions; his philanthropy in the *Peace* seems largely rustic, as for instance in his appeasement by Trygaeus at vv. 192-3, where he alters his harsh tone in response to the offer of a piece of meat, disregarding the special urban terminology of the credentials listed by Trygaeus.[52] Nevertheless, his support for the excavation of Peace is finally won with a promise of civic cultic titles, with the decisive addition of a golden drinking-cup. Trygaeus has been telling Hermes about an alleged conspiracy on the part of the Sun and the Moon to abandon Greece for the barbarians: this will endanger the gods' food supply, and Hermes' assistance in securing peace for the Greeks would therefore be in his own best interest.[53]   What more directly influences Hermes is the list of honors to be granted him for his compliance; the golden drinking-cup offered him only supplementarily clinches the deal:

TP. . . . Καὶ σοὶ τὰ μεγάλ' ἡμεῖς Παναθήναι' ἄξομεν
     πάσας τε τὰς ἄλλας τελετὰς τὰς τῶν θεῶν.
     Μυστήρι' Ἑρμῇ. Διπολίει'. Ἀδώνια·
     ἄλλαι τέ σοι πόλεις πεπαυμέναι κακῶν
     Ἀλεξικάκῳ θύσουσιν Ἑρμῇ πανταχοῦ.
     Χἄτερ' ἔτι πόλλ' ἕξεις ἀγαθά. Πρῶτον δέ σοι
     δῶρον δίδωμι τήνδ'. ἵνα σπένδειν ἔχῃς.
EP. Οἴμ' ὡς ἐλεήμων εἴμ' ἀεὶ τῶν χρυσίδων.

TRYG: . . . And we shall celebrate in your honor the Great
                Panathenaea,
          As well as all the other rites of the gods: in honor of Hermes
          The Mysteries, the Dipolieia, and the Adonia;
          And the rest of the cities, delivered from their troubles,
          Will sacrifice to Hermes the Warder-off of Evils,
                everywhere.
          And you will have still other boons. But first
          I give you this gift, that you may make libations.
HERM: Oh, how I do ever feel for golden vessels! (vv.418-425)[54]

Hermes' price, finally, is a mundane artifact, a gold plate or cup, one that may lend the elegance of symposiastic luxury but is here essentially just the occasion for a piece of animistic buffoonery on a par with Dicaeopolis' threats against the charcoal in the *Acharnians*, vv. 331 ff., and the women's anxieties about the wineskin in the *Thesmophoriazusae*, vv. 689 ff.[55] What is effected in the end by the rustic Hermes' appropriation of the various civic festivals is not a revolution in socio-economic life, but a regression to a primitive time before the rise of the need for money: the romance of a utopia, a free feed, an imaginary symbiosis with the beneficent rustic life-world.[56] The imagery with which Trygaeus greets the emerging goddess and her attendants (vv. 520-55) is full of the language of the good old days, of agricultural abundance and rustic celebration, and not of gold and riches.[57] There is of course mention of money as such in the *Peace*, but it is limited for the most part to jokes on Trygaeus' part concerning the desperate straits that have prompted his excursion (vv. 119-21, 169-72, 253-4, and 374-5); significantly, upon Trygaeus' return to Earth, his Slave dismisses the gods in monetary terms: Οὐκ ἂν ἔτι δοίην τῶν θεῶν τριώβολον, / εἰ πορνοβοσκοῦσ' ὥσπερ ἡμεῖς οἱ βροτοί (vv. 848-9, "I wouldn't give three obols for the gods any longer, if they pimp the way we mortals do"). The gods are ruled defunct and outside the system of exchange, even as that system is made largely unnecessary by the restoration of idyllic, "old" Peace. There are of course also the sickle-maker's remarks, at vv. 1199-1202 and ff., on the financial improvement in his business since the restoration of peace, and the weapon-maker's complaints about the decline in his (vv. 1210 ff.). But Trygaeus soon shows that his restored Golden Age operates according to an alchemical or magical rather than a monetary economy, one whereby commodities are transformed or sublated directly one into another, without an intermediary exchange-value stage.[58] The hymenaeal song that ends the comedy places the play back firmly into an ahistoric, pre-monetary countryside.[59] When Trygaeus exhorts the Chorus at the beginning of the exodos to "pray to the gods to grant wealth (πλοῦτον) to the Hellenes, and to provide us all equally with lots of barley and wine, and figs to munch, and women to bear children for us," vv. 1320-5, the uncanny allegorical force of the eponymous figure of the *Plutus* is missing; instead the word seems to be a transparent synecdoche for the agricultural goods listed.[60]

Thus in the *Peace* Hermes is overhonored with cultic titles stolen from the deposed and defunct gods and bribed with a piece of valuable handicraft, a commodity but nevertheless a primitive exchange item; he is to be maintained in the restored Golden Age since he has been revealed as an avatar of the ancient rustic order.[61] In the *Plutus*, on the other hand, he is himself sublated, erased but preserved in a new form: divested of almost all of his cultic functions (although he is the single one of the old gods to be kept on at all in the new dispensation) and supplanted (or perhaps supplemented) by a more sophisticated monetary system: not quite the *crédit mobilier* but a step towards establishing exchange-value as finally transcendent of use-value and rendering at least potential the social equality made possible by such a system.[62] Marx writes, in a discussion of the *Nicomachean Ethics*, of the developing interest in and understanding of this phenomenon as the fourth century wore on:

Aristotle himself was unable to extract this fact, that, in the form of commodity-values, all labour is expressed as equal human labour and therefore as labour of equal quality, by inspection from the form of value, because Greek society was founded on the labour of slaves, hence had as its natural basis the inequality of men and of their labour-powers. The secret of the expression of value, namely the equality and equivalence of all kinds of labour because and in so far as they are human labour in general, could not be deciphered until the concept of human equality had already acquired the permanence of a fixed popular opinion. This however becomes possible only in a society where the commodity-form is the universal form of the product of labour, hence the dominant social relation is the relation between men as possessors of commodities.   Aristotle's genius is displayed precisely by his discovery of a relation of equality in the value-expression of commodities.   Only the historical limitation inherent in the society in which he lived alone prevented him from finding out what 'in reality' this relation of equality consisted of.[63]

What will become clear in the following discussion of the *Plutus* is that the ground is there laid for the representation of just such an equality, even as the discontent felt by Aristophanes' audience at contemporary social inequalities is defused or recontained by means of the very strategies of fantasy that gratify that same audience's desire for pleasure.

Hermes appears in the *Plutus* in a role far less central than the one he fills in the *Peace*. The entire scene, vv. 1097-1170, one of a series of tableaux following the establishment of Wealth, now no longer blind, is a modified iambic trimeter stichomythy with Chremylus' slave Karion; it forms a calm set-piece between the slapstick bawdiness of the Old Woman and her Young Man and the conventional scene of a destitute Priest, one that merges with the sexual episode to end the comedy.   As in the *Peace*, Hermes is at first present in his messenger-of-the-gods aspect, specifically as the bearer of threats from Zeus to overweening mortals.   The language is reminiscent of the scene from the *Prometheus Bound* referred to above (vv. 994 ff.) where Hermes relays Zeus's threats, reminiscent indeed as well of the god's communication of War's plan to grind up the cities of Greece in a mortar at *Peace* vv. 228 ff.   Here, however, there is a twist to the reception given the threats, since Hermes appears after the realization of the Great Idea and is not needed as an accomplice in its performance. After some perfunctory stage business, the exchange proper begins:

EP.   Ὁ Ζεὺς. ὦ πόνηρε. βούλεται
         εἰς ταὐτὸν ὑμᾶς συγκυκήσας τρύβλιον
         ἀπαξάπαντας εἰς τὸ βάραθρον ἐμβαλεῖν.
KA.   Ἡ γλῶττα τῷ κήρυκι τούτων τέμνεται.

HERM: Zeus, you wretch, wants
          To mix you all together up into
          The same bowl, and hurl you to the deep.
KARI: One cuts off the tongue of the bearer of such news.

                                            (vv. 1107-10)

Here Hermes' threats are met immediately with derision, as against
Peace vv. 228 ff., where Trygaeus despairs upon hearing of War's plan.
The derision goes to the extreme of suggesting violence to the god, a
violence also reminiscent of that practiced on the sacrificial victim (cf.
Peace v. 1060: Ἡ γλῶττα χωρὶς τέμνεται, "One cuts off the tongue
separately," spoken by Hierocles to Trygaeus and his Slave as they
sacrifice to Peace; cf. also *Birds* v. 1705).[64]   Karion does not in fact
offer violence to the god, but listens instead to Hermes' complaint of
deprivation under the new regime, one in which mortals no longer need
to sacrifice to the gods. He is admiring of Hermes' self-centeredness in
caring only for his own welfare amid the general divine crisis (EP. Καὶ
τῶν μὲν ἄλλων μοι θεῶν ἧττον μέλει, / ἐγὼ δ' ἀπόλωλα
κἀπιτέτριμμαι. ΚΑ. Σωφρονεῖς, "HERM: I'm not so concerned
about the other gods, / But I've had it, I'm screwed.[65] KARI: Sensible
of you"), and elicits from the god a nostalgic remembrance of the
offerings once proper to Hermes. Soon however Karion is back to his
raillery, forcing Hermes into the unusual role of recalling his past
beneficence to mortals with an eye to extracting material favors from
them -- a sort of reverse *do ut des*. But Karion refuses all of Hermes'
fawning and exacts from him instead an earnest of his desertion from
the Olympian ranks. Significantly, the witticism with which Karion
responds to Hermes' readiness to leave the gods for a better life among
the newly rich mortals styles this desertion "urban" (ἀστεῖον), an
adjectival form of the name for the Greek town proper, as against the
surrounding fields; it possesses approximately the same aesthetic
nuance, as well as what might be called the same semantic opacity, as
the English doublet "urban/urbane."[66]

ΚΑ. Ἔπειτ' ἀπολιπὼν τοὺς θεοὺς ἐνθάδε μενεῖς;
ΕΡ. Τὰ γὰρ παρ' ὑμῖν ἐστι βελτίω πολύ.
ΚΑ. Τί δέ; ταὐτομολεῖν ἀστεῖον εἶναί σοι δοκεῖ;

KARI: Then you wish to desert the gods and stay here?
HERM: Well, things are going much better with you.
KARI: So! You think desertion is witty, do you? (vv. 1148-50)

The word is used in mockery, of course, as a bathetic send-up of a sort
of "dulce et decorum est pro patria mori" *avant la lettre*; indeed, Hermes
caps Karion's perverted sentiment with the pragmatically unpatriotic

Πατρὶς γάρ ἐστι πᾶσ' ἵν' ἂν πράττῃ τις εὖ, "The fatherland is wherever one prospers" (v. 1151). There follows (vv. 1152-63) a series of suggestions on Hermes' part for the possible roles he might play in the new mortal economy. These roles are all traditional aspects of the god, institutionalized either in poetry, or in the very fabric of city-life. They are: Στροφαῖος, the Hinge-God or herm, posted outside a house's outer door; Ἐμπολαῖος, the Commerce-God; Δόλιος, the God of Craft and Deceitfulness, one of his commonest titles in tragedy as in comedy; Ἡγεμόνιος, the Guide-God, dream-bringer and psychopomp; and Ἐναγώνιος, the Games-God, addressed under this aspect by Aeschylus and Pindar among others.[67] Karion rejects each suggestion but the last, perverting the titles instead into *jeux d'esprit*: he plays on the twisty turpitude of the first, glosses the second with the vulgar παλιγκάπηλος or "retailer of imported produce," pulls a straight face at the suggestion that deceit will play any part in the "simple ways" (ἁπλῶν τρόπων) to come, and reduces the complex role of Hermes in the supernatural, the oneiric, and the communicative (or "hermeneutic") to a joke on the god of Wealth's restored vision (vv. 1153-60). The last of the epithets, Ἐναγώνιος or Games-God, Karion accepts: he is won over by Hermes' especially lavish cozening, but has the last word even so, as he transforms that cult-title too into little more than a form of livery.[68] The passage runs in full:

> EP. Ἐναγώνιος τοίνυν ἔσομαι. Καὶ τί ἔτ' ἐρεῖς;
> Πλούτῳ γάρ ἐστι τοῦτο συμφορώτατον.
> ποεῖν ἀγῶνας μουσικοὺς καὶ γυμνικούς.
> KA. Ὡς ἀγαθόν ἐστ' ἐπωνυμίας πολλὰς ἔχειν.
> Οὗτος γὰρ ἐξηύρηκεν αὑτῷ βιότιον.
> Οὐκ ἐτὸς ἅπαντες οἱ δικάζοντες θαμὰ
> σπεύδουσιν ἐν πολλοῖς γεγράφθαι γράμμασιν.
> EP. Οὐκοῦν ἐπὶ τούτοις εἴσίω;
> KA.   Καὶ πλῦνέ γε
> αὐτὸς προσελθὼν πρὸς τὸ φρέαρ τὰς κοιλίας.
> ἵν' εὐθέως διακονικὸς εἶναι δοκῇς.

HERM: The Games-God? What do you say now?
      For it's most advantageous for Wealth
      To set up artistic and athletic contests.
KARI: How good it is to have a lot of surnames!
      He's found himself a livelihood with that one.
      No wonder all our judges often rush
      To inscribe their names in many rolls.
HERM: Then it's agreed, I go in?
KARI: Yes, and wash the tripes
      Carefully at the well yourself,

To show right off you're a useful fellow. (vv.1161-70)

But Hermes Games-God does not last long in that aspect: he is
quickly reduced (vv. 1168-70) to carrying out the sacrificial porter's
duties that were burdening Karion at the play's beginning.[69] The scene
that follows, and which ends the play, has been criticised by
commentators for its lackluster, anti-climactic tone;[70] it is true that the
joke that ends the play, at vv. 1204-7, immediately before the
Choryphaeus' valedictory two-line hortative, is weak. It is a mere pun
on the polyvalence of the word γραῦς, which can mean "old woman"
or "skin on boiled milk," as the Old Woman of the earlier scenes helps
to carry offertory pots (χύτραι) into Chremylus' house for the
dedication of Wealth, and it is observed that, in this exceptional case,
the "scum" is on the *bottom* of the pot, rather than on the *top*.

But this anemic coda does serve to recall two themes. One is the
means of dedication rejected at *Peace* vv. 923-4 as fit only for "damned
little Hermes," recalled here by the pots intended for Wealth, onto
which attention is focused through this rather labored play on words.
The other is the plight of the Old Woman, who has been promised the
love of the Young Man at v. 1202, but whose predicament -- she is
undesirable now as a lover now that all are rich and no longer in need
of money in return for gigolo services -- is re-emphasized with this
likening to skin on boiled milk.[71] The new state of social relations
parodied in the interaction of the Old Woman and her erstwhile swain is
crucial to the utopian transformation of society envisioned in the
Plutus, and will be discussed below, as will the means of dedication
chosen. Where it leaves Hermes is more simply put: the God of
Exchange has been definitively displaced by the new dispensation,
which, if not the *crédit mobilier*, at least suggests the possibility of a
new theory of value based on labor, as sketched by Marx in the passage
from *Capital* quoted above. Whereas in the *Peace* Hermes is
overestimated, however ambivalently, with his commercial and
criminal aspects firmly in place (or perhaps assimilated to the rural
landscape) as the play closes, in the *Plutus* he has been supplanted by a
sort of ethico-economic revolution. He began in the *Peace* as the
tender of the gods' pots (σκευάρια) and ended as the possessor of all
their honors; in the *Plutus* he begins as a suppliant amongst the
mortals and ends as the attendant to their novel sacrifices. The role of
Hermes in the *Peace* is unmasked as that of the ancient god of rustic
exchange in an economy of scarcity and class disparities, and he is
thereby re-affirmed in this position; with Chremylus' new dispensation
of wealth in the *Plutus* to all who deserve it (i.e., to those who were
formerly poor and therefore virtuous), a new, more sophisticated
economy has come into play, based no longer on bare need and
craftiness, but on ethical considerations of value.[72]

Peace and Wealth: Allegory, Recontainment, Possibility

At the same time, this dream of equality of labor is short-circuited or "recontained" by the continuing traces of slavery and unfreedom marring Chremylus' utopia. Indeed, unfreedom is inscribed in the very image or allegory of Wealth as presented in the *Plutus*, which will now be considered against the central allegory of the *Peace* and against the allegory of Poverty also contained in the *Plutus* in order to show how Aristophanes simultaneously works his subtle critique and his insistent maintenance of the status quo.

The term "allegory" as used above is perhaps in need of a brief exegesis. Theorists of medieval, renaissance, and modern literature have tended to reserve its field to that of the parable or enigma, the encoded text that manages to tell two quite distinct stories at once, one manifest and the other latent.[73] Scholars of classical literature, despite enjoying first-hand usufruct of the principal texts for such a definition,[74] have tended to be looser in their use of the term, allowing a certain slippage between "allegory" and "personification" (προσωποποιία, a "making of a mask" or πρόσωπον, translated directly by the Latin *persona*), the rhetorical and dramatic practice of giving imaginary voice and countenance to a fictive or dead person, an idea, or an inanimate object.[75] The resistance of critics of modern literatures to extend the term "allegory" to such a practice has to do with a wish to distinguish clearly between metaphor and allegory and not simply to posit allegory as an extended metaphor.[76] This resistance can perhaps be seen as a reaction to the systematic critical undervaluing of allegory as a form since the middle ages, culminating in unsympathetic treatment by Goethe and Hegel, and brought back to sophisticated currency by Walter Benjamin, among others.[77] Personification considered by these new lights, then, resembles exactly the rejected model of the extended metaphor: "Man kann formulieren," writes Gerhard Kurz in *Metapher, Allegorie, Symbol*, "daß (viele) Personifikationen auf der *Reifikation* metaphorischer Bedeutung beruhen,"[78] where "reification" describes the bringing to life of an inanimate object or concept through its insertion in a specific grammatical context.[79] Such a "reification" lacks for modern theorists the productive ambiguity of the proper allegory, which is capable of a polyvalence of interpretation by virtue of its two independent yet interconnected levels, its "text" and its "pretext."[80]

It will become clear, however, that the rhetorical process at work in the Aristophanic comedies under consideration here is indeed capable of a polyvalent interpretation, albeit one that tends rather to exhaust than to amplify the interconnection of text and pretext: the novel bringing to life of the newly reified forms of relations constituting Wealth, in other words, draws on a previously existing mythical personification. The literary bringing to life of an abstraction, or of a social institution, performed as it was within a traditional society, can be seen as a response to social conditions changing under the pressures of history, a response that lends to the reified form of social relations (in the case of the *Plutus*, a burgeoning money economy personified by the god of Wealth) a certain mechanical novelty borrowed from the old systems of traditional superstition.[81] We may call these figures allegorical insofar as they admit of more than one reading: a meliorative interpretation, stressing the new chances for the individual's control of and participation in prosperity, and a pejorative interpretation, emphasizing the degree to which the figure reformulates certain features of the former system, and thus effectively recontains revolutionary energies. In the case of the *Plutus*, these varying interpretations will depend largely on the degree to which the figure of Wealth crosses the line between a simple metaphor for the empowering equality of an economy that recognizes the value of labor, and the monstrosity of a semi-autonomous, wandering currency, finally undecidable in ethical terms and inextricable from the history of slavery and unfreedom from which it springs.

In a commentary on Marx's *Economic and Philosophical Manuscripts*, Terry Eagleton produces this striking gloss:

> Capital is a phantasmal body, a monstrous Doppelgänger which stalks abroad while its master sleeps, mechanically consuming the pleasures he austerely forgoes. The more the capitalist forswears his self-delight, devoting his labours instead to the fashioning of this zombie-like alter ego, the more second-hand fulfilments he is able to reap. Both capitalist and capital are images of the living dead, the one animate yet anaesthetized, the other inanimate yet active.[82]

While the economic situation of Chremylus and his companions in Aristophanes' comedy is certainly not that of the modern capitalist, it will be seen that the figuration of that situation shares some features with the description offered by Eagleton here. It remains only to contrast the figures of Peace and Wealth as represented in the two eponymous plays to begin to demonstrate these features.

Peace and the Countryside

Katherine Lever, a principal advocate of allegorical readings of Aristophanes' personifications,[83] has divided the relevant characters of the Aristophanic corpus into three categories: silent figures, such as the Σπονδαί or Truce of the *Knights*, Εἰρήνη, Ὀπώρα and Θεωρία or Peace, Harvest and Festival of the *Peace*, and Βασιλεία or Royalty of

the *Birds*;[84] speaking embodiments, such as Δῆμος or The People of
the *Knights*, Πόλεμος and Κυδοιμός or War and Panic of the *Peace*, the
two Arguments (Δίκαιος and Ἄδικος Λόγοι) of the *Clouds*, and
Πλοῦτος and Πενία or Wealth and Poverty of the *Plutus*; and human
characters with significant names, such as Δικαιόπολις or Just City of
the *Acharnians*, and Πραξαγόρα or Effective-in-the-Market of the
Ecclesiazusae.[85] Such a classification may help to suggest the didactic
nature of all of these characters, grouping them as it does according to
their relative ability to speak and thus to relay a message. In the case
of the latter two groups the manifest message is explicit, literally
spoken by the characters so designated, as well as being suggested by
their reception in their various dramatic contexts. In the case of the
first group, the mute characters, the significance of their figuration
relies entirely on their respective contexts, and on the reactions of the
comedies' other *dramatis personae*.[86]

Peace, Harvest, and Festival are obviously such silent characters.[87]
Their participation in the action of the *Peace* is, as noted above, limited
to their rescue by Trygaeus and company from War's clutches at vv.
520 ff., Harvest's espousal to Trygaeus at vv. 706 ff., Peace's serving
as a means of descent to Earth at vv. 725-8, Festival's presentation to
the Council at vv. 846-909, the sacrifice to Peace at vv. 922-1126,
including the discomfiting of the ἀλάζων or charlatan character
Hierocles, and Trygaeus' formal marriage to Harvest at vv. 1316-end.
They are uniformly treated as passive instruments of use and
enjoyment, most egregiously in the long passage of sexual *double
entendre* with which Trygaeus hands over Festival to the Council at
vv. 884-909.[88] Indeed, as noted above, there is some suggestion that
the figure of Peace herself was just that, a "'gigantic figure' . . .
probably only the head and bust of the goddess, so disposed that its
mouth was on a level with, and could talk into, Hermes' ear."[89]
Harvest and Festival seem to require live representation,[90] if only to
provide objective correlatives to the obscenities at vv. 891-2, 1339 and
elsewhere.

The passage in which Peace, Harvest, and Festival are finally dragged
up out of their cave by Trygaeus and his somewhat diminished
Panhellenic band (vv. 520 ff.) is of great interest, introducing as it does
the salient features of Peace as allegory. Trygaeus greets the emerging
figures with a formal speech of welcome and olfactory description,
interrupted twice by the stock buffoonery of Hermes:

TP. Ὦ πότνια βοτρυόδωρε, τί προσείπω σ' ἔπος·
Πόθεν ἂν λάβοιμι ῥῆμα μυριάμφορον
ὅτῳ προσείπω σ'· Οὐ γὰρ εἶχον οἴκοθεν.
Ὦ χαῖρ'. Ὀπώρα, καὶ σὺ δ', ὦ Θεωρία·
οἷον δ' ἔχεις τὸ πρόσωπον, ὦ Θεωρία·

οἶον δὲ πνεῖς, ὡς ἡδὺ κατὰ τῆς καρδίας,
γλυκύτατον, ὥσπερ ἀστρατείας καὶ μύρου.
EP. Μῶν οὖν ὅμοιον καὶ γυλιοῦ στρατιωτικοῦ;
TP. Ἀπέπτυσ' ἐχθροῦ φωτὸς ἔχθιστον πλέκος.
Τοῦ μὲν γὰρ ὄζει κρομμυοξυρεγμίας,
ταύτης δ' ὀπώρας, ὑποδοχῆς, Διονυσίων,
αὐλῶν, τραγῳδῶν, Σοφοκλέους μελῶν, κιχλῶν,
ἐπυλλίων Εὐριπίδου --
EP. Κλαύσαρα σύ
ταύτης καταψευδόμενος· οὐ γὰρ ἥδεται
αὕτη ποητῇ ῥηματίων δικανικῶν.
TP. κιττοῦ, τρυγοίπου, προβατίων βληχωμένων,
κόλπου γυναικῶν διατρεχουσῶν εἰς ἀγρόν,
δούλης μεθυούσης, ἀνατετραμμένου χοῶς,
ἄλλων τε πολλῶν κἀγαθῶν.

TRYG: O Mistress Grape-Producer, in what terms shall I address you?
Where am I to get a ten-thousand-amphora word
With which to address you? For I haven't any at home.
O hail, Harvest, and you too, o Festival.
What a face you have, o Festival.
And what a breath, how sweet it is to my heart,
Extreme sweet, like military exemption and myrrh!
HERM. You don't mean she smells like a kit-bag?
TRYG. Fie on the wretched satchel of a wretched man!
For he smells of oniony belches,
While she smells of harvest, welcome, the Dionysia,
Flutes, tragedies, the songs of Sophocles, thrushes,
The versicles of Euripides --
HERM.   You'll get in trouble for
Such slander; she doesn't like
A poet who makes legalistic speeches.
TRYG. -- of ivy, the wine-strainer, bleating sheep,
Women's breasts as they run to the field,
Of drunken slave-girl, upturned jug,
And lots of other good things. (vv. 520-538)

There are two textual problems in the above passage, cases in which the manuscript readings are unclear or ambiguous, and where editors have wanted to make emendations. Meineke reads Εἰρήνη φίλη, "dear Peace," for the repetition of ὦ Θεωρία or "o Festival" at v. 524; Blaydes suggests ὦ φίλη θεός, "o dear goddess." The assumption of corruption comes from the oddness of Trygaeus' seeming praise of the goddess's two attendants at the expense of much mention at all of the goddess Peace herself.[91] Similarly, at v. 530, van Leeuwen reads ὀπώρας or "of harvest" as a gloss that has made its way into the text, and suggests βοτρύων, "of grape-bunches." There is some confusion in the text, to be sure: if ὀπώρας is a gloss on ταύτης, how can vv.

530 ff. be read as a reference to Peace at all, no matter how many emendations? Platnauer *ad loc.* complains that "[t]o say that Peace smells of her own attendant, Harvesthome, or even of harvest is very strange;" van Daele and Reckford adapt by simply giving the word a broader translation in this instance than they do when it appears as a name ("la saison des fruits" and "autumn-time" respectively).[92] More serious problems than this synaesthetic potpourri are perhaps the simple ungainliness of the repeated names and the change of Trygaeus' reference from Festival at v. 525, to Peace at v. 530. Furthermore, the list of "odors" at vv. 530-2 seems in fact better suited to Festival than to either of the other two figures, stressing as it does elements of the dramatic festivals (Dionysia, flutes, tragedies, Sophoclean lyrics, Euripides' epyllia). Yet Hermes' bantering interruption at v. 532 makes it clear that the list is motivated partly by the hopes of the bathetic laugh for which it can be played, and when Trygaeus resumes, at vv. 535-8, the items have become resolutely rustic, the props of the comic country-side. Wine, animals, sex: the stage is thus set in the fields or ἀγροί.

After a brief meta-theatrical interlude, in which Trygaeus and Hermes turn to the audience to observe the effects of the goddess's return on the various elements of Greek society ranged there (vv. 538-49), Hermes invites Trygaeus to disband the Attic farmers, who have proved the ablest helpers in the rescue. Trygaeus instead leads off a hymn of praise to the goddess Peace and to the country-side, in which the two are linked in the farmers' nostalgia. Trygaeus begins:

> ΤΡ. Ἀκούετε λεῴ· τοὺς γεωργοὺς ἀπιέναι
> τὰ γεωργικὰ σκεύη λαβόντας εἰς ἀγρὸν
> ὡς τάχιστ' ἄνευ δορατίου καὶ ξίφους κἀκοντίου·
> ὡς ἅπαντ' ἤδη 'στὶ μεστὰ τἀνθάδ' εἰρήνης σαπρᾶς.
> Ἀλλὰ πᾶς χώρει πρὸς ἔργον εἰς ἀγρὸν παιωνίσας.

> TRYG. Oyez folk! Let the farmers depart
>   With their farmers' gear for the field
>   As quick as they can without spear nor sword nor javelin.
>   For all is now replete even there with good old peace.
>   Now all to work, to the field: but first a paean.   (vv. 551-5)

The word translated "good old" at v. 554, σαπρᾶς, is glossed variously as synonymous with ἀρχαῖος, "ancient," or as equivalent to "rotten," here with the specifically positive sense of the word found in the German *Edelfäule*, French *pourriture noble*, or English "noble rot," all terms from the realm of viticulture.[93] (Whatever the sense, the word recurs significantly at *Plutus* v. 323 and elsewhere, where it sums up all that is to be *rejected* in Chremylus' new regime.)   Platnauer assertively argues against taking the word as a παρὰ προσδοκίαν or bathetic joke, and translators have for the most part followed this counsel.[94] At any rate, here and *passim* in the following song there is an explicit continuum between Peace and all that burgeons, mellows and (nobly) rots.

The association of Peace with the country-side appears to have been standard for comedy, if the evidence of two fragments is significant. One, fragment 109, said to be from Aristophanes' lost Γεωργοί or *Farmers*, seems to represent a husbandman's prayer to Peace, calling for an end to war and a return to the activities of vine-dressing, drinking, and eating. Peace is given the epithet "exceeding rich" (βαθύπλουτε), and is associated with a "little oxen-team." The other, fragment 294, said to come from the disputed "second *Peace*,"[95] seems to introduce yet another allegorical figure, Γεωργία or "Husbandry," who claims to be the "trusted nurse, housekeeper, colleague, executor, daughter and sister of Peace, friendly to all humans."[96]

This association of peace-time and the rural life is made negatively explicit further on in the *Peace*, when Hermes details the effects war has been having on the Attic populace. In response to the Choryphaeus' question as to the whereabouts of the goddess until her rescue, Hermes delivers a mock disquisition on the causes of the Peloponnesian War, which has been waged since 431 B.C.E. and looks now, in 421, to be over, at least temporarily, thanks to the Peace of Nicias. Hermes' speech foregrounds to a grotesque degree the rivalrous ambitions of Pheidias and Pericles, and stresses (illogically, as Platnauer notes *ad loc.*) the role of money in the outbreak and escalation of the conflict: Pheidias' venality (v. 605), the Athenian tribute-states' fear of war-levies and their consequent hiring of Spartan mercenaries (vv. 619-22), and the Spartans' murderous love of profit (vv. 623-4), all are named as causes of the war. The chief victims are identified as the farmers, whose produce has had to serve as fodder for trireme crews engaged in reprisals against land sorties (vv. 625-7).[97] Finally Hermes makes plain the most deleterious effect of the war, the movement of the country-people to the city, the internal migration that is everywhere in the *Peace* in the process of being magically reversed amid the ubiquitous refrain of "to the field."[98] His description highlights the social alienation and class antagonism wrought by this displacement, as well as further insisting on the generally bad effects of money and demagoguery on the fortunes of the "working poor," the πένητες:

Κἀνθάδ' ὡς ἐκ τῶν ἀγρῶν ξυνῆλθεν οὐργάτης λεώς,
τὸν τρόπον πωλούμενος τὸν αὐτὸν οὐκ ἐμάνθανεν.
ἀλλ' ἅτ' ὢν ἄνευ γιγάρτων καὶ φιλῶν τὰς ἰσχάδας
ἔβλεπεν πρὸς τοὺς λέγοντας· οἱ δὲ γιγνώσκοντες εὖ

τοὺς πένητας ἀσθενοῦντας κἀπορῦντας ἀλφίτων.
τήνδε μὲν δικροῖς ἐώθουν τὴν θεὸν κεκράγμασιν.
πολλάκις φανεῖσαν αὐτὴν τῆσδε τῆς χώρας πόθῳ.
τῶν δὲ συμμάχων ἔσειον τοὺς παχεῖς καὶ πλουσίους.
αἰτίαν ἂν προστιθέντες. ὡς φρονεῖ τὰ Βρασίδου.
Εἶτ' ἂν ὑμεῖς τοῦτον ὥσπερ κυνίδι' ἐσπαράττετε·
ἡ πόλις γὰρ ὠχριῶσα κἀν φόβῳ καθημένη.
ἅττα διαβάλοι τις αὐτῇ. ταῦτ' ἂν ἥδιστ' ἤσθιεν.
Οἱ δὲ τὰς πληγὰς ὁρῶντες ἃς ἐτύπτονθ'. οἱ ξένοι.
χρυσίῳ τῶν ταῦτα ποιούντων ἐβύνουν τὸ στόμα.
ὥστ' ἐκείνους μὲν ποῆσαι πλουσίους. ἡ δ' Ἑλλὰς αὖ
ἐξερημωθεῖσ' ἂν ὑμᾶς ἔλαθε.

And then, when the working folk had converged from the fields,
They did not realize how they had been sold out;
But deprived of marc and fond of their dried figs,
They looked to the orators. Now these, knowing well
How weak and desperate for bread were the poor,
Yet drove off this goddess here with raucous cries,
As often as she might reappear in longing for this land;
And they vexed the fat and rich amongst the allies,
With the accusation that each was of the party of Brasidas.
And you would tear him to shreds like a pack of dogs.
For the city was pale and crouched with fear,
And eagerly snapped up whatever slander was offered her.
But the foreigners, who saw what blows she suffered,
Stopped up the mouths of these trouble-makers with gold --
And so they became rich, while you failed to notice
How Greece was was emptied out. (vv.632-47)

War breeds shortages, which engender displacement of rural elements to the city, which in turn tempts demagogues to exacerbate class tensions by pitting poor against rich.[99] And yet Aristophanes does not put a program for any particular social or economic change into Hermes' mouth (remember that this is the god of the old countryside), but rather has him instead sketch the simple need for a return to the way it was, to the field, to an earlier division of labor, space, and resources. There is no suggestion of noble or romanticized poverty, of course: the chorus eventually refers to itself as πρὸ τοῦ πεινῶντες, "those who formerly went hungry" (v. 1312). But the difference between city and country is upheld and even strengthened by the concentration in the figure of Peace and her attendants of so many vestiges of rural life, mixed with rituals that regulate the correct commerce of city and country (the dramatic festivals, for instance, which draw attendance at specified times and at specified locations, either city or country, and which serve to reinforce notions of decorum and to socialize the young). The wedding train that ends the comedy, with its cries of "bring out the bride" and "bring back the tools to the field" (τὴν νύμφην ἔξω τινὰ δεῦρο κομίζειν and τὰ σκεύη πάλιν εἰς τὸν ἀγρόν, vv. 1316 and 1317), continues and completes this general movement outwards and away from the venal city.

Plutus and the City

In "The Ideology of Aristophanes' *Wealth*," David Konstan and Matthew Dillon examine what they identify as two strands in the economic argument of Aristophanes' comedy and explore the contradictions arising from this ambivalence of position. Their discussion focuses on the apparent co-existence in the play of "two quite different conceptions of the nature of want and sufficiency," that of "unequal social distribution," whereby dishonest people grow rich at the expense of the honest poor, and that of "universal scarcity, as a result of which all alike are more or less indigent."[100] Their consideration of these conflicting conceptions leads them to read Aristophanes' solution to his play's problem as a relatively straightforward and traditional comic vision of utopia. Aristophanes' skillful presentation of the god of Wealth as both blind and errant, they contend, allows the poet to bridge the gap from a "social conception" of the injustice of unequal distribution to a "natural conception" of scarcity and bounty, and thereby to "dissolve the issue of exploitation and inequality into a vague nostalgia for a golden age, a nostalgia which is catered to with comic exuberance in the utopian finale of the play."[101] The "utopian finale" they refer to is the scene of the Old Woman's discomfiture, mentioned above in the discussion of Hermes' role in the *Plutus*. Konstan and Dillon make the following comments:

> The scene of the old lady and her young lover, or rather, former lover -- for now that he has resources of his own, thanks to Plutus, he need no longer sell his favors to the crone -- would seem to be celebrating economic autonomy, at least so far as its import for the themes we have been investigating is concerned. From another point of view, the grotesque and bawdy humor is simply a manifestation of that early exuberance that is natural to festive comedy. What Mikhail Bakhtin identified as the essential features of Rabelaisian humor -- the holiday inversion of social hierarchy; the valorization of the body and its nether functions; the abandonment of the classical moment, the poised perfection of youth, for processes of birth and decay; fecundity amplified to the absurd degree of pregnant old hags, closing the circle of death and procreation -- these features are the heart and soul of Aristophanic laughter.[102]

The *Plutus*, however, stands at some remove from that "heart and soul," not merely chronologically, but also aesthetically.[103] Apart from a couple of Karion's scandalous remarks in his parody of a tragic messenger speech (vv. 699 and 706),[104] the *Plutus* is perhaps one of the least scatological of Aristophanes' plays, certainly innocent of the tendency to "*nostalgie de la boue*" ascribed by Whitman to the *Peace*.[105] As for the "processes of birth and decay," the *Plutus* is relatively restrained too in its sexual humour, tending to assign such imagery to the period preceding the cure and appropriation of the god of Wealth, rather than to the Golden Age that ensues, as the *Peace* does in its analogous stages of rediscovery and rededication of the godhead.

In fact, in a number of places, the *Plutus* explicitly rejects the folkloric rusticity prized by the *Peace*, indicating that Chremylus' Golden Age is of another kind altogether from Trygaeus'. This rejection is made clear by the repeated and pointed disclaimer throughout the play of that earthily desirable quality of noble rot evoked by the word σαπρός at *Peace* v. 554. In the *Plutus*, the word becomes virtually synonymous with ἀγροικός or rural, provincial, outdated, a far cry from the evident valorization of over-ripeness, fecundity, and indeed Rabelaisian decay expressed by the word in its context in the *Peace*. A review of the word's appearances in the *Plutus* will make obvious that play's manifest position vis-à-vis the vision of a rustic Golden Age, and set the stage for a consideration of the ambiguous utopia represented instead by its own central allegory, that of Wealth.

The word's first use in the play is at vv. 322-5, where Chremylus appears to Karion and the Chorus after the announcement of Wealth's theophany. He is transformed already by the god's presence, and has adapted his speech accordingly:

Χαίρειν μὲν ὑμᾶς ἐστιν. ὦνδρες δημόται.
ἀρχαῖον ἤδη προσαγορεύειν καὶ σαπρόν·
ἀσπάζομαι δ' ὁτιὴ προθύμως ἥκετε
καὶ συντεταμένως κοὐ κατεβλακευμένως.

To give you a "hail," my fellow demesmen,
Would be old-fashioned and stale [σαπρόν].
Instead it's "enchanté, kissy-kissy" for your stout-hearted,
Strenuous, punctual arrival.

Whereas Trygaeus after the recovery of his goddess bids his Chorus of demesmen hie to the field with the promise that all there is now full of Εἰρήνη σαπρά or "good old/nobly rotten Peace," here Chremylus consigns those same good old days to the linguistic dust-bin, opting instead for a new, more urbane idiom to suit his new, more urban lifestyle.[106]

The second occurrence of the word is at v. 542, in one of Chremylus' ripostes to Poverty in the course of their agon. Poverty has been listing the benefits she bestows via the crafts, her contention being that only lack of money inspires their invention. Chremylus responds with a vision of the miserable early mornings necessitated by just this lack, and adds a note on some of the impoverished accoutrements of this life:

Πρὸς δέ γε τούτοις ἀνθ' ἱματίου μὲν ἔχειν ῥάκος· ἀντὶ δὲ κλίνης
στιβάδα σχοίνων κόρεων μεστήν. ἢ τοὺς εὕδοντας ἐγείρει·
καὶ φορμὸν ἔχειν ἀντὶ τάπητος σαπρόν·

Yes, and what's more, instead of a cloak you've rags; instead of a bed
You've a reed-pallet full of bugs to keep you awake;
And instead of a rug you've a rotten mat. (vv. 540-2)

Here the ideas expressed by σαπρός are linked explicitly with the very mise-en-scène of the life of working poverty, the rounds of drudgery and discomfort associated with farm-labor.[107]

The third appearance of the word bridges the gap between this sordid vision of poverty and the miraculous era of opulence ushered in by the healing of Wealth; again, the context is a description of household items. Karion notes the changes in his master's home after Wealth has been welcomed in by Chremylus' wife:

Ὀξὶς δὲ πᾶσα καὶ λοπάδιον καὶ χύτρα
χαλκῆ γέγονε· τοὺς δὲ πινακίσκους τοὺς σαπροὺς
τοὺς ἰχθυηροὺς ἀργυροῦς πάρεσθ' ὁρᾶν.

Every vinegar-cruet, little plate and pot
Has become bronze; the rotten little trenchers
For the fish have turned to silver -- it's plain to see! (vv. 812-14)

This juxtaposition of desuetude and silver makes clear the degree to which the utopia of the *Plutus* is mediated by the standards of a certain culture, by precious metals and currency: this is definitely not the pastoral scene of the *Peace*.

The two final occurrences of a form of the word σαπρός in the *Plutus* come in the context of the Young Man's rejection of his former lover, the Old Woman; both are instances of abuse of the latter, references to her age and relative "freshness." In the first, in what van Leeuwen and van Daele maintain is an aside to the audience, Chremylus mocks her tears at the heartless Young Man's abandonment with the verb σήπομαι, conveying only the negatively rotten aspect of the word σαπρός:[108]

ΓΡ. ὑπὸ τοῦ γὰρ ἄλγους κατατέτηκ'. ὦ φίλτατε.

48   *The Visible God*

ΧΡ. οὔκ, ἀλλὰ κατασέσηπας, ὥς γ᾿ ἐμοὶ δοκεῖς.

O.W. I've just melted away with the pain, my dearest man.
CHR. Seems to me you've rotted away, rather.   (vv. 1034-5)

The second of these abuses of the Old Woman, and the final occurrence
of a form of σαπρός, comes from the Young Man himself, as
Chremylus urges him to overcome his revulsion and be reconciled with
the Old Woman. Their exchange is metaphorical and synaesthetic, as
the Young Man plays on her age and alleged promiscuity, and
Chremylus likens her instead to a vintage:

ΝΕ. οὐκ ἂν διαλεχθείην διεσπλεκωμένη
    ὑπὸ μυρίων ἐτῶν γε καὶ τρισχιλίων.[109]
ΧΡ. Ὅμως δ᾿ ἐπειδὴ καὶ τὸν οἶνον ἠξίους
    πίνειν, συνεκποτέ᾿ ἐστί σοι καὶ τὴν τρύγα.
ΝΕ. Ἀλλ᾿ ἔστι κομιδῇ τρὺξ παλαιὰ καὶ σαπρά.
ΧΡ. Οὐκοῦν τρύγοιπος ταῦτα πάντ᾿ ἰάσεται.

Y.M. I wouldn't have intercourse with a woman who's been banged
     By all these thousands upon thousands of years.
CHR. Nevertheless, since you rated the wine worth
     Drinking, you must drink down the lees too.
Y.M. But the lees are mighty ancient and mouldy.
CHR. Then surely a wine-strainer will cure all that.   (vv. 1082-7)

Here, finally, the word is used in an explicitly agricultural context, one
in which the stress on the lees draws interesting intertextual attention
to the root of Trygaeus' name (τρύξ), and ironically makes of his
elegiac mention of a wine-strainer, one of the items in his synaesthetic
list of the smells of Peace (*Peace* v. 535), the mere butt of a rude
joke.[110]

Thus, despite Konstan and Dillon's contention that the *Plutus* tends
towards the same sort of rustic utopia as is visible in the *Peace*, and
their recourse to the abuses hurled at Chremylus and his side-kick
Blepsidemus by the figure of Poverty to prove the characters'
imaginary return to an antediluvian era,[111] it seems evident that the
comedy itself is less bucolic in the utopia it fashions. Certainly the
final dedication of the god of Wealth, in the opisthodomos of the
Parthenon or Erechtheum,[112] on the Acropolis in the middle of Athens,
establishes his civic and urban centrality firmly (vv. 1191-3).
Furthermore, there is some suggestion that the *Plutus* was in fact
meant to be staged within imaginary view of the Acropolis, that is,
near this central urban space, and not merely leading to its invocation
at the play's end.[113]   And despite some borderline anti-city ribbing of
the Sycophant, at vv. 900 and 902 ff.,[114] the movement of the *Plutus*

seems to be inwards, towards the οἶκος and the πόλις, the family-home and the city, as opposed to the centrifugal movement of the *Peace* noted above. Where the final scenes of the *Peace* featured a procession out of the house and into the country-side, the exodos of the *Plutus* describes a procession into the opisthodomos or inner quarters of the Acropolis, in a realm in which that civic space has become somehow co-extensive with Chremylus' own house.[115] Indeed, Wealth's first entrance into his benefactor's abode following the restoration of his eye-sight (vv. 788-801) is the occasion for an almost reverent meditation on the propriety of guest-host relations and gift-exchange, as well as a comment on the decorum of comic stage-conventions. Truly, this is a play preoccupied with inner and outer space, with changing manners, and with mobility and stasis.

But of course the direction of these preoccupations is the reverse of that of the *Peace*. In the *Plutus* a lone, wandering, exiled male god of rough and unprepossessing countenance is healed, ennobled, and established in a fixed, interior place, the better to serve the luxury of his handlers. In the *Peace*, an attractive trio of female figures is set free from captivity and returned to a rugged male landscape[116] of work and artisanship. The utopia of the *Plutus* is that of a currency literally fixed in place and of the abolition of scarcity, and it announces this novelty with the confection of a male god objectified through his entrance into the female space of the home, yet still not deprived of his status as speaking subject;[117] the *Peace*, on the other hand, promises essentially a return to the rigid class-divisions obtaining before the war, with the single bonus of a cease-fire. But the particular way in which Wealth is represented in the *Plutus*, the extent to which he is still implicated in a system of exploitation and enslavement, indicates the way this utopian fantasy has been sabotaged with the flaws that will defuse it and thus recontain its revolutionary energies.

That the figure of Wealth in the *Plutus* can be read as an allegory of money as such, and not simply as "wealth in corn,"[118] is evidenced by the jokes made about him upon his epiphany to Chremylus and Karion and in the arguments used by the pair to convince the god of his supremacy. In a comment on vv. 202 ff., in which Wealth defends himself against allegations of his cowardice, van Daele maintains that the figure represents the rich themselves, notoriously craven in their precautions.[119] But in fact Wealth speaks only impersonally about the house (οἰκία) into which the robber penetrates, leaving unspoken his own relation to the actions described, save as the victim of slander. Later on, at vv. 234 ff., Wealth replies to Chremylus' invitation to him to enter *his* house and make it "full of money" (ἡ γὰρ οἰκία / αὕτη 'στὶν ἣν δεῖ χρημάτων σε τήμερον / μεστὴν ποῆσαι καὶ δικαίως κἀδίκως, vv. 231-3) with a vision of his anxieties that makes clear the extent to which he materially personifies money:

'Αλλ' ἄχθομαι μὲν εἰσιὼν νὴ τοὺς θεοὺς
εἰς οἰκίαν ἑκάστοτ' ἀλλοτρίαν πάνυ·
ἀγαθὸν γὰρ ἀπέλαυσ' οὐδέω αὐτοῦ πώποτε.
'Ην μὲν γὰρ ὡς φειδωλὸν εἰσελθὼν τύχω.
εὐθὺς κατώρυξέν με κατὰ τῆς γῆς κάτω·
κἄν τις προσέλθῃ χρηστὸς ἄνθρωπος φίλος
αἰτῶν λαβεῖν τι σμικρὸν ἀργυρίδιον.
ἔξαρνός ἐστι μηδ' ἰδεῖν με πώποτε.
'Ην δ' ὡς παραπλῆγ' ἄνθρωπον εἰσελθὼν τύχω.
πόρναισι καὶ κύβοισι παραβεβλημένος
γυμνὸς θύραζ' ἐξέπεσον ἐν ἀκαρεῖ χρόνου.

But by the gods how wearisome it is
Every time I enter a completely new house:
For no good ever comes of it for me.
Example? If I happen into a miser's house,
He buries me immediately below the ground;
Even if some honest man, a friend of his, should come
And ask him for a little tiny bit of silver,
He denies he's ever seen me.
And if by chance I happen to enter a madman's home,
It's thrown away on whores and dice
I go out the door, in no time, naked. (vv. 234-44)

Here Wealth describes himself as the very stuff of currency: hoarded, begrudged, spent recklessly. This has been his fate at the hands of the unjust, whom it had been his lot to frequent owing to the punitive blindness imposed on him by Zeus (vv. 87-91).

Wishing to reverse this situation and win wealth for themselves and their friends, Chremylus and Karion try to convince Wealth of his power, which they claim is superior to Zeus's: after all, they argue, the Olympian's reign is supported principally by silver (v. 131), its value expressed in monetary terms as a variable of Wealth's status (vv. 124-6).[120] In one example after another, the pair reveals that money lies behind every human interaction and experience as well, whether religious (vv. 133-43), aesthetic (vv. 144-6 and 168), production-relational (vv. 147-8), sexual (vv. 149-59), artisanal (v. 160-7), adventurous (vv. 181-3), or military (vv. 184-5). Finally, they make explicit the sequestering of Wealth's representational sphere by listing all of the material and spiritual goods of which humans can have a satiety, excluding only money from their account (vv. 188-96). The list is bathetic, in that it mingles the serious with the vulgar (music and candies, honor and cakes, for instance): it manages to convey a vast congeries of affects, skills, and foods, and effectively brackets Wealth as money from the standard attributes of the Aristophanic utopia. For those attributes are utopian exactly by virtue of the fact that the comic fantasists *can* finally get enough of them.[121] In the case of money, such a total appropriation of material reality is in fact impossible, because the emptiness of the absolute token of exchange is such that a surfeit cannot be imagined. A greater amount can always be projected, as Chremylus explains to Wealth:

σοῦ δ' ἐγένετ' οὐδεὶς μεστὸς οὐδεπώποτε.
'Αλλ' ἢν τάλαντά τις λάβῃ τρισκαίδεκα,
πολὺ μᾶλλον ἐπιθυμεῖ λαβεῖν ἑκκαίδεκα·
κἂν ταῦθ' ἀνύσηται, τετταράκοντα βούλεται,
ἢ οὔ φησιν εἶν' αὐτῷ βιωτὸν τὸν βίον.

But no one has ever had enough of you.
Should someone receive thirteen talents,
He's all the more eager for sixteen.
Once he's got that, he wants forty,
Or life's not worth the living, he says. (vv. 193-7)

It is of course Chremylus' desire for his house to be full (μεστή) of Wealth that motivates him throughout the comedy; the above parable stands nevertheless as a cautionary tale or as the reality principle against the play's central utopia, which is as riven by contradiction as it is by impossibility.

What the reification of wealth in the form of a wanderer cured and contained seems to represent is freedom from want and humiliating dependence on wage-earning; what it does instead is re-inscribe the economy of slavery and unfreedom directly into the texture of the ostensibly new regime. In his exchange or agon with Poverty, Chremylus makes clear that his projected Golden Age, so far from abolishing wage-labor or working poverty (that constellation of ideas surrounding the words πενία and πόνος), will actually reinforce it, as those who formerly had to labor can now hire servants:

ΧΡ. λῆρον ληρεῖς· ταῦτα γὰρ ἡμῖν πάνθ'. ὅσα νυνδὴ κατέλεξας
οἱ θεράποντες μοχθήσουσιν·
ΠΕ.   Πόθεν οὖν ἕξεις θεράποντας;
ΧΡ. 'Ωνησόμεθ' ἀργυρίου δήπου.

CHR. You're talking rubbish! For all those tasks you've been mentioning,
     Why, our servants will do them.
POV.   And just where will you get servants?
CHR. We'll buy them with silver, of course. (vv. 517-9)

Chremylus is deaf to Poverty's rationalizing arguments about the relative risks of slavetrading in an economy of abundance.[122]   He will buy slaves as he pleases, because he controls Wealth.

And indeed, the relationship between Chremylus and Wealth is in at least one place sketched in explicit terms of proprietorship. When Karion has finished his messenger speech describing the healing of Wealth, and has announced the advent of the god himself, Chremylus' Wife expresses her pleasure at the news thus:

ΓΥ. Νὴ τὴν Ἑκάτην, κἀγὼ δ' ἀναδῆσαι βούλομαι
      εὐαγγέλιά σε κριβανιτῶν ὁρμαθῷ
      τοιαῦτ' ἀπαγγείλαντα.
ΚΑ.   Μή νυν μέλλ' ἔτι,
      ὡς ἄνδρες ἐγγύς εἰσιν ἤδη τῶν θυρῶν.
ΓΥ. Φέρε νυν, ἰοῦσ' εἴσω κομίσω καταχύσματα
      ὥσπερ νεωνήτοισιν ὀφθαλμοῖς ἐγώ.

C.W. By Hecate, I want to award you with a garland
       Of pastries for these good tidings
       You've just brought.
KAR.   Well don't wait:
       The men are even now near the doors.
C.W. Come now, I'll go inside and bring out the largesse
       As for newly-purchased eyes. (vv. 764-9)

The word Chremylus' Wife uses of the largesse she intends to throw at Wealth, καταχύσματα, is explained by a scholiast as the typical gifts given to a newly-purchased slave;[123] she drives the point home with the παρὰ προσδοκίαν of "newly-purchased eyes." There is a moment of suspense for the Wife later on, after Wealth arrives and seems to reject the idea of the καταχύσματα, at vv. 788-94: "Veretur mulier," glosses van Leeuwen *ad loc.*, "ne dona oblata deus spernat vel inter familiares recipi nolit." But in fact Wealth is merely anxious about decorum, and is quite willing to accept his gifts inside.

So Ploutos, the harbinger of freedom from toil, comes to resemble a symbol for the servitude from which he seemed at first the salvation. An adequate recontainment of the energies for change expressed in this vision of an equitable redistribution of monetary resources is effected by this turn, in which the salvational object is revealed to be a ruse. The burlesque of the Old Woman that closes the play sets the seal on this strategic recontainment, as she comes to realize that her very sexual life has been dependent on the uneven distribution of money: her Young Man is a gigolo, and no longer needs her patronage. Of course, both she and the destitute priest will eventually be assimilated into Chremylus's economy, but not before they have been made to feel the painful extent of their new dependence. The fixing of currency, its settling into a static form as Wealth is reified and invested as a deity, defeats the hopes that had caused that deity to arise in the first place. Free circulation turns out to be its most effective state, and it is exactly this that is impeded by the sudden bounty. If there are vestiges of nostalgia for the sort of rural free feed, for the orgiastic utopia of the *Peace*, they are largely negative. The pot that the Old Woman carries in on her head as the play ends recalls the χύτρα of another Old Woman, the one in Karion's messenger speech (vv. 672 ff.): just as that woman's food is stolen by the slave who now controls Wealth, so this woman's sexual gratification has been jeopardized by the grotesqueries of financial autarky. Konstan and Dillon's point, that the play works by confusing the ideas of unequal social distribution and universal scarcity, is apposite. Wealth healed and fixed in place turns out to be no wealth at all: for a currency to be effective, there must be some lack. Thus the idea of redistribution is defused by the playwright's ridicule; in the form of the uncanny squalor forever underlying the freshly healed god of Wealth, furthermore, the very notion of a monetary free feed, a ripping-open of the mainsprings of wealth, is dangled before the audience and then snatched back. And this ambivalent representation was already available to Aristophanes in the scandalously ugly portrait of Ploutos, outcast and denatured son of Demeter, to be found in the archaic tradition.

Aristophanes' last preserved comedy has in modern times been reviled as somehow least like him, perhaps because the glorious baroqueries of his other comic fantasies are so conspicuously absent from this depiction of an economic utopia stripped to the bone. And yet the play enjoyed a Byzantine flourishing at the head of schooltexts, and was printed first in Nicodemus Frischlin's edition presented to the Holy Roman Emperor Rudolf II in 1586. The *Plutus* may have been medievally showcased for exactly that paucity of scurrilous incident that has led more recent and more jaded readers to bracket it; it may also have appealed to an age that was preoccupied with allegory, and increasingly given to couching its religious and political agendas in the semaphor of classical prestige.[124] In any case, Aristophanes' specter of an imaginary redistribution of wealth was to recur often, in radically different ideological clothing every time, to haunt the powers of old Europe and to be vilified or heroized anew. The lineaments would alter somewhat, but the basic features, squalor, vagrancy, foreignness, unfreedom, incompleteness, immorality, ambiguity, infidelity: these were to remain the tokens of the satirical allegorizing of money, in need of healing, re-education or conversion as the cause might warrant.

Notes

[1] See the discussion in Cedric H. Whitman, *Aristophanes and the Comic Hero* (Cambridge: Harvard Univ. Press, 1964), 5 ff. More recently, see Lowell Edmunds, *Cleon, Knights, and Aristophanes' Politics* (Lanham: Univ. Press of America, 1987); Malcolm Heath, *Political comedy in Aristophanes* (Göttingen: Vandenhoeck & Ruprecht, 1987); and Kenneth J. Reckford, *Aristophanes' Old-and-New Comedy* (Chapel Hill: Univ. of North Carolina Press, 1987), particularly pp. 285-363. An important study of the ambivalent socializing agenda of Aristophanes' utopianism can be found in Carrière (1979); see too Rösler (1986): 25-44.

[2] See Thomas Gelzer, *Der epirrhematische Agon bei Aristophanes* (Munich: C. H. Beck, 1960), 10 ff.

[3] Carrière (1979) 110.

[4] Van Daele calls him "le vigneron athénien" in the "Notice" to Victor Coulon and Hilaire van Daele, *Aristophane* vol. 2 (Paris: Les Belles Lettres, 1985; reprint), 89; Whitman (1964) 104 ff., however, calls Trygaeus the "civic" hero of the last city- (or πόλις-)based play. As will be discussed below, the civic is of course a strong theme in the *Peace*: Whitman's dichotomy here is however civic/supernatural, as embodied in the pair Dicaeopolis/Pisthetaeros, rather than urban/rural; since he does not treat the *Plutus* comprehensively, and indeed consigns it implicitly to the heuristic limbo of middle comedy, it is hard to say what he would make of the pair Trygaeus/Chremylus.

[5] Overturned, but evidently assimilated: see *Plutus* vv.1189-90, and discussion below.

[6] Fantasy means to σωτηρία or salvation in the rest of the corpus include: a separate peace for market transactions, as in the *Acharnians*; a change of despots, as in the *Knights*; wings for escaping to Νεφελοκοκκυγία, or Cloud-Cuckoo-Land, as in the *Birds*; a trans-gendering of the political process, as in the *Lysistrata* and the *Ecclesiazusae*; or an ethico-literary renaissance, as in the *Frogs*.

[7] On the relative complexity of the *Peace* in particular see the excellent discussion in Thomas K. Hubbard, *The Mask of Comedy: Aristophanes and the Intertextual Parabasis* (Ithaca: Cornell Univ. Press, 1991), 140-156. Hubbard cautions thus: "Those who criticize the *Peace* for lack of conflict and dramatic tension . . . do not give sufficient attention to the revolutionary nature of Trygaeus' actions; the plot of the *Peace*, though not as complex as that of the *Clouds* or the *Wasps*, is no less dramatic than that of the *Birds*, and in many ways served as a model for that play. . . ," p. 142n9. It is the purpose of my work to question neither the dramatic tension nor the revolutionary nature of the *Peace*, but rather to determine just what kind of revolution is represented and how it may be compared with that represented in the *Plutus*.

[8] This quasi-magical property might perhaps be likened to that of Pierre Bourdieu's *symbolic capital*: see the discussion of this concept, and of its role in another ancient poetic economy, in Leslie Kurke, *The Traffic in Praise: Pindar and the Poetics of Social Economy* (Ithaca: Cornell U. P.,

1991), 36.

[9] M. I. Finley, *Economy and Society in Ancient Greece*, ed. Brent D. Shaw and Richard P. Saller (New York: Viking Press, 1982), 185-186.

[10] Finley, *The Ancient Economy*, Sather Classical Lectures 43 (Berkeley and Los Angeles: Univ. of California Press, 1973), 20-21: "The one Greek attempt at a general statement [of the use of the word *oikonomia* to mean the management of public revenues] is the opening of the second book of the pseudo-Aristotelian *Oikonomikos*, and what is noteworthy about these half a dozen paragraphs is not only their crashing banality but also their isolation in the whole of surviving ancient writing." And see Victor Ehrenberg, *The People of Aristophanes: A Sociology of Old Attic Comedy* (Oxford: Basil Blackwell, 1951), 248: "It is typical of the working of the Greek mind that even at a time [= the early fourth century B.C.E.] when the importance of economic factors had become obvious and their impact on social life far stronger than before, the problem of wealth and poverty was essentially regarded as a moral question. Whatever the specific social or economic issue, its influence on the community was primarily one of individual morals. This is probably the chief reason why the Greeks never succumbed to an economic interpretation of political and social life." Ehrenberg is speaking here specifically about the milieu in which the *Plutus* was produced. K. J. Dover, in his *Aristophanic Comedy* (Berkeley and Los Angeles: Univ. of California Press, 1972), 209, goes so far as to suggest that the *Plutus* "is less about economics and sociology than about magic, fantasy and the supernatural." A more explicitly Marxist treatment of the moral issues implied by the play's peculiar "economics" can be found in David Konstan and Matthew Dillon, "The Ideology of Aristophanes' Wealth," *American Journal of Philology* 102 (1981): 371-394. Perhaps the seminal historical-philological work on Greek attitudes towards poverty and wealth is Jacob Hemelrijk, Πενία en Πλοῦτος (Amsterdam: Blikman & Sartorius, 1925). More recently see Vincent J. Rosivach, "Some Athenian Presuppositions About 'the Poor'," *Greece and Rome* 38, no. 2 (October 1991): 189-198; and for a comparative literary-historical overview, see Gerhard Hertel, *Die Allegorie von Reichtum und Armut: Ein aristophaneisches Motiv und seine Abwandlungen in der abendländischen Literatur* (Nürnberg: Hans Carl, 1969).

[11] See however Finley (1982) 179: "There were [in the ancient world] no proper credit instruments -- no negotiable paper, no book clearance, no credit payments. The desperate search of the 'modernisers' among economic historians of antiquity for something which they can hold up with pride against, say, 15th-century Toulouse or Lübeck, is sufficient proof. Barring some odd and dubious text here and there, the best they can produce is the giro system for corn payments in Hellenistic Egypt. There was money-lending in plenty, but it was concentrated on small usurious loans to peasants or consumers, and on large borrowings to enable men to meet the political or other conventional expenditures of the upper classes. Only the bottomry loan was in any sense productive, and it was invariably restricted in amount and usurious in rate, as much an insurance measure spreading the high risks of seaborne traffic as a proper credit instrument.

Similarly in the field of business organisation: there were no long-term partnerships or corporations, no brokers or agents, no guilds -- again with the occasional and unimportant exception. In short, both the organisational and the operational devices were lacking for the mobilisation of private capital resources."

[12] M. M. Austin and Pierre Vidal-Naquet, *Economic and Social History of Ancient Greece: An Introduction* (London: B. T. Batsford, 1977), 150.

[13] Louis Gernet, "'Value' in Greek Myth," trans. R. L. Gordon in Gordon (1981) 113-114.

[14] Peter W. Rose, *Sons of the Gods, Children of Earth* (Ithaca: Cornell Univ. Press, 1992), 20n35.

[15] On Athenian scorn for banausic work, see for example Xenophon *Oeconomicus* 4.2-3, Plato *Republic* 495D, and Aristotle *Politics* 1258b35-39 and 1337b8-17. See too the discussion in Josiah Ober, *Mass and Elite in Democratic Athens: Rhetoric, Ideology, and the Power of the People* (Princeton: Princeton Univ. Press, 1989), 12.

[16] Hemelrijk (1925) 147. The citation is from the German abstract that follows Hemelrijk's Dutch text.

[17] Hjalmar Frisk, *Griechisches etymologisches Wörterbuch*, 2 vols (Heidelberg: Carl Winter, 1970), and Pierre Chantraine, *Dictionnaire étymologique de la langue grecque: Histoire des mots* (Paris: Klingsieck, 1980), s.v. πένομαι, both citing Hemelrijk's data among various other ancient sources, relate the semantic progress of the word πένης from early ideas having to do with *labor*, especially domestic ("häuslich" or "ménager"), to a later association with *poverty* (Hesychius, for example, gives πτωχή as a synonym for the feminine form πένησσα), to the point that o-Ablaut forms of the πεν- stem have displaced derivations of πτωχός to mean indigence or want in modern Greek. *Plutus* vv. 553 ff. is important for its distinction of πένης from both πλούσιος *and* πτωχός. See also the discussion of terms in Ober (1989) 194-196.

[18] Hemelrijk (1925) 140.

[19] But see Rosivach (1991) 196-197n5 for disagreement with Hemelrijk over the fastness of the distinction to be drawn between πένητες and πτωχοί: Rosivach argues (with references to the tragedians and the orators) for a figurative use of the latter word to refer abusively on occasion to the former.

[20] Ehrenberg (1951) 243.

[21] Ehrenberg (1951) 242-243, citing Cratinus 208, Euripides *Suppliants* v. 742 and fr.235, and Lysias 27.10, as well as numerous places in Aristophanes.

[22] Austin and Vidal-Naquet (1977) 150.

[23] E. David, *Aristophanes and Athenian Society of the Early Fourth Century B.C.* (Leiden: Brill, 1984), 3.

[24] That Wealth is an urban god in Aristophanes' *Plutus* is suggested by the sorts of characters upon whom he bestows his favor (vv. 149-180), and perhaps by the fact that Karion must be sent to collect the peasant-chorus "in the fields" (ἐν τοῖς ἀγροῖς, v. 224), implying that the main scene is not set in the country-side. The repeated refrain of "to the fields" in the

Peace, meanwhile, is to be accounted for perhaps by the play's initial and never quite abandoned supernatural setting: that is to say, neither on rural nor on urban earth. See the discussion of this scenic dynamics in Pavlos Sfyroeras, *The Feast of Poetry: Sacrifice, Foundation, and Performance in Aristophanic Comedy* (Ph.D. diss., Princeton University, 1992), abstract in *Dissertation Abstracts International* 53 (1992-93): 2357A, where it is argued that the change of scene from Olympus to earth is ritually necessary, albeit obscure. See now too Sfyroeras, "What Wealth has to do with Dionysus: From Economy to Poetics in Aristophanes' *Plutus*," *GRBS* 36, no. 3 (1995): 231-61. Van Daele, in the "Notice" to the play in Coulon and van Daele, *Aristophane* vol. 5 (Paris: Les Belles Lettres, 1930), 76, summarizes thus: "Le campagnard Chrémyle, sur ses vieux jours, se demande avec inquiétude ce qu'il doit faire de son fils: le destinera-t-il à suivre l'exemple paternel, à vivoter aux champs en peinant dur et en restant honnête, ou à devenir un vaurien pour se faire une existence riche et facile *à la ville*." Emphasis supplied.

[25] For all the goddess's virtue and originary beauty, of course, the *Peace* is by no means free of squalor; indeed, the play opens with a scene of scatological proportions rivalled only, perhaps, by that of Blepyrus' *toilette* in the *Ecclesiazusae*. Both Jeffrey Henderson, in his *The Maculate Muse: Obscene Language in Attic Comedy* (New Haven: Yale Univ. Press, 1975), and DuBois (1988), despite some peculiar misreadings in the latter, have much to say about the specific grotesqueries of the *Peace*. It should be clear that for the purposes of the present discussion a paramount distinction between the *Peace* and the *Plutus* lies in the initial reception of the plays' eponymous allegories by their respective *dramatis personae* and the subsequent treatment they receive at the hands of these latter (i.e., lusty celebration of Peace as is, or careful healing to remove the taints of Wealth's squalor). See the intriguing discussion of the celebration of scatological and sexual imagery in the *Peace* in Hubbard (1991) 140-144, and its uses in marking a transition in the comedy's psycho-sexual decorum.

[26] "[U]t Helena illa vel Penelope, sic Pax prodit, οὐκ οἴη· ἅμα τῇ γε καὶ ἀμφίπολοι δυ' ἕπονται, Opora et Theoria, fructuum auctumnalium abundantium laetaque sollemnia promittentes," J. van Leeuwen, *Aristophanis Pax cum prolegomenis et commentariis* (Leiden: Sijthoff, 1906), ad loc.

[27] Ehrenberg (1951) 235.

[28] Johann Gustav Droysen, *Des Aristophanes Werke* (Leipzig: 1881; third reprint of Berlin 1835-8 edition), 353n1. Droysen is drawing here on the evidence of a scholion to Plato *Apology* 19c, to the effect that the goddess Peace was represented in Aristophanes' production by a statue, or κολοσσός.

[29] Droysen (1881) 407n1. Droysen's observation turns on a variant reading of *Plutus* v. 267, where the god of Wealth is being described by the slave Karion, who says either that he is "mangy" (ψωρόν), or that his foreskin has been drawn back (ψωλόν), with the possible meaning "circumcised." Van Leeuwen, in his *Aristophanis Plutus cum prolegomenis*

et commentariis (Leiden: Sijthoff, 1904), ad loc., reads van Herwerden's emendation ψωρὸν instead of VR's ψωλὸν, acknowledging the consequent *hapax* in the Aristophanic corpus but arguing for a set-up for the Coryphaeus' comic mishearing of the word as σωρὸν. He finds ψωλὸν awkward: "inepte, sive *libidinosum* interpreteris (sic schol., cf. vs. 294), sive *recutilum* (vid. ad Ach. 161)." Most of all he seems led by the apparent *double entendre* of Karion's feigned doubt ("οἶμαι") as to this eminently visible state! It is hard to know what to take van Leeuwen to task for first: his phallic logic, or his deficient sense of comic understatement. At any rate, the burden of textual evidence seems to point to ψωλὸν as a likelier choice for Aristophanes than the never-used ψωρὸν (Bergk, in his 1857 edition, prints ψωλὸν); and Dover in *Greek Homosexuality* (Cambridge: Harvard Univ. Press, 1978), 129 ff. assembles loca where the retraction of the foreskin (whether through circumcision or sexual excitement) simply draws comic attention to the indecorously revealed male member. Droysen's ugly anachronisms enjoy no such textual support. See too Holzinger's forceful arguments ad loc.

[30] Ehrenberg (1951) 233n7. See more recently Gabrielsen (1986): 99-114. See also Marc Shell's more involved theoretical discussion of 'Visibility and Invisibility,' and their role in the Herodotean and Platonic origins of money, tyranny, and philosophy, in his *The Economy of Literature* (Baltimore: Johns Hopkins Univ. Press, 1978), 30-36. Most germane to the present argument is Shell's assertion, based on studies by Fritz Pringsheim, Walter Jones, and Louis Gernet, that increasingly in the fourth century "the Greeks (and especially the landed aristocracy) feared the *ousia aphanes* [= invisible property]. To them, the development of money seemed to threaten not only the material basis of their wealth but also their mode of thought," p. 35. The last claim is connected to Shell's central argument, which likens money to language as homologously symbolizing (and similarly consciousness-constructing) systems. Compare Charles Mauron, *Psychocritique du genre comique* (Paris: J. Corti, 1964), 114-115, on fifth-century class structure: "L'aristocratie, en qui s'incarnait l'esprit politique avant Périclès, se détériore sous l'effet de trois facteurs: moeurs licencieuses, argent et sophistique. Les paysans s'appauvrissent; au contraire, les marchands et les artisans, quoique toujours travailleurs et non capitalistes, s'enrichissent et forment la classe dominante, de plus en plus guidée par des considérations économiques individuelles. Les hommes qui comptent dans cette classe moyenne, sont surtout soumis à deux des facteurs qui altèrent l'aristocratie: l'argent et la sophistique, cette dernière étant alors l'art de gagner de mauvais procès, mais entrainant une virtuosité dans *le maniement des concepts, cette monnaie mentale universelle.*" Emphasis supplied.

[31] Ehrenberg (1951) 233-234.

[32] See the brief discussion of contemporary religious views in Dover (1972) 33: "If it is right to regard the treatment of the gods in comedy as a means by which man hits back at the superhuman powers which dominate the world, the religious standpoint and the political standpoint of comedy can be treated as two species of the same genus. . . ."

[33] On the significance of the god Hermes to ancient Greek thought in general, and to notions of space and movement in particular, see the pivotal article of Vernant, "Hestia-Hermès: Sur l'expression religieuse de l'espace et du mouvement chez les grecs," in Vernant, *Mythe et pensée chez les grecs: Études de psychologie historique* (Paris: Maspero, 1965), 97-143; see too the Vernant-influenced study of the *Hymn to Hermes* in Laurence Kahn, *Hermès passe: ou les ambiguïtés de la communication* (Paris: Maspero, 1978). Other important (if divergent) mythological studies of Hermes include Norman O. Brown, *Hermes the Thief* (New York: 1947) and Karl Kerényi, *Hermes der Seelenführer* (Zürich: 1944).

[34] Indeed, apart from Poseidon and Iris in the *Birds* and Dionysus and Pluto in the *Frogs*, he is one of the very few immortals represented at all in the extant corpus.

[35] *Clouds* vv. 1508-9, assigned to the Choryphaeus by Beer; invocations at *Acharnians* v. 816, *Knights* v. 297, *Frogs* vv. 1126, 1138, 1144, and 1145, *Thesmophoriazusae* vv. 977 and 1202.

[36] Vernant (1965) 100.

[37] See discussions of the Hermes scene in D. J. Conacher, *Aeschylus' Prometheus Bound: A Literary Commentary* (Toronto:Univ. of Toronto Press, 1980), 68-73, and in Vernant and Vidal-Naquet, *Myth and Tragedy in Ancient Greece*, trans. Janet Lloyd (New York: Zone Books, 1990), 272.

[38] Kahn (1978) 166. Compare Jean-Christoph Agnew, *Worlds Apart: The Market and the Theatre in Anglo-American Thought 1550-1750* (Cambridge: Cambridge Univ. Press, 1986), a study of theater and the market in late renaissance English and American society, for a more sublunary appraisal: "The difficulty that exchange in and for the market presented was that it necessarily involved the crossing of boundaries; there was then a pointed logic in the appropriation of Hermes as a patronal deity by the merchants, or 'professional boundary-crossers,' of antiquity," p. 22.

[39] Among those of his cult-titles extant in the Aristophanic corpus are: ἀγοραῖος (of the market), δόλιος (trickster), ἐμπολαῖος (commercial), ἐναγώνιος (gamesman), ἐριούνιος (of uncertain meaning: Droysen has "ruhesegnend," Rogers renders the word "Helper," and van Daele translates "le Secourable"), ἡγεμόνιος (guide: cf his role as psychopomp or leader of souls to the underworld), and νόμιος (pastoral or legal). See too Burkert (1985) 184 on Hermes' ambivalence: "Hermes sends profit in the market place as *agoraios*, but escorts the dead as *chthonios* or *psychopompos*," and see Vernant (1965) 99-100 for a catalogue of Hermes' various aspects, what Vernant calls "ce foisonnement d'épithètes."

[40] Burkert (1985) 156; he goes on to stress the complex nature of the god: "That a monument of this kind [= the *herm*, understood as an inheritance of Mycenaean phallic culture] could be transformed into an Olympian god is astounding. In effecting this transformation, narrative poetry combined two motifs: the widespread mythical figure of the trickster who is responsible for founding civilization, and the epic role of the messenger of the gods. . . ." (Here he renders a more conservative estimate of the same over-determination of the god's origins suggested by Cicero in *De natura deorum* III 22.) By this description Hermes is both champion of the human

world and representative of the divine. Burkert goes on to call Hermes "a rival of Prometheus, the artful bringer of fire," p. 157, lending an interesting turn to the scene from the *Prometheus Bound* mentioned above.

[41] Peter W. Rose, *Sons of the Gods, Children of Earth* (Ithaca: Cornell Univ. Press, 1992). See the "Introduction: Marxism and the Classics," pp. 1-42, in which Rose acknowledges a debt in the formulation of his approach to such Marxist and neo-Marxist scholars as Mikhail Bakhtin, Antonio Gramsci, Louis Althusser, and most especially Fredric Jameson.

[42] Rose (1992) 33.

[43] A method later revised in Jameson, *The Political Unconscious: Narrative as a Socially Symbolic Act* (Ithaca: Cornell Univ. Press, 1981).

[44] Rose has been criticized for the perceived difficulty of his style, and the questionable fit of some of the more post-modern varieties of neo-Marxism he discusses with the ancient objects of his study: see for example the review by Kirk Ormand in *Bryn Mawr Classical Review* 3/6 (1992): 474-480. Nevertheless Rose's signal contribution, recognized by Ormand as such particularly in the chapters on the *Iliad* and the *Philoctetes*, is to have applied the Jamesonian "double hermeneutic" to Classical texts, and this innovation is crucial to my discussion here.

[45] Marx (1973) 110.

[46] Terry Eagleton, *The Ideology of the Aesthetic* (Oxford:Basil Blackwell, 1990), 198-9.

[47] But see Ehrenberg (1951) 147: "Hermes was the god of trade. In comedy he is called Empolaios, 'engaged in traffic and commerce', and Agoraios, 'belonging to the market'. He was, above all, the god of small tradesmen and hucksters, and so is derided as a 're-retailer' [παλιγκάπηλος, translated above as 'retailer of imported goods']. As Dolios and Strophaios a deceitful and shifty god, he was the patron of all dubious methods of business. He was, however, more than the god of trade. We shall not take into account all his functions, important as they were: some of them are also mentioned in comedy; he is the god of herds and flocks, the doorkeeper, the god who shows the way, or the god of games. The part, however, which he plays in the *Peace* is of immediate relevance to our questions. The god from whom the chorus asks help is a god of peace, humane and bountiful, and when directing 'like a good craftsman' the work of excavating the goddess of Peace, he is thought of as the god of craftsmanship." It is hard to square this resolutely sunny picture of the god with his initial behaviour towards Trygaeus, particularly at vv. 361-382. The sense of Hermes' role as go-between is rendered sinister as he threatens to bring about Trygaeus' death by exposing him to Zeus and the corporal punishment announced for any would-be saviors of Peace.

[48] For discussion of the diminutive form "-ιδιον" in the Aristophanic corpus in uses other than Hermes' name, see Dover (1968) in his note on *Clouds* v. 80, where the suffix appears in Φειδιππίδιον and is termed by Dover a "wheedling diminutive." Sommerstein (1982) in his note on *Clouds* v. 237 calls Σωκρατίδιον, or "little Socrates," an "affectionate diminutive" and agrees that "the tone is wheedling;" he compares *Peace* v. 382.

[49] Van Daele translates here "mon petit Hermès," while rendering the diminutive at v. 924 simply "un méchant petit Hermès."

[50] The term is from Whitman (1964) passim, and is his designation for the wish-fulfilling motor-force of the Aristophanic plot.

[51] On this last aspect, see particularly vv. 392-4, where the chorus addresses Hermes as ὦ φιλανθρωπότατε καὶ μεγαλοδωρότατε δαιμόνων; van Daele translates pointedly "ô le plus humain et le plus libéral des dieux."

[52] Vv. 190-1: Τρυγαῖος Ἀθμονεύς, ἀμπελουργὸς δέξιος. / οὐ συκοφάντης οὐδ᾽ ἐραστὴς πραγμάτων. "Trygaeus the Athmonian, skilled vineyard-worker, neither a sycophant nor a meddler [= lover of public affairs]." These last two categories of behavior, as made clear in Edmunds (1987) 17 ff., are connected specifically, and pejoratively, with urban political life.

[53] The loose, almost dreamlike associations of this logic are typical of Aristophanes; as van Daele suggests ad loc. vv. 414-5, the reference to cosmic reorganization is included for the sake of a dig at recent reforms of the Athenian calendar: compare *Clouds* vv. 607 ff.

[54] The festivals promised Hermes are, of course, to be appropriated from Athena, Demeter, Zeus, and Aphrodite, respectively. They are here termed "civic" because of their special importance for city life at Athens: Burkert (1985) 232 calls the Panathenaea "the birthday festival of the city," despite its Panhellenic tendencies, and at pp. 285 ff. notes the obvious associations of the Mysteries of Eleusis with Athens. The Dipolieia, of course, were held in honour of Zeus specifically in his civic (Πολιεύς) aspect; the Adonia, a woman's festival, is perhaps included for piquancy.

[55] Platnauer's edition of the *Peace* (Oxford: Oxford Univ.Press, 1964) contains the observation ad loc. that "χρυσίδων ('gold plate') is put παρὰ προσδοκίαν for some such word as ἱκετῶν." That the wine-skin scene is not, of course, simply a piece of stage business but a skillful parody of Euripidean preoccupations and Greek gender roles in general is made clear in Zeitlin (1981) 183-4.

[56] See Whitman (1964) 110 for good remarks on the reverse food-imagery of the play, comparing it to the changes in the comedy's olfactory vocabulary: "The imagery of food makes a similar progress from the beginning to the end, from the ghastly fare of the beetle to the splendid marriage feast. More specifically, it goes from the dung cakes of the opening line to the wedding cakes of the last, cakes which go 'wandering around alone,' waiting to be eaten." Hubbard (1991) 144 offers a more involved analysis of the play's imagistic progress: remarking on the fact that the dung beetle is abandoned among the gods to subsist on 'Ganymede's ambrosia,' Hubbard writes that this "signals . . . the movement from scatological interests, such as the dung beetle and his food, to sexual ones, not only Ganymede but Opora and Theoria as well. Freud has identified the transition from the anal-erotic to the Oedipal as a crucial stage in infantile development, but the Greeks were more likely to think in terms of masculine development from passive, pathic sexuality to active, genital sexuality." The *Peace* then might be said to display (both

temporally and spatially) a range of polymorphously utopian delights.

[57] The actual terms in which Trygaeus voices his salutation are interesting, and will receive further discussion below.

[58] See Whitman (1964) 111: "Trygaeus well-nigh literally turns swords into ploughshares -- the crest into a feather duster, the spear into a vine prop, the breastplate into a chamberpot. . . ."

[59] See Whitman (1964) 110 on the rural rhythm of the play's chief refrain: "This movement back toward the country is accented by the frequent repetition of the words, εἰς ἀγρόν, 'to the field'; the phrase, or its close equivalent, recurs roughly a dozen times. . . ."

[60] Wealth as a ritual or mythological figure has a somewhat marginal place anyway: the product of the *hieros gamos* of Demeter and Iasion, he is as such possibly associated with the Eleusinian Mysteries, where he is said to represent "wealth in corn." "Wealth proper is the produce of the corn harvest that banishes poverty and hunger. Vase paintings from the fourth century show a boy with a horn of plenty between the Eleusinian goddesses, surrounded in one case by sprouting corn ears -- Plutos personified," Burkert (1985) 108 and 288. Sculptural iconography even shows Wealth in at least one case, a statue by Kephisodotos, as a little child borne up by Peace (see Hertel [1969] 85n2, illustration 1). At any rate, the wealth of the present passage seems hardly even to bear that much allegorical significance.

[61] There remains, of course, v. 924, in which Hermes is "rather casually dismissed," Whitman (1964) 115, but this is perhaps just a verbal reflex of Hermes' darker aspects, as mentioned above; his last appearance in the comedy (v.726) is in an authoritatively benign role, as opposed to the actual demotion he suffers in the *Plutus*. Burkert (1985) 189 notes of Greek mortal-immortal relations in general that "only rarely is the god invoked with the title Lord, despota, the word a slave uses to his owner." Hermes is twice so addressed in the *Peace*, at vv.385 and 399, by the Chorus.

[62] Agnew (1986) 21, acknowledging the work of Norman O. Brown among others, writes, "Hermes himself came into being as a rustic deity but was gradually urbanized when the locus of trade shifted from the countryside to the *agora*. . . ." Agnew's speculation misses the important point that Hermes as deity of exchange is already ancient, so that any transition to the urban or monetary marketplace is prefigured in the young trickster and huckster god of the *Homeric Hymn* anyway. Vernant (1965) 131 makes this transformed continuity clear: "Les Grecs, en pleine économie marchande, n'auront pas de mal à reconnaître, sous les traits de leur dieu du commerce, la figure de l'ancien dieu des bergers: dans le mouvement de l'argent qui sans fin se reproduit lui-même par le jeu des intérêts, ils verront encore le croît du bétail se multipliant à intervalle régulier."

[63] Marx, *Capital*, vol. 1, trans. Ben Fowkes (New York: 1977; reprint), 151-2. The passage is quoted in a slightly different form also in Vernant (1988) 262-3n9. Compare Louis Gernet in Gordon (1981) 145-146 on this same epistemic shift: "it was left to Plato and Aristotle, neither of them friends of the mercantile economy, to construct a theory of money-as-sign and money-as-convention. That was a logical theory, since of course these

philosophers were interested only in the aspect of exchange and circulation (and they forgot or failed to understand that metal money had been very early used in a kind of religious 'trade' to settle debts. . . ." According to Gernet, what Plato and Aristotle left out of their account was the continued functioning of the mythological superstructure in the economic base, thus replaying exactly the occultation of significance to which Marx refers in *Capital.*

[64] See Benjamin Bickley Rogers' note ad loc., in his edition with translation of the *Plutus* (London: Heinemann, 1907), where he stresses the joke on Hermes' aspect as patron of heralds, and thus recipient of the tongue at sacrifices, and the resulting play on the ethic dative τῷ κήρυκι.

[65] See van Daele ad loc. on ἐπιτέτριψαι at *Peace* v. 369.: "le mot est à double entendre."

[66] See an explicit contrasting of "urban" and "rustic" in the aesthetic sense in Aristophanes *Fragment* 685 (= Hall and Geldart ΑΔΗΛΩΝ ΔΡΑΜΑΤΩΝ fr. 685): διάλεκτον ἔχοντα μέσην πόλεως / οὔτ' ἀστείαν ὑποθηλυτέραν / οὔτ' ἀνελεύθερον ὑπαγροικοτέραν. See too the aesthetic use of ἄγροικον at *Plutus* v. 705, in a scatological context with resonance for the contrasting milieux of our two plays. I owe the observation of the term's "semantic opacity" to Richard P. Martin.

[67] My exegesis of these cult-titles is indebted to Rogers' note ad loc to *Plutus* vv. 1153 ff.

[68] In this Karion is following Hermes' own earlier flattering self-debasement at v. 1136: ἆρ' ὠφελήσαις ἄν τι τὸν σαυτοῦ φίλον: "Won't you help your own dear fellow at all?" Karion responds, effectively, "I'm a rogue and you're another." Contrast the appropriate use of these terms of rustic sodality at v. 631, where the Choryphaeus uses them to Karion.

[69] And as became clear in the *Peace*, where Hermes is in fact *over*honored with cult prestige, the lubriciously figurative "Games" celebrated on the occasion of the union of the Council (βουλή) with Festival (Θεωρία) are notable secondarily for Hermes' *absence* (*Peace* vv. 886-906).

[70] See most poignantly van Leeuwen (1904) ad loc., for whom this is a sorry way for Aristophanes to leave the stage forever: "Pudet poetae inepto ioco fabulam claudentis et nobis qui nunc vivimus, ut olim spectatoribus, veluti valedicentis. Quanto festiviorem vividioremque exitum habebant Equites vel Aves!"

[71] Robert Lamberton has suggested to me that the skin on boiled milk is delicious, and therefore desirable; thus he contradicts both the evidence of one's own childhood experience with such a substance, as well as the obvious spatial sign-system at work here in Aristophanes' text (that is, the indication of a movement from above to below) to indicate the comedy's transvaluation of the Old Woman, who had heretofore only been "enjoyed" by the Young Man for her exchange value but who has now been thrown back upon her empty (sexual) use value.

[72] David Konstan and Matthew Dillon, in "The Ideology of Aristophanes' Wealth," *American Journal of Philology* 102 (1981): 371-94, describe the situation at the end of the Plutus succinctly (p. 383): "Hermes' skills and duplicity were appropriate in the reign of scarcity; now, in the kingdom of

plenty, there is employment only for his marginal, festive aspect." My analysis here differs with some of the conclusions of this excellent article; see a fuller discussion in the final section of this chapter.

[73] See Angus Fletcher, *Allegory: The Theory of a Symbolic Mode* (Ithaca: Cornell Univ. Press, 1975; reprint) and Gerhard Kurz, *Metapher, Allegorie, Symbol* (Göttingen: Vandenhoeck & Ruprecht, 1982); in both works the debt to Freud's *Interpretation of Dreams* is explicit.   On the issue of allegorical readings of ancient literature with special reference to Aristophanes see the interesting note on *Peace* vv. 43-46 (a discussion of the possibility of likening the dung beetle to the Athenian demagogue Cleon) in Hubbard (1991) 141n6: "Although much neglected, this passage is extremely important for students of ancient literary criticism.   It proves that ancient audiences were expected to interpret Comedy, and by extension we can infer other forms of drama, in symbolic and allegorical terms. . . ."

[74] See among others Demetrius Phalereus *On Style* 99, and Quintilian *Inst. Orat.* 8.6.44.

[75] See Karl Reinhardt, "Personifikation und Allegorie," in *Vermächtnis der Antike,* ed. Carl Becker (Göttingen: Vandenhoeck & Ruprecht, 1966); Leiva Petersen, *Zur Geschichte der Personifikation in griechischer Dichtung und bildender Kunst* (Würzburg-Aumühle: Konrad Triltsch, 1939); Katherine Lever, "Poetic Metaphor and Dramatic Allegory in Aristophanes," *The Classical Weekly* 46 (1953): 220-223; Hans-Joachim Newiger, *Metapher und Allegorie: Studien zu Aristophanes,* Zetemata 16 (Munich: C. H. Beck, 1957); and Hertel (1969) passim.

[76] Such is the implication of the passage from Quintilian cited above: "ἀλληγορία, quam inversionem interpretantur, aut aliud verbis aliud sensu ostendit, aut etiam interim contrarium, prius fit genus plerumque continuatis translationibus. . . ." Quoted also in Kurz (1982) 33.

[77] See for discussion Kurz (1982) 52-5 particularly and 27-64 generally. See too Hertel (1969) 5-7 for a consideration of this shift with explicit reference to the classics in general, and to Aristophanes in particular. Burkert (1985) 184 is lapidary: "The personification of abstract concepts is a complicated and much disputed matter. . . . The later art of rhetoric treated it as an artistic device, and as such it was seized on all too eagerly by allegorical writing down to the age of the Baroque." The whole section in Burkert (1985) from which the preceding is cited, "The Special Character of Greek Anthropomorphism," pp. 182-9, is of interest to the present discussion.

[78] Kurz (1982) 57. Emphasis supplied.

[79] "Der Satz *Ein Gerücht ging durch die Stadt* ist eine metaphorische Äußerung.   Wird das Prädikat wörtlich verstanden und durch weitere Handlungsverben fortgesetzt, dann erhält das Subjekt die Rolle eines Akteurs," Kurz (1982) 57.

[80] See Kurz (1982) 27-33 and 40-42.

[81] See, however, Karl Reinhardt's comments on Jacob Grimm's romantic-euhemerist derivation of deities from personifications, in which he condemns also the "humanist" tradition of laying stress on the theatrical materiality of the "personification"-process: "Doch eins war der späteren

Praxis wie der späteren Theorie entschwunden: daß die Personifikationen des Theaters und der Fabel ursprünglich und eigentlich Götter waren! Daß der Personifikation der Bühne der Gott selbst unter der Maske vorausging; daß allein als Götter all dergleichen zur Person geworden und nicht umgekehrt als Person zu Göttern. Hätte man nicht besser getan, dieses Zusammenhanges sich bewußt, anstatt von einer Personifikation von vornherein von einer 'Deifikation' zu reden? Wort und Begriff der Prosopopöie, gleich Personifikation, ist die Erfindung einer Zeit, die den Zusammenhang mit Sinn und Ursprung dessen, was es zu erklären galt, verloren hatte. Man sah in den Göttern des Theaters statt der Götter nur noch deren Masken, πρόσωπα, 'Personen'," Reinhardt (1966) 9.

[82] Eagleton (1990) 200.

[83] Lever (1953) 223: "In [Aristophanes'] hands poetic metaphor reached the heights of dramatic allegory. . . ."

[84] See more recently the discussion of mute female characters in Aristophanes in Bella Zweig, "The Mute Nude Female Characters in Aristophanes' Plays," in *Pornography and Representation in Greece and Rome,* ed. Amy Richlin (New York: Oxford Univ. Press, 1992), 73-89.

[85] Lever (1953) 221.

[86] Compare Kurz (1982) 39-40 on "implikative Allegorie" and "explikative Allegorie."

[87] Reckford (1987) 5 describes the two "handmaids" of Peace as "Autumn Harvest" and "Festive Sightseeing," and notes that "for the emotional flavor, I translate them as Thanksgiving and Holiday." He stresses the fact that they are "personifications," as if Peace herself were a well-established goddess. Yet Burkert notes that, apart from her inclusion in the iconography, Εἰρήνη is a relative late-comer to Greek religion. In a discussion focusing on the Hellenistic period, he writes: "The decisive break-through of personifications into the realm of cult had taken place earlier, in the fourth century: increasingly, statues, altars, and even temples were erected for figures such as Eirene, Peace, and Harmonia, Concord; even Demokratia could not be forgotten. . . . All this, of course, is more propaganda than religion. The arbitrariness of the cult foundations could not be concealed; the profusion of robed female statues of an allegorical character arouses no more than dusty, aesthetic antiquarian interest," Burkert (1985) 186. Aside from questioning his too-ready distinction between religion and propaganda, one might take issue with Burkert's judgement regarding the interest of the allegorical, although the allegation of "aesthetic" value is certainly praising with faint condemnation.

[88] Whitman (1964) 114 calls the passage "a masterpiece of montage;" Henderson (1975) 64-66, the product of another age, speaks of gang rape.

[89] Platnauer (1964) xiii, where reference is made to the scholion to Plato cited also by Droysen. Hans-Joachim Newiger, "Retraktionen zu Aristophanes' 'Frieden'," *Rheinisches Museum* 108 (1965): 242, is definitive in his assertion of Peace's representation by a prop: "Wenn noch jemand bezweifelt, daß die Göttin -- im Gegensatz zu anderen ebenfalls stummen Personen -- durch eine Puppe dargestellt wurde: ihr wird mit feierlichem Gebet am Altar ein Opfer dargebracht; eine Veränderung ihres

Standorts ist seit ihrem Erscheinen (520) durch nichts indiziert; sie muß von 520 bis zum Schluß an derselben Stelle stehend gedacht werden; die ἵδρυσις einer Statue (oder Heiligtums) ist ein normaler kultischer Vorgang. Der einmal herbeigeführte Friede bleibt bis zum Ende auf der Bühne, um durch sein Dasein den neuen Zustand darzustellen; Theoria und Opora werden, ihren 'Bedeutungen' entsprechend, aus der Handlung hinausgeführt."

[90] Whitman (1964) 112 makes coy remarks on the "minor, but enthusiastic, philological controversy" of participation by naked courtesans or ἑταῖραι in the comedies; see now the important discussion in Zweig in Richlin (1992) 73-89. Zweig's argument is persuasive, and her central thesis, that the manipulation of nude women (or their representations) on the ancient comic stage was less about festival than about repression, troubling; nevertheless she does ultimately leave the question as to whether actual nude ἑταῖραι were employed to play the roles unanswered, and indeed moot: see particularly her conclusions at pp. 85-88.

[91] In support of the emendations of v. 524 to refer to Peace rather than to Festival, it may be noted that further on, at v. 617, the Choryphaeus in conversation with Hermes calls Peace εὐπρόσωπος, a possible echo of the term used in v. 524, and set off in that place from the address to Festival by a δέ.

[92] Coulon and van Daele (1985) ad loc.; Reckford (1987) 5. Obviously the implicit distinction made here between word and name is heuristic and imported, yet it responds well, it seems to me, to the relatively lax allegorical exigencies of the scene and indeed of the play, in which the trio of Peace, Harvest, and Festival is so closely construed as to allow for just such semantic blurring. And see Burkert (1985) 184 on the slippage of abstractions and god's provinces: "the extreme thesis that there were originally no abstractions at all, . . . only demonic powers experienced as person-like, ignores the facts of the Indo-European languages at the least."

[93] Chantraine, s.v. σήπομαι, notes the oinological use of the term as its single favorable connotation: "dit de vielles gens dans un sens péjoratif, mais parfois, en bonne part, d'un vin vieux." Jean Taillardat, *Les images d'Aristophane* (Paris: Les Belles Lettres, 1965), § 56, claims that the word was used unironically of a vintage wine, and that its metaphorical use to denote an old person occurs only in comedy. Note that the word is used in just this negative sense at *Peace* v. 698, suggesting that its earlier appearance is not entirely unironic.

[94] See for example Coulon and Van Daele (1985), Droysen (1881), and van Leeuwen (1906), all ad loc.

[95] The anonymous third argument to the extant *Peace* claims that Eratosthenes, the third-century Librarian at Alexandria, was in doubt about whether the *Peace* had been simply restaged or entirely rewritten. The problem stems from citations of lines by other writers, ostensibly from Aristophanes' *Peace* but not to be found in the extant text. See discussion in van Daele's "Notice" in Coulon and van Daele (1985), and in the "Prolegomena" to van Leeuwen (1906).

[96] τῆς πᾶσιν ἀνθρώποισιν Εἰρήνης φίλης / πιστὴ τροφὸς ταμία συνεργὸς ἐπίτροπος / θυγάτηρ ἀδελφή·

[97] κᾆτα τἀκείνων γε κέρδη τοῖς γεωργοῖς ἦν κακά· / αἱ γὰρ ἐνθένδ' αὖ τριήρεις ἀντιτιμωρούμεναι / οὐδὲν αἰτίων ἂν ἀνδρῶν τὰς κράδας κατήσθιον. There is some confusion about the exact implicature of events (whether the farmers' fig-trees were devastated principally by Athenian naval commandeering, or by Spartan slash-and-burn ground sallies, as seems to be the suggestion at vv. 628-9, or whether indeed it is *Spartan* farmers under discussion), but the charge of enrichment of cynical politicians at the expense of the rural population is clear enough.

[98] See vv. 552, 555, 563 (where Herwerden would read οὐ σαπρόν, which is overruled by citations in Suidas and Athenaeus), 569, 585, 1202, 1329, and 1389.

[99] And implicitly, country against city: for the taxiarchs are said to be prejudiced against the land-workers and in favour of the city-folk in the matter of conscription, *Peace* vv.1172-90.

[100] Konstan and Dillon (1981) 372.

[101] Konstan and Dillon (1981) 393.

[102] Konstan and Dillon (1981) 381-2.

[103] See van Leeuwen (1904) xiii ff. for a discussion of the style of the *Plutus*, including an equivocating rejection of any charge of senility being laid against its author.

[104] A speech that Eduard Fraenkel, in *Beobachtungen zu Aristophanes* (Rome: Edizioni di Storia e Letteratura, 1962), 154, significantly assigns to the one scene of the play "die noch ganz des Aristophanes würdig ist."

[105] Whitman (1964)108.

[106] Van Leeuwen (1904) ad loc. notes that Chremylus here "magis exquisito salutandi verbo utitur," and significantly compares Socrates' use of the same word at *Clouds* v. 1145, as well as the Young Man's at *Plutus* v. 1042, where the novelty of the word is made concrete by the *Old* Woman's incomprehension. Rogers ad loc. adduces Lucian's citing of Plato's objection to this same "old-fashioned" greeting, thereby strengthening the suggestion of another Aristophanic take-off on everything new-fangled.

[107] See the Sycophant's one-two response to the Just Man's inquiring as to his profession: ΔΙ. Γεωργὸς εἶ; ΣΥ. Μελαγχολᾶν μ' οὕτως οἴει; (= Q: Are you a farmer? A: Do you think I'm that crazy?) Farm labor is thus juxtaposed explicitly, and negatively, with city labor.

[108] Chantraine (1980) and Frisk (1970) s.v. σαπρός both view it as an a-Ablaut form of σήπομαι, the latter word seeming to be restricted to the negative aspects of corruption and rot.

[109] There is some controversy over the odd image, although most manuscripts preserve the reading (S has a capitalized Ἐτῶν, suggesting the genitive plural of ἔτης rather than ἔτος, according to Coulon). Rutherford and Willems emend ἐτῶν γε to τε τῶνδε; see however van Leeuwen (1904) ad loc., who compares a fragment of Philetaerus for the usage, and points out that ἔτης "neque Aristophanea est, neque si esset, huc conveniret."

[110] There is also perhaps in the idea of "curing" an ironic take on Chremylus' earlier exchange with Blepyrus (vv. 406-8), in which the latter suggests retaining a physician to cure Wealth's blindness, and the former protests that the city lacks both the salary and the expertise (Τίς δῆτ'

ἰατρὸν ἐστι νῦν ἐν τῇ πόλει· / οὔτε γὰρ ὁ μισθὸς οὐδέν ἐστ' οὔθ' ἡ τέχνη.). The tools of the country-side have now been pressed into metaphorical service, as the city has found its cure.

[111] "To be sure, Penia endorses a world that is at the opposite pole from that inaugurated by Plutus in the finale of the play. Plutus restores the original prosperity of an age preceding Zeus, while Penia, insisting that Zeus too goes poor, dismisses the picture of Olympian splendor drawn by Chremylus and Blepsidemus as a Cronus-like dimness (*Kronikais lemais*, 581), playing on the common idea of Cronus as an old man, but alluding also, no doubt, to their purblind faith in the golden age over which that god was believed to have presided," Konstan and Dillon (1981) 385. Konstan and Dillon fail however to mention that Zeus is himself cited by Chremylus at vv. 1189-90 as being present αὐτόματος or "of his own free will" at the feast that ends the play and ushers in the new dispensation, thus suggesting a post-Olympian, rather than pre-Olympian, era. There is however the scholiast tradition of identifying this Zeus with Plutus himself, against which see Rogers (1907) ad loc.

[112] Scholiasts disagree over whether the opisthodomos meant was that of Athena Polias or of Athena Parthenos, that is, whether it belonged to the Erechtheum or to the Parthenon. There is evidently no trace of such a vault in the remains of the Erechtheum, whereas the opisthodomos of the Parthenon is still extant. At any rate both buildings would provide equally central civic spaces.

[113] See Rogers (1907) ad loc. on vv. 771, Wealth's formal address after returning from the precinct of Asclepius: "The Scholiast explains Παλλάδος κλεινὸν πέδον [= Athena's famous plain] by τὴν ἀκρόπολιν [= the Acropolis], and no doubt rightly; for πέδον is very frequently used to denote sacred ground, and no word could more fitly express the 'flat oblong' top of the Acropolis which was the special home and sanctuary of Athene." Stephanus Byzantinus emends and glosses succinctly: κλεινὴν πόλιν (τὴν ἀκρόπολιν δηλονότι).

[114] "Borderline" because the interchange between the Just Man and the Sycophant in which the remarks fall could just as easily be read as a criticism of the Sycophant's *particular* relationship to the city, and not as a blanket condemnation of city-life.

[115] See Konstan and Dillon (1981) 383: "The priest himself prepares to abandon Zeus and remain with Chremylus (1186-87), *whose house now has something of the status of a city.*" Emphasis supplied.

[116] See Loraux in Reverdin and Grange (1993) 209-211 on the specific maleness of the ἀγροί in the *Peace*.

[117] On subjectivity and speech see again Zweig in Richlin (1992) 73-89. Zweig is particularly evocative in her comparison of Aristophanic comic technique with the distribution of "speaking parts" in twentieth-century pornography, 85-89. It might perhaps be added, in the case of the *Plutus*, that it is precisely in the making visible of the wandering, speaking god of Wealth (his exposure to the eyes of his owners, even as he is given back the means to reciprocate that view) that his problematic *subjectivity* is exposed. And this is entirely in keeping, as it happens, with the generally

ambivalent history of the money form.

[118] Burkert (1985) 108.

[119] As Coulon and van Daele (1985) ad loc. explain, "la richesse ici, c'est d'abord Ploutos lui-même, si peureux (v. 198) et si hésitant; ce sont aussi les riches en bloc, toujours en souci de leur argent, tremblant à la pensée qu'ils pourraient le perdre, et obligés de prendre mille précautions pour le garder. . . ."

[120] Compare *Peace* vv. 848-9, where a similar turn of phrase is used to disparage the gods; in the *Plutus* this expression (in effect, "I wouldn't give sixpence for it") is rendered literal by the particular personification in question.

[121] See Carrière (1979) passim for extended discussion of this dynamics.

[122] It is notable that Trygaeus' rural utopia also contains slaves, although of course no mention is made of their acquisition (*Peace* vv. 537 and 1002). Carrière (1979) 259, in connection with a fragment of one of Cratinus' contemporaries, notes:"La disparition de l'esclavage ne se conçoit que si le monde présent devient magique ou si on se reporte à un temps très ancien."

[123] Interestingly, the word is also used of the offerings made to a bride as she is first brought into the house of her husband: see discussion in Vernant (1965) 103n23 and at 137-8 on the Chaeronean custom (reported by Plutarch) of casting out Hunger and ushering in Wealth in its stead. Once again, compare here this play's centripetal action with the centrifugal movement of the *Peace*.

[124] On the later rise of allegory see Maureen Quilligan, *The Language of Allegory* (Ithaca: Cornell Univ. Press, 1979), 13-24, and Walter Benjamin, *The Origin of German Tragic Drama*, trans. John Osborne (London: New Left Books, 1977). Rudolf Pfeiffer, *History of Classical Scholarship from 1300 to 1850* (Oxford: Oxford Univ. Press, 1976), 28, in a remark on fifteenth-century Italian translations of the *Plutus*, notes both an increasing interest in allegory and a growing moralism, from as early on as Hellenistic times and the Byzantine recensions of Aristophanes, as possible reasons for the eventual medieval preference for the play.

Chapter 2

The Masks of Money:
Plautus' *Aulularia* and *Trinummus*

Only comedy accorded the allegorical the rights of citizenship in the secular drama; but when comedy moves in seriously, then the consequences are unexpectedly fatal.

Walter Benjamin

Prologue

Virtually all of the twenty-one extant comedies of Plautus concern money in some fundamental way, with an insistence not always attributable to their Hellenistic templates:[1] and yet scholarship has tended to treat money's role in the Plautine corpus discretely and functionally, rather than as a general signifying element in a code relevant to the particular Roman republican milieu of the plays' composition.[2] The work most thoroughly devoted to the centrality of the theme in the Plautine corpus, Monique Crampon's *Salve lucrum*, is a concordance to "le vocabulaire de la richesse et de la pauvreté tel qu'il se présente dans le corpus le plus ancien de la langue latine,"[3] and limits itself mainly (apart from brief concluding remarks on Roman social history) to a structuralist investigation of a closed semantic field.

Part of the problem of Plautine interpretive focus in general, and not only as regards the importance of money in the plays, is due to the well-known *aporia* concerning the Roman-historical relevance of these texts and the consequent divide in scholarship between philological and sociological approaches. Florence Dupont, in her influential *L'acteur-roi*, has warned scholars away from the twin dangers of reading anything other than the plots of Greek new comedy into Plautus' Latin versions, and of attempting to psychologize what should thereby

emerge only as static, "mythological" characters.[4] She reserves
particular disdain for psychoanalytically-oriented critics like Charles
Mauron, author of *La psychocritique du genre comique*, who is by her
lights guilty of both cardinal sins by imputing Oedipal motivations to
the characters of Roman comedy, characters whom he also fails to place
in their properly rigid, new comic contexts.[5] Dupont is nevertheless
prepared to grant that Mauron's analysis of Plautine comedy holds at
least a grain of interest, if not novelty: for she herself has already been
at work classifying the personages of the Roman comic stage in a
functionalist manner akin to Mauron's superimposition of comedies, in
order to extract their archetypal narratological patterns.[6] Dupont is
even prepared to accept Mauron's talk of the triumph of the pleasure
principle over the reality principle as enacted in comedy, but only so
long as her own structural-sociological terms are substituted for
Mauron's Freudian meta-psychological. She writes:

> Mais à partir des analyses de Mauron, on peut proposer une
> interprétation qui substitue aux principes de plaisir et de réalité ainsi
> qu'à l'Œdipe qui les accompagne, deux pôles de comportement social: le
> repliement sur le privé et le déploiement dans la convivialité. Deux
> termes abstraits mais qui dans l'Antiquité correspondent à une réalité
> concrète: l'homme appartient à sa famille et maison (*oikos*), et cet
> *oikos* lui impose des devoirs d'économie et même d'accumulation. Mais
> il appartient aussi à un groupe social, cité ou village.   Cette
> appartenance lui impose des devoirs de consommation et de
> dissipation. Car la consommation en commun, les dons de femme,
> d'argent, de nourriture sont des façons obligatoires d'appartenir à cette
> communauté. Les deux comportements sont complémentaires: il faut
> accumuler pour pouvoir dépenser et ne pas trop dépenser pour pouvoir
> continuer à accumuler. La dualité jeune/vieux fortifie cette polarité
> sociale.[7]

What the psychoanalytic literary critic calls the triumph of the pleasure
principle over the reality principle, then ("Triomphe 'magique' du
plaisir dit encore Mauron et le théâtre serait cette magique"[8]) becomes
in Dupont's model just another in a series of border-skirmishes in the
ongoing social war between the young male comic protagonist's desire
for expenditure ("la dépense") and sociability, and the old male comic
protagonist's insistence on zealous stewardship of property. "Que les
uns ou les autres l'emportent, c'est la ruine de la société: soit
disparition de l'*oikos* comme cellule sociale par sa dissolution
économique, soit éclatement du groupe social en *oikoi* disséminées et
repliées sur elle-mêmes."[9]
    Such a dialectics of expense and retention, however, of usufruct and
accumulation, whether or not it is couched mythologically, in a
Roman version of a defunct Greek form, or burlesquely, in the

persistence of prohibition- and rejuvenation-themes in Aristophanes, or didactically, in fourth-century economic manuals, depends for its intelligibility on a certain relevance to the society to which it addresses itself. In the case of the Plautine *palliata*, plot dynamics and personages may have been borrowed from Greek new comedy, but the verisimilitude of the actual Roman productions requires that there be a minimum of identification (beyond simple technical translation) with the terms of the situations embroiling those personages. Dupont insists on the Aristotelian element of verisimilitude ("le vraisemblable") in her comparison of Greek new comedy with Attic tragedy: "Le *muthos* comique a ceci de particulier qu'il est un faux, une fiction vraisemblable à la différence du *muthos* tragique qui est vrai mais invraisemblable;"[10] and indeed, further on Dupont does seem to suggest a parallel between Roman new comedy and Attic tragedy, at least in their respective uses of *cantica* and *stasima*, as might befit two mythological forms similarly opposed, in their non-verisimilitudinous deployment of character, to the experimental-classificatory style of Greek new comedy.[11]   Yet Dupont never actually claims that the personages of Roman new comedy have the same holographic quality as do the figures of Attic tragedy, that they and their history can be reconstructed whole from the merest particle of their representation. There is after all a great difference between stock types like the buffoon and the schemer, who act predictably in any given situation insofar as they follow their characteristic destiny, and figures like Agamemnon and Antigone, whose behavior is conditioned by a destiny already circumscribed by a store of robust if occasionally contradictory particulars in other tellings.[12]   "Dave et Géta," Dupont rightly points out, "ne reproduisent pas des types d'esclaves romains pas plus que Phédria n'est un jeune patricien, et Chrémès un vieux sénateur;"[13] but they are also not, for all that, endowed with such impressive and well-known histories that their presenter can afford to dispense with an explanatory prologue.

In other words, the compulsory rites of belonging to the community represented in Greek new comedy ("des façons obligatoires d'appartenir à cette communauté"), that is, shared consumption, gifts of women, money, and food, must be assimilable by the Roman audience, too, in the absence of a true-but-improbable *muthos* that might provide the comedy's personages with history and motive.   No doubt Dupont is correct in reconstructing the *palliata* as a sort of period piece or costume drama, a staging for Roman republican delectation of "une Grèce hors du temps et de l'histoire, cette Grèce créée par la Néa et qui ne prétendait à aucun réalisme."[14] But it is just as sure that it is only in such a mythologized yet banal quotidian that one may glimpse the operation of an uncanny fantasy, a make-believe in which ostensibly foreign characters speak one's own language and make reference to

familiar institutions. As Dupont says, in defense of her *caveat* against
the scholarly will to seek directly reflected topicality in Plautus:
"Lorsque la comédie interférera avec le réel, ce sera toujours le masque
comique qui servira à interpréter une réalité et non celle-ci qui servira de
référent au masque comique."[15]   This pronouncement at least
acknowledges that there may have been such a thing as 'the real' to
which Plautus had interpretive access; it may indeed go a good deal
further, opening up as it does the possibility of a reading that takes
into account the productively distorting effects of the theatrical mask,
that most crucial element in the Roman culture of spectacle.[16]

Barred from divining direct historical relevance, the critique of
Plautus must have recourse to some touchstone of shared experience,
lest it founder in formalist irrelevance.[17]   It will be my project in this
chapter to locate such a touchstone for the broader discussion of the
changing representation of wealth in ancient comedy by bringing to
bear a certain set of critical assumptions on the texts of the two plays
of Plautus arguably most concerned with money and its representation.
Chief among these assumptions is the conviction that, despite their
two-dimensional stock nature, the personages of Roman new comedy
had to depend for their intelligibility on a measure of psychological
verisimilitude: as noted above, their presenter could not very well rely
on a cycle of popular oral narratives to flesh out the vicissitudes of his
play's action.   Psychological   verisimilitude   in   storytelling,
furthermore, depends for its reception on its audience's minimal
familiarity with the social conditions and relations of power in which
its themes are embedded, lest the estranging effect of foreign milieu and
habit become wholly alienating rather than pleasantly diverting.
Finally I will assume that such verisimilitude, the sense that a given
action or reaction is inevitable or characteristic, relies most
fundamentally on a chain of fantasy associations underlying social life:
for in what other register could it be felt that events that are contrary to
fact, that have actually taken place neither in historical reality nor in
story and myth, yet satisfy a certain logic?

In an attempt to examine the mutations wrought on allegories of
wealth by Roman new comedy I turn in the following chapter from the
Marxist analysis of imagery to a method of reading based in part on the
ideas of Jacques Lacan, perhaps the century's most influential and
innovative theoretician of the Freudian mechanism of fantasy.   This
turn is contingent upon the texts at hand.   For whereas the overtly
fantastical nature of the Aristophanic inventions seems to call for a
materialist reading to bring to light the relations of power buried under
their grotesqueries, the apparently realist surface of the Plautine
situation may be found to yield most fruitfully to an interpretation that
applies pressure upon the fantasy structures dissembled by Roman
comedy's characteristic masks.   In the course of that interpretation, I

will suggest that the allegorical representation of wealth in the two plays of Plautus most focused on money, and its significance, are indeed stranger and more sinister than the full-blown burlesque of Aristophanes' *Plutus*, a play that might at first glance seem to have said the last comic word on the subject of money.

Roman New Comedy and the Masks of Money

"Roman civilization has three ages," writes the influential nineteenth-century French historian Jules Michelet, in the preface to his *History of the Roman Republic*: "The *Italian*, or national age, ends with Cato the elder. The *Greek* age, commenced under the influence of the Scipios, produces as its fruit in literature, the age of Augustus. . . ."[18] That Plautus rides the cusp of the first two of Michelet's Roman ages (the third is the "*Oriental*" age, culminating in the baptism of the Empire) is a matter of historical record. Just what may have been Plautus' particular stakes in the alleged early second-century conflicts between Roman nativist and philhellenist tendencies, as exemplified respectively by Cato and the hellenizing Scipionic circle, however, continues to occasion debate.[19] Furthermore, the age ushered in by the Scipios and perfected under Augustus was by no means a mere return to classical Athens but a hybrid, apocryphally to be known as Hellenism,[20] a great age of translation and reception.[21] That Rome itself should somehow never have had a Roman age is symptomatic of the readings proposed below. There I will propose that, in the figure of the Sycophant who adorns his *Trinummus*, Plautus foreshadowed the decentered subject of post-modern parlance, with its revelation that the ego is not master in its own house. Plautus delivers with his Trinummus the unsettling lesson that the mastership and expanding wealth that were Rome at the beginning of the second century B.C.E. rested on an uneasy balance of centripetal nationalism and centrifugal adventuring, and yet that this mastership was itself definitively to be located in neither nationalism nor adventuring, but rather in the mask forever veiling the site of power.[22] That this mask was theatrical both in the strict sense of belonging to the Roman comic and tragic theaters of the day and as the property of a continuous cultural display instrumentalized by Roman society is of course the central claim of Florence Dupont's *L'acteur-roi*; it will be my purpose in this chapter to focus rather more narrowly on the *economic* masks of two products of the Roman comic tradition.

This comic tradition, however disjointed, presupposed a certain cultural continuity between Greek new comedy and its burgeoning Roman offshoot. "Roman Comedy took Middle and New Comedy (rather than Aristophanes) for its model," notes Paul Shaner Dunkin in *Post-Aristophanic Comedy:*

perhaps, not alone for simple reasons of approximate contemporaneity, but also because second-century Rome was in a stage of development roughly analogous to that of fourth-century Greece. Here as in Greece the struggles of the classes through many years had ended in the surrender of aristocrats and commons to capitalists; and an exhausting imperialistic war had just been concluded.[23]

A quality of retrenchment links the two ages: fourth-century Greece, and particularly Athens, after the Peloponnesian Wars (to which period, of course, the *Plutus* belongs), and second-century Rome after the Punic and Macedonian Wars. Still, despite these parallels, it is the innovations of Plautus, his contributions of anachronistic or culturally jarring Roman material to the *mise-en-scène* of his Greek models, that came to constitute a discrete field of scholarly research during the high age of modern classical studies.[24] Indeed, the Plautine corpus, by a sort of hermeneutic sleight of hand, functions for philologists both as an index of the continuity of Greek culture in the Hellenistic world, and as a mirror of the youthful flexing of Rome's hegemonic muscle.[25] But as has been pointed out, the specific Romanness of Plautus only emerges against this appreciation of the Hellenistic.[26] A play of differences in these intensely social texts allows the rhetorical, psychological and economic lineaments of both periods to be glimpsed.

It will be, then, my assumption in this chapter that the text of Plautus can be read both as a variation on themes inherited from Greek ancient, middle, and new comedy, and as a critique of contemporary Roman politics. By taking as my object of study the two plays of Plautus most centrally concerned with money and property, the *Aulularia* and the *Trinummus*, I will focus on the role of wealth in these comic commentaries. For if Aristophanes' statue of Peace, exhumed and refurbished, his god of Wealth, sight restored and established in a cult, and even the pot of gold of Plautus' *Aulularia*, finally put to social use, all represent a sort of healing of the gap between the representation of value and the fantasy of its immanent presence, then the strange figure of the Sycophant in the *Trinummus*, unveiled as a hoax yet uncannily still somehow possessed of the ability to make good on his promise of wealth and patrimony, warns against a too-comfortable belief in the possibility of such a healing. Behind this Sycophant, I will argue, stands the prologue's figure of Inopia, daughter of Luxuria, as a sign of the poverty present at all times in wealth, and as a reminder of the lack that ever shadows opulence.

At the same time, the Sycophant's status as the ploy of Megaronides in the interests of Philto (both characters associated with the nativist, conservative ideology of a Cato[27]) and as the actual bearer of the wealth of Lesbonicus' father Charmides, whose financially triumphant return from abroad suggests the cosmopolitan, philhellenic, Scipionic counter-pole to such an ideology, effects a dismantling of both contemporary Roman positions.[28] The Sycophant's failure to carry out his assignment may be read allegorically, as a discrediting of the hollowly hypocritical ways of Cato, at the same time as the obstinate quality of his departure from the stage signals the inability of the Scipios to control the cultural and material wealth they had seemingly mastered. Furthermore, the resistance of the Sycophant to being resolved into a symbol of the pastoral landscape, a cult-figure, a medium of exchange or even a rhetorical trope (which last recuperation might be pleaded for his double, Inopia) reveals the obstinate nature of some substance at work in the comic image of society, something which cannot be dissolved but which is necessary for the continued play of language and commerce.

It must of course be noted that the economic language of price and value is always intimately connected with the social setting of comedy, however much the comic text may problematize the interrelation of the two. Marie Delcourt, in a discussion of exaggerated slave-prices in Latin comedy, observes prudently: "La comédie nous donne presque toujours des cas exceptionnels, mais l'exception est toujours psychologiquement fondée et il n'y a aucun prix excessif qui n'apporte une indication sur un caractère."[29] The language of money in the comic tradition nevertheless resists costuming more stubbornly than do the Hellenistic social conventions and rhetorical postures that are otherwise the stuff of comedy, and which quickly adapt their older selves to the new garments made for them. The Sycophant's threadbare costume fails to hide the fact that he is neither coin of the realm nor foreign currency, but a strange intermediate object, whereas the *sententiae* of the many purveyors of wisdom in the *Trinummus* easily pass from their former Greek to their present Roman milieu. This is not to say that financial and economic signifiers become unrecognizable in their passage from Greek to Latin, and from fourth- or third- to second-century B.C.E., but merely that they serve better than purple rhetorical set-pieces to point up the difficulty with which certain elements are preserved in the comic tradition, and to suggest their particularly close connection to the object cause of desire at work in comedy.

The persistent importance of economic signifiers such as money and property is of course also to be sought in their political significance. In the case of Plautus, and of the period of composition of the two plays under consideration, as noted above, what was at stake politically was the stand-off between Cato's republican populism and Scipio's aristocratic elitism. In whatever direction Plautus' sympathies may "actually" have fallen, the *Aulularia* and the *Trinummus* dramatize and problematize the issues at stake in the politics of the day: the alienability of property, the importance of money for the construction of social class, and the connection between riches (or poverty) and ethics.[30]   As was the case in Aristophanes' *Plutus*, the *Trinummus'* hope of a positive or progressive social change in which wealth will be mobile, invisible, justly distributed, and thus available to all is at once excited and dashed: the meta-theatricality of the Sycophant's providential appearance reduces him to a nihilism of buffoonery, and the poverty of his representation is thus revealed. For I will show that the two Plautine comedies also call into question, particularly through their different uses of the conventions of the prologue, the very status of theatrical allegory and dramatic personification.

The *Aulularia* and the *Trinummus*: Species of Allegory

The plots of both comedies can be briefly sketched. The *Aulularia* opens with a prologue spoken by the *Lar familiaris*, the tutelary deity of the old man Euclio's house. This figure reveals the presence of a treasure in the house, a pot (*aula*, hence the play's title) of gold, which was hidden by Euclio's grandfather from Euclio's father, to whom the grandfather left instead only a small piece of arable land. The treasure, subsequently withheld from Euclio in turn by the house-spirit, has at last been made known to him by this same deity, so that it may be used as a dowry for Euclio's pious daughter Phaedria. Phaedria has shown her devotion to the Lar, unlike her father and her grandfather, and has thus won its assistance. Meanwhile, she has also been raped and impregnated by her young neighbor Lyconides; his wealthy uncle Megadorus, ignorant of her rapist's identity, is currently requesting her hand in marriage without dowry, so as to spare the apparently impoverished Euclio the expense of providing one. Megadorus' sister Eunomia, however, has learned of her son's assault of Phaedria, and is determined to procure her for Lyconides. This finally ensues, despite Euclio's indifference to his daughter's condition and his preoccupation with his pot of gold and its security. This pot of gold is nevertheless eventually stolen, by Lyconides' slave Strobilus, who hopes in vain to use it to purchase his freedom. The *Aulularia* ends in fragments, so that it is not possible to know whether Euclio ever retrieves his treasure from the now contrite Lyconides, who has confiscated it from his slave, or whether, now repentant of his avarice, Euclio himself offers it finally to Lyconides to keep as a dowry.

The *Trinummus*, meanwhile, concerns the wastrel Lesbonicus, who has squandered his father Charmides' estate; this latter is now away on business, attempting to recoup the spent wealth. Accordingly, the play is introduced by the allegorical personage Luxuria, or "Debauchery," who explains the coming action and consigns her equally allegorical daughter Inopia, or "Scarcity," to Charmides' home. It then transpires, as the action of the play commences, that Lesbonicus' guardian,

Callicles, has just saved Charmides' home (and the treasure hidden within it, which he holds in trust for Charmides, and the existence of which he has prudently not communicated to his ward) by purchasing it for himself: Lesbonicus, in his efforts to procure more capital, had put it up for sale. The purchase exposes Callicles to the disapprobation of his crony Megaronides, who suspects him of thus duping his protégé. Callicles, however, reveals to Megaronides the secret of the treasure, and makes clear the consequent necessity of his transaction. Meanwhile Lesbonicus' friend Lysiteles, hoping to aid Lesbonicus in his apparent penury, offers to marry his sister without dowry, and thus relieve him of her upkeep. Lesbonicus, however, suddenly conscious of public opinion, refuses this dishonorable solution to a part of his financial woes and resolves instead to sell off the last remaining item of his father's estate, a piece of arable land. His slave Stasimus prepares himself for probable penury and military service at his master's side, by attempting to retrieve money he had lent in the forum. To prevent the sale of the land, meanwhile, and realizing that his charge cannot simply be apprised of the treasure's existence, Callicles arranges at the suggestion of Megaronides for a stranger to present himself to Lesbonicus as having come from his father Charmides, and to give him the dowry, to be taken in fact from the treasure, as if provided by Charmides. The Sycophant who is chosen for the job (for which he is to receive three *nummi*, or small coins,[31] hence the play's title[32]) is however foiled in his mission by the coincidental return from a successful voyage abroad of Charmides, who chases him away in consternation. He confronts his friend Callicles with accusations of perfidy, but is soon mollified with explanations. All ends felicitously with the marriage of Lysiteles to Charmides' daughter, provided now with a proper dowry, and of Lesbonicus to Callicles' daughter.

Both plays take as their leitmotif a hidden treasure: indeed, the comedy of Philemon that provides the immediate material for the *Trinummus* is called in Greek the Θησαυρός, or *Treasure*;[33] yet only in the *Aulularia* is the hoard literally at the center of the action, thus claiming the protagonist's attention wherever he goes, motivating most of his actions, and being moved among the three scenic landmarks of the stage (Euclio's house, the temple of Fides, and the grove of Silvanus) in order to prevent its theft. In the *Trinummus* the treasure stays in Charmides' house, which Callicles goes so far as to purchase in order to prevent the treasure's falling into foreign hands.

The figures who speak the prologues of the two plays are also significant.[34] The Lar familiaris, or genius of the house, who opens the *Aulularia*, is a spirit consonant with the constant occupation of a house by a given family. "Der *familiai Lar pater*," explains the Pauly-Wissowa, s.v., in reference to the term's appearance at Plautus'

Mercator v. 834, "wird völlig zum Exponenten des ganzen Hauswesens, dessen Mehrer und Schützer er ist, . . . so daß man sich zum Verkauf der Lar-Bilder nur unter schwerem Zwange entschließt . . . und ihren gewaltsamen Verlust schwer beklagt . . . und sie zum Zeichen verzweifeltster Trauer auf die Strasse wirft." There is indeed a sense in which the Lar can be said to share the house with the family;[35] so that despite Naudet's reduction of the Lar's function to the strictly technical, it is entirely appropriate that this play concerning the fetishization of property be given its overture by property's very apotheosis.[36] The Lar's tone is measured and stately, as befits the spirit of a house long-occupied, and the guardian of a treasure hidden for generations ("ego Lar sum familiaris ex hac familia / unde exeuntem me aspexistis. hanc domum / iam multos annos est cum possideo et colo / patri avoque iam huius qui nunc hic habet," vv. 2-5[37]). That the Lar sets in motion the events of the comedy, which then unfold according to the inevitable logic of Euclio's already existing character, is indicative of the almost organic implication of the treasure, the family property, and the figure of the old miser, who is both conditioned by and conditioning of his immediate situation, in a non-contingency that will contrast sharply with the chance occurrences of the *Trinummus*.[38]

For the *Trinummus* does indeed have quite a different opening, a more vividly theatrical scene in which two allegorical figures, Luxuria and Inopia, share the stage and exchange lines. There is movement (Inopia, or Scarcity, is ushered into Charmides' house), relation (Inopia is said to be the daughter of Luxuria, or Debauchery), and meta-theatrical self-consciousness (Luxuria cites Plautus as the present play's author, names the *Treasure* of Philemon as the playwright's Greek source, and details Plautus' innovations). The figures themselves seem to have arisen out of the chaos of the young Lesbonicus' mismanagement of his patrimony. Far from having long inhabited the house of Charmides, as the Lar has that of Euclio ("hanc domum / iam multos annos est cum possideo . . . ," *Aul.* vv. 3-4, "I've occupied this house for many years now"), they are announced as newcomers: implicitly, as the inventions of Plautus ("primum mihi Plautus nomen Luxuriae indidit; / tum hanc mihi gnatam esse voluit Inopiam," *Trin.* vv. 8-9, "Plautus, first of all, gave me the name Debauchery; then he wanted my daughter to be Scarcity"); and explicitly, as Luxuria has only recently helped ("me adiutrice," v. 13) Lesbonicus squander his money, this recent change of fortune being indeed the reason for the industrious Charmides' departure (vv. 108-115), and as Luxuria is now moving out and installing her daughter Inopia in her stead (vv. 14-15).

There is no sense, then, in the prologue of the *Trinummus* of a symbiosis or even of a dialectic of character and fortune, as there is in the prologue of the *Aulularia*. In the *Aulularia*, as maintained above, the Lar familiaris, the house and property of Euclio's grandfather, the treasure hidden within, and Euclio himself, are all part of a complex centred on greed, nativism, and xenophobia. To the extent that the Lar can be said to represent the house of Euclio, to the extent that he is a metonym for that place, he may be considered a species of allegory, or symbolic representation of an actual state of affairs. Perhaps better, however, the Lar might be thought of as the metaphor of Euclio's very retentiveness and exclusiveness, a metaphor, however, which is also somehow determining of what it represents. The Lar simultaneously pulls the strings in the play's plot, and reflects the retentiveness of Euclio, by withholding from him his treasure in accordance with an already determined stingy character, one passed down for generations. For it should not of course be overlooked that the Lar is the supernatural agent of Euclio's (grand)father, and as such constitutes a symbolic function of his (dead) father's legacy. In Lacanian psychoanalytic terms,

> the non-coincidence of symbolic and real father means precisely that some 'non-father' (maternal uncle, the supposed common ancestor, totem, spirit -- ultimately the *signifier* 'father' itself) is 'more father' than the (real) father. It is for this reason that Lacan designates the Name-of-the-Father, this ideal agency that regulates legal, symbolic exchange, as the 'paternal *metaphor*': the symbolic father is a metaphor, a metaphoric substitute, a sublation [*Aufhebung*] of the real father in its Name which is 'more father than father himself', whereas the 'non-sublated' part of the father appears as the obscene, cruel and oddly impotent agency of the super-ego.[39]

Euclio's imaginary household, the fantasy of the father's integrity through his gift of the magical pot of gold, is complete and intact. He will brook no alterations to its fabric: not a cobweb is to be removed, not even Good Fortune, a possible bar to Euclio's enjoyment of his treasure, a sort of third disrupting the original dyad Euclio has reconstructed for himself, is to enter (*Aul.* vv. 85-100).[40] In the *Trinummus*, Inopia does indeed enter the house of Charmides, hardly as a temporarily alienable metonymy for, or partial object of, that house as site of the subject's integrity (as in the case of Euclio's Lar), but rather as a metaphorical emanation of the young Lesbonicus' behavior.[41] She is a figure trumped-up for the occasion out of the barely veiled animation of the words that might be used to describe the actual state of affairs in Charmides' house at this particular juncture in its history, and not an enduring emblem of the house's particular character.[42] Like the figure of Penia or Poverty in the *Plutus* of Aristophanes, Inopia is without cult. Indeed, Jean-Marie André notes the non-allegorical use of the doublet "luxuria-inopia" in other plays of Plautus, and reduces its typical action to an almost Aeschylean formula: "Consommation, débours, endettement, engendrent le mécanisme *luxuria-inopia*."[43] Luxuria, the more positive member of the couple, is herself "conçue comme moteur de l'économie de consommation sous toutes ses formes."[44] Thus these figures seem transparent masks for the economic mechanisms at work in the *Trinummus*, a play that reflects the growing pragmatism of the Roman political and economic scene.[45] It will be seen, however, that there is another dimension to the figure of Inopia, to her personification of lack giving rise to the masquerade that ends the comedy.

Prosopopoeia and Personification Reconsidered

The mechanism whereby the allegorical effect of the figures of Luxuria and Inopia, and of the Sycophant, is achieved in the *Trinummus* might be called "personification," the especially Latin term (from *persona*, "mask," but literally, "that through which voice is given") for what is in Greek called προσωποποιία (from πρόσωπον meaning "mask" also, but with the etymological sense of "that which is in view"), or "prosopopoeia," and which will be reserved for the device at work in the *Aulularia*. The pot of gold recalls the mute statue of the Aristophanic goddess Peace, animated by the venerating regard of the farmers; the Lar familiaris, whose effects are felt by the play's characters but who speaks only to the audience, represents a middle stage in the progress, through Luxuria and Inopia's passage into rhetorical presence in the action of the *Trinummus*, to that play's full-blown meta-theatrical representation of the father's money, personified by the Sycophant. This last figure, given voice and autonomous existence, is a new, uncanny version of the Aristophanic god of Wealth, who also speaks but to whom principally regard is given, in the form of his own restored sight and his establishment in a city cult. He too is a stage on the way to Plautus' representation of the money form, for despite his effective critique of the fantasy of immanent wealth propagated in the *Peace*, the god of Wealth is nevertheless enshrined at the close of the *Plutus*, and thus reassimilated to the ideology of autochthony represented by the goddess of Peace.

What Plautus effects hereby, in his representation of the fantasied object cause of desire, is a change of trope from the *Aulularia*'s mute and inanimate pot of gold called into life through being viewed and addressed by Euclio, to the *Trinummus*' garrulous, independently mobile Sycophant, put up to his task of impersonation by Callicles: that is, from prosopopoeia to personification. Leiva Petersen relates the lineage of the Greek and Latin terms for allegory and personification more or less unproblematically, but notes that it was only with the rise of republican Rome (the period of Plautus) and its increasingly important reception of Hellenistic forms that it began to be possible to construe allegorical figures as literary-rhetorical and thus distinct from cult-religious:[46] in other words, to allow the priority of artistic fabulation over deistic hallucination, of contingent invention over cultural tradition. That the *Aulularia* and the *Trinummus* of Plautus in some sense replay the shift from a conception of prosopopoeia founded on the apperception of a godhead, the Lar familiaris, to the device of personification arising from the material conditions of lived experience, the figures of Luxuria and Inopia, and later, the burlesque of the Sycophant, is an assumption of this chapter more important than any strict distinction between the two terms. In the chapter on Aristophanes, the *Plutus'* use of allegory was found to be a subtle critique of the values at play in the *Peace*. Here the heuristic distinction of prosopopoeia and personification is proposed as a means of comparing the sorts of incarnations, reifications and representations the *Aulularia* and the *Trinummus* themselves construct.

More indirectly, though no less importantly, these representations may be seen to have developed from the two Plautine comedies' composition in a historical milieu, the early second century B.C.E. at Rome, defined in large part by the contemporary conflict between Italian nativism and patrician Hellenizing. In particular, the attacks on Scipio's aristocratic circle carried out by Cato and his followers after 189 B.C.E., charging the general with failure to turn over the booty won in his campaign against Antiochus, are suggested in the motifs of retentive greed and false appearances, as well as of occasional populist moralizing, that run through both of the plays; at the same time, Cato's own hypocrisies as a populist orator and republican nativist who was not averse to abusing power for his own ends[47] help to inform the complicated cynicism with which the false coin of the Sycophant is unveiled by the very guarantor of the wealth he actually brings.[48]

It will be seen, then, when the two comedies are compared according to these theoretical pre-assumptions (the persistence of economic motifs in new disguises, and the distinction between prosopopoeia and personification as one of a certain psychological progress and as replayed by Plautus in the two plays under consideration) that the *Trinummus* performs in effect an unmasking of its own technique of personification. Through a meta-theatrical debunking of this technique as the hired Sycophant, disguised as the bringer of wealth from afar, is unmasked as a fraud by the very guarantor of his actual wealth, the *Trinummus* delivers a subversive critique of money and mobile wealth. In addition, and from the outset, what is put into question by means of the many forms of wealth, patrimony, hidden treasure, dowry, and mercantile gain, that are put into play in the course of the two comedies is indeed the value of money itself, the ostensibly transparent bearer of value that can also conceal itself by introducing a gap between its bearer and its value, its use and its exchange, its form and its significance. Plautus' discovery of money in the masked figure of the Sycophant tends toward the confusion of language and money, and works to the detriment of the latter, understood as the sign of imperfection, discordance, treachery, and the disjuncture of appearance and reality. And just as in the case of the *Plutus*, a double hermeneutic will reveal in the *Trinummus* an ambivalence with regard to money and its representation, a view of money both positive and negative, as a liberation and as a scourge, "good mother" and "bad mother." And indeed, only a consideration of money that takes into account these various social valences, its modalities and forms, its instrumentality in both giving and removing value, has the possibility of realizing money's power for social change, even as it runs the risk of assigning money to the place of the marginal, the rejected, and the uncanny.

The *Aulularia*: Fetishism and Prosopopoeia

The action of the *Aulularia* turns on the old man Euclio's failure to realize the social utility of his inherited pot of gold. Despite the intentions of the Lar familiaris in revealing to him the secret of the treasure, Euclio refuses to grant it as a dowry for his daughter Phaedria, and thus allow her to take up a position in society and bear a legitimate child.[49] This recalcitrance on the part of an old man is of course a stock function of what David Konstan, quoting Northrop Frye, calls Roman comedy's "blocking characters;"[50] but Jachmann points out importantly, in his polemical defense of the play's Menandrian heredity, the special nature of Euclio's inability to share the treasure, his obsessive miserliness.[51] Euclio is evidently not only unwilling to make social use of his treasure (that is, to exchange it against a proper future for his daughter Phaedria), he is in fact also in some way ignorant of the treasure's utility: that its use-value consists precisely in its exchange-value, and not in any inherent or immanent character. This is in part revealed by his resolution, early in the play, to attend a municipal welfare hand-out despite his anxieties for his treasure's safety; if he didn't go, he reasons, he would be suspected of not needing the hand-out, and thus of having money already (vv. 105-110). The few *nummi* he is to receive from the *magister curiae* (local council president), therefore, become merely a device for distracting the community's attention from his more substantial assets: a vicious circle, in other words, in which money's only use is the defense of itself, not the advancements or gains to be had from putting it into social play.[52]

What might be called Euclio's fetishistic relationship to his pot of gold is well demonstrated in the manner in which he refers to it in asides during his exchange with Megadorus, whom he mistakenly believes to be after the treasure. His paranoia at a fever pitch, Euclio transfers the pot of gold from its most recent hiding-place in his house, to the temple of Faith or *Fides* that shares the stage with the scene-buildings. He is to move it again, a hundred lines later, this time to the Grove of Silvanus, a forest deity, in the now correct belief that the slave Strobilus is plotting to rob him. The exchange with Megadorus, however, who only wishes to prepare himself for his wedding to Phaedria and to get drunk with his teetotaling father-in-law to be, shows the precise extent of Euclio's pathology:

MEG: ego te hodie reddam madidum, si vivo, probe,
     tibi cui decretum bibere aquam.
EUC: scio quam rem agat:
    ut me deponat vino, eam adfectat viam.
      post hoc quod habeo ut commutet coloniam.
      ego id cavebo; nam alicubi abstrudam foris.
      ego faxo et operam et vinum perdiderit simul.
MEG: ego, nisi quid me vis, eo lavatum, ut sacrificem.
EUC: edepol ne tu, aula, multos inimicos habes
      atque istuc aurum quod tibi concreditum est.
      nunc hoc mihi factum est optimum, ut te auferam,
      aula, in Fidei fanum; ibi abstrudam probe.
      Fides, novisti me et ego te: cave sis tibi,
      ne ut inmutassis nomen, si hoc concreduo.
      ibo ad te fretus tua, Fides, fiducia.

MEG: I'm going to get you properly drunk today, as I live,
     You who have sworn to drink only water.
EUC: I see what he's up to:
     He's behaving this way just to stun me with wine;
     Then what I have will change its residence.
     I'll foil that plan: I'll hide it elsewhere.
     I'll make sure he squanders both his effort and his wine.
MEG: Unless you need me for anything, I'll go wash up for the
                 sacrifice.
EUC: By Pollux, pot, but you've got a lot of enemies!
     Both you and the gold entrusted to you.
     Now the best thing for me to do is to take you,
     Pot, to the Temple of Faith; there I'll hide you properly.
     Faith, we know each other: be careful
     Not to change your name once I've entrusted this to you.
     I come, Faith, filled with confidence in you. (vv. 573-586)

Notable in this exchange is Euclio's address to the pot of gold, which not only brings it to life, but bestows upon it particularly human attributes like having a place of residence, making enemies, and being entrusted with gold. In fact, there is some suggestion of historical topicality in the actual words chosen by Plautus for Euclio's fears about the pot's changing location: while Hildyard, in the notes to his edition, protests the catechresis of a pot full of gold addressed in terms appropriate to "a people *seeking a new home*,"[53] Stockert points out that the period following the Roman campaigns in Greece, Spain, and the Middle East (mid- to late-190s B.C.E.) would have seen just such migrations of people and establishments of colonies in and around the Roman world, thus rendering the trope particularly vivid and actual.[54] Euclio further elaborates this imputation of uniquely human properties to the pot of gold by distinguishing explicitly between it and the treasure it holds, which is said to have been entrusted to it ("quod tibi concreditum est," v. 581), and which is equally the target of the pot's many imagined enemies ("multos inimicos habes / atque istuc aurum," vv. 580-581). Euclio's relationship therefore is as much with the vessel holding his wealth as with the gold itself, which, because forever to be withheld from circulation, is reduced to a sort of pure value, indeed fetishized by Euclio, through the process of prosopopoeia just discussed, into an animate, magical being, an imaginary bulwark against the poverty in which he continues to live and that in some sense defines him.

The foregoing use of the term fetishism in this regard, in connection with a commodity (the pot of gold), relies on Marx's well-known formulation of the concept of "commodity fetishism" in the first volume of *Capital*. There are indeed notable similarities between Euclio's conjuring of the pot into life and the transformation described by Marx in that famous evocation. The crucial passage is the following:

> There is a physical relation between physical things. But it is different with commodities. There, the existence of the things *quâ* commodities, and the value-relation between the products of labour which stamps them as commodities, have absolutely no connexion with their physical properties and with the material relations arising therefrom. There it is a definite social relation between men, that assumes, in their eyes, the fantastic form of a relation between things. In order, therefore, to find an analogy, we must have recourse to the mist-enveloped regions of the religious world. In that world the productions of the human brain appear as independent beings endowed with life and entering into relation both with one another and the human race. So it is in the world of commodities with the products of men's hands. This I call the Fetishism which attaches itself to the products of labour, so soon as they are produced as commodities, and which is therefore inseparable from the production of commodities.[55]

The situation in which Euclio finds himself is closest in fact to the terms of Marx's religious analogy, in which life is given to fantastical hallucinations: because of course Euclio hasn't the slightest intention of allowing his pot of gold to enter into relation with any other commodities, much less so with any other men.

Euclio's peculiar relation to his pot of gold more closely resembles that developed by the Marxist-Lacanian Slavoj Zizek as "fetishism *stricto sensu*," a belief in one's privileged access to an object with magical properties of which others are unaware. Zizek outlines this phenomenon in the course of his Lacanian exegesis of totalitarian power in *For They Know Not What They Do: Enjoyment as a Political Factor*, his pathbreaking analysis of post-Cold War Europe. Zizek differentiates "three modes of disavowal of castration," a distinction germane to the present discussion because of the obsessive character of Euclio's fear and the imaginary compensation he has constructed in response to it: symbolic control over his daughter's sexual life through the imaginary medium of his treasure. Marie Delcourt has already drawn attention to the imagistic logic at work in Euclio's dealings with the world by pointing out the metaphoric correspondence of the pregnant Phaedria with Euclio's pot of gold: "Une image souterraine, étonnament efficace, rapproche dans l'inconscient la marmite enceinte d'or et la fille grosse de l'enfant qui assurera au vieux la continuation de sa lignée."[56] Euclio significantly does not see this correspondence, which blindness allows Plautus the *coup de théâtre* (to be adapted later by Molière) of Lyconides and Euclio confronting each other on the two different topics, each thinking the other is referring to his own obsession (*Aul.* vv. 733-760). Euclio has in other words supplied himself with an imaginary entity (the pot of gold brought to life) in the face of the ostensible economic violence practiced on him by society; he can no more part with "his" goods (imaginarily pot of gold, symbolically dowry for his daughter) than he can recognize the symbolic compensation offered him by that same society in the form of the posterity to be enjoyed through a potentially legitimate grandson.

Zizek's schema, in which castration stands in for the loss of prestige experienced by a poor man in a society dominated by male power and wealth, may help to elucidate this interplay of fetishism and personification in Euclio's imaginary relationship with his pot of gold. Zizek terms his three modes of disavowal of castration the "traditional," the "manipulative," and the "totalitarian," and he illustrates them with recourse to examples drawn from the theatrical milieu. Euclio's mode will be seen to be the totalitarian, the most complete rejection of the reality of the subject's powerlessness in the face of society. The first example, illuminating what Zizek calls "traditional" disavowal, concerns a Hopi initiation rite, in which children are shown their own fathers and uncles hidden behind terrifying masks, masks that are at a certain point removed to reveal the familiar kin behind them. The naive belief of the children in the power of the masked figures is thus transformed into a symbolic faith in the masks themselves, which thus compensates for the loss of authority invested by the child in the imaginary figures of all-powerful gods or parents by supplying a strictly symbolic-functional authority *which is nothing more than the mask itself.*[57]

Zizek's second example, chosen to illustrate "manipulative" authority, is drawn from a legend in which Casanova personifies a wizard in order to impress a young woman. In the course of his prestidigitations, however, a storm actually breaks out, and despite his knowledge that he can hardly have conjured it up, Casanova is nevertheless frightened, and takes refuge in his own trumped-up magic circle. The seducer is thus caught up in the same naive belief he has been trying to engender in his young female prey, without thereby being able to transform that belief for himself into a symbolic faith in his own mask, since for that to occur, he would have to experience it through the mediation of his audience, and that is the one thing he cannot risk doing. He is thus trapped in his own personification, unable to recognize its symbolic-functional quality.[58]

The final illustration given in Zizek's exegesis, to illustrate fetishistic disavowal *stricto sensu,* is hardly an illustration at all, and is the one that best exemplifies Euclio's characteristic behavior. It is merely the description of the relation to an object in which the object itself incarnates or embodies, through the magical powers frankly attributed to it, the refutation of the knowledge that there is actually no power immanent in the subject, that the castration has always-already taken place as a condition of the subject's coming into being. "For the fetishist, therefore," explains Zizek,

> his other, 'ordinary people', are not simpletons, suckers whom it is necessary to exploit, but simply ignorant: the fetishist has privileged access to the Object, the significance of which 'ordinary people' overlook; his position is thus in some sense the very opposite of the manipulator Casanova, since he is primarily himself that which appears in the eyes of 'ordinary people' a simpleton, convinced of the exceptional value of the chosen Object.[59]

This final form of the "disavowal of castration" may at first seem not apt to the character of Euclio, since he is exactly convinced that the others *do know* the worth of his object. On closer inspection, however, it becomes clear that it is just this fear of being robbed that reveals the nature of Euclio's fetishistic attachment to the pot of gold, an attachment that has more to do with its symbolic or magical qualities than with any particular social use. This may be elucidated with a final reference to "commodity fetishism" formulation and its relation to Euclio's case. Zizek has taken care, earlier in his book, to complicate the traditional Marxian notions of reification and reflection in the following way:

> It is not sufficient to ascertain that in capitalism, relations between individuals apear in a reified form, as relations between things; the crucial point is that the relationship of individuals towards "things" is reflected back in the relationship between individuals, which is why the necessary reverse of "reification" is "personification", the process by means of which "things themselves assume the shape of "persons" (capital becomes the capitalist). This second, "squared" reflection where the first reflection -- "reification" ("things instead of people") -- is reflected back into "people" themselves constitutes the specificity of the dialectical self-relationship.[60]

The "process by means of which 'things' themselves assume the shape of 'persons'," called here "personification" by Zizek, is what is meant in the present discussion by prosopopoeia, with exactly the crypto-religious undertones given that process by Marx in the above citation from *Capital*, and in just the form in which Euclio enacts it.[61] What Euclio fails to complete, however, what he cannot perform, stuck as he is in his antique pre-capitalist condition, is the crucial manœuver of the capitalist, who recognizes in the commodity-fetish the quintessence of human labor, the surplus to be credited to him, and who thus reifies his relations with other humans even as he personifies his relations with the object. In this sense Euclio operates according to only one half of the dialectical relationship described by Zizek, in that he enacts the reverse of reification by conducting a relationship with a pot of gold, *only to the exclusion of other human beings.* Euclio behaves thus like the fetishist described by Zizek in the above-cited discussion of totalitarian power, with the added complication of his paranoia as to the treasure's security, his conviction, not that others are equally aware of the pot's magical properties, but that they wish to steal it from him.[62] This fear on Euclio's part represents in fact the very process structuring his fetishization of the pot: that is to say, his refusal to allow it to enter the circulation of goods and currency (and indeed women) proper to patriarchal, civilized society is embodied in the peculiar relationship he has to it as object-come-to-life. His fear, then, that the pot will be stolen, that is, liquidated, exchanged, given up in return for his daughter's marriage, can be seen as merely a symptom of that relationship, or indeed as the tic that is constitutive of his attachment to an inert object insofar as he is incapable of relations with other humans.

In the course of the play, however, Euclio is forced to renounce his attachment to the fetish object and to enter into relations, social and economic, with his community. The end of Euclio's imaginary relation with the fetishized pot of gold comes about, significantly, as a result of the intersection of an episode of prosopopoiea and the presence of another human: specifically, when the slave Strobilus overhears Euclio beseeching the goddess of Faith not to betray the deposit he has made in her temple (vv. 608-623). This leads only indirectly to Strobilus' stealing the gold, of course, for he will have to wait to get his hands on it until it has been moved to the Grove of Silvanus (vv. 701-712). But it is the specific character of Euclio's acting out of his fears for the fetishized object, his address of the goddess of Faith as the imaginary embodiment of the temple spirit with whom he has deposited his treasure, that allows the listening slave Strobilus to discover the existence of the gold and to trace its whereabouts.

Euclio's address of the goddess of Faith takes over from his earlier prosopopoiea of the pot itself; he now imagines the gold being entrusted to Faith ("tuae fidei concredidi aurum; in tuo luco et fano est situm," v. 615, "I have deposited the gold to your trust; it is placed in your grove, in your temple"), whereas before he had used the same construction of the gold's being entrusted to the pot ("edepol ne tu, aula, multos inimicos habes / atque istuc aurum quod tibi concreditum est," vv. 580-581, "By Pollux, pot, but you've got a lot of enemies! / Both you and the gold entrusted to you").[63] It is as if the pot and the temple spirit were equally animated by his regard and his address, indeed capable of a hand-off of his treasure between them. It must be remembered, too, that in the prologue the Lar uses this very construction of its own role in the affair: "sed mihi avus huius obsecrans concredidit / thesaurum," vv. 6-7, "Now his grandfather deposited with me in secret a treasure."

This implied homology of the Lar, the pot, and the goddess of Faith, as animate depositary and/or prosopopoeic addressee, turns on Euclio's agency in recognizing these various figures, or rather, recognizing the last two named, since it is his daughter Phaedria whose pious respect for the Lar wins him the treasure. Euclio's agency, then, as noted above, represents the internalization of his contingent relation to his patrimony and its magical appearance: he seems to be operating in accordance with his own character, rather than as a puppet whose strings are pulled by the Lar. This is of course because the Lar is at once cause of and metonymy for this very character.

The *Trinummus*: Personification and Unmasking

The foregoing discussion would risk, of course, psychologizing Euclio out of his symbolic function as exemplar of a particular rhetorical stance over against the sign of money, were it not the case that comedy is exactly the privileged site of the intersection of psychology and rhetoric, as well as the staging of their mutual undoing. One need think only of the ἀλάζονες or imposters of

Aristophanes, those figures like Lamachus in the *Acharnians*, or the Paphlagonian in the *Knights*, whose rhetorical excesses unravel to reveal their sorry characters. Wolfgang Rösler connects ancient comedy's origins both with the ritualized abuse typical of carnival or religious procession, and with the formal ridiculing of local politicians for the enlightenment of the suffrage.[64] Thus obscenity and devotion share the stage with the unmasking of the claims of power and the frail human forms underlying them, in a process that is sublated but not absent in the Roman inheritance of Greek middle and new comedy.[65] In particular, of course, this discordance played itself out in second-century Rome on the level of the financial sign, as the increasing wealth of the Republic made all the more compelling those comic figures who called into question the stability and representative integrity of the token of wealth, money.

As I move in my discussion from the *Aulularia* to the *Trinummus* it should become clear that such a questioning is what is in play, and that the connection between money and language as expressed theatrically is not an idle one. Money is staged as a sign in both comedies, a sign of presence or absence of means, power, the father; as well, money is used to stage the comedies' conflicts, for it is money, or what it represents, that already structures those conflicts, insofar as it is both a mask for and a construction of the social relations within which those conflicts are played out. Money arises in the lack that makes possible, or indeed necessary, symbolic exchange, the absence or scarcity of things to be bridged with a fantasy transitional object.

Once again, the intervention of Slavoj Zizek may elucidate this process. In his seminal *The Sublime Object of Ideology*, in which he elaborates a synthesis of the Hegelian and the Lacanian theories of ideology, Zizek writes that the difference between the two schools "corresponds to the one which distinguishes the Freudian from the Marxian notion of fetishism: in Marxism a fetish conceals the positive network of social relations, whereas in Freud a fetish conceals the lack ('castration') around which the symbolic network is articulated."[66] Whereas the pot of gold in the *Aulularia* tends to conceal the relations it represents (patrimony, father's amassing of wealth, mobility of women) by virtue of its fetishized status as an object called into life through Euclio's hallucinations, the money represented by the Sycophant in the *Trinummus* will operate according to the logic of the Freudian fetish once it has encountered the symbolic network: that is to say, once its personified fraudulence has been revealed by the very guarantor of its meaning.

What is at first striking about the two comedies under discussion here is the degree to which they follow the same narrative pattern. Both begin with supernatural prologues announcing changes in fortune as constitutive of the comedies' actions; both concern a secret patrimony in the form of a hidden treasure, juxtaposed with a publicly acknowledged piece of arable land; both turn on the charitable ambitions of a man with regard to marriage, foiled temporarily for financial reasons by the guardian of the young woman in question; both involve as sub-plot a slave's fortunes in connection with his master's financial condition; both contain set-pieces decrying the expenses involved in romantic courtship and marriage (*Aul.* vv. 501-533; *Trin.* vv. 235-255); and both feature scenes of mutual non-recognition or misunderstanding (*Aul.* vv. 731-776; *Trin.* vv. 843-997).

On the levels of plot and of construction the plays thus seem to form a doublet.   And yet there is a fundamental difference in their motivational structure: while the object causing all the fuss in the *Aulularia* is a pot of gold, at the heart of the *Trinummus'* action there is instead a void, an absence.   The treasure left by Charmides in the care of Callicles in the *Trinummus* is not, strictly speaking, the cause of the play's state of affairs, in the sense that Euclio's new-found wealth causes him to shun all company for fear of being robbed, and thus actually to bring about his own destitution through his eccentric relation to the treasure.   In the *Trinummus* it is rather Lesbonicus' sudden self-inflicted penury, combined with the withholding of his father's treasure through the paternal proxy Callicles, that brings about his sale of the house, the discomfiture of his guardian Callicles through malicious gossip, and the charitable offer of his friend Lysiteles to marry his sister without dowry.   These events in turn lead to his decision to liquidate the last of his estate, and to Callicles' resolve to provide him with a dowry through the agency of the disguised Sycophant.

The object cause of the *Trinummus*, then, is a lack; this is signalled from the outset by the choice of the allegorical figures who introduce the play.   Luxuria or "Debauchery" is shown departing; this is the spirit of expense or dissemination already lost who ushers in the almost completely silent Inopia or "Scarcity," the barely present sign of Luxuria's own having-been.   Expense and destitution co-exist: or rather, the first is the condition for the latter.   In Plautus' cosmology Luxuria is actually the mother of Inopia, a cruelly ironic play on the Greek commonplace whereby interest on money is called its child or τόκος;[67] perhaps we may even read here a genealogy in the tradition of Socrates' evocation of Poverty and Ingenuity (Πενία καὶ Πόρος) as the parents of Desire (Ἔρως; see Plato *Symposium* 203b ff.).[68]   In the *Trinummus*, meanwhile, it is Lesbonicus' ingenuity in satisfying his desires which has brought forth poverty: his expenditure is most frequently described in metaphors of eating.[69]   There is a suggestion, in Stasimus' ironic riposte at vv. 414-415, that Lesbonicus imagines his money somehow to be of immortal stuff ("nisi tu immortale rere esse argentum tibi"): that is to say, his desire for the lost object constantly overgoes any possible satisfaction, oral or sexual, in its quest for the deathless body of the treasure, of the fantasied primal mother, withheld by his father.

In contrast to the immanent plenitude of the Lar who opens the *Aulularia*, all that is immanent in the prologue of the *Trinummus* is the lack already at work within expenditure,[70] the child "Scarcity" born out of the mother "Debauchery," a mother whose readiness to propel her daughter on to fulfill her already assigned duty stands at the head of the play like the negative reflection of the staunch Lar, his homestead and its available treasure, the home into which not even Bona Fortuna is to be admitted (*Aul.* v. 100), so complete is it; all this against Lesbonicus' home, already being abandoned by the lack-engendering Luxuria as the *Trinummus* begins.[71]

As noted above, Inopia or "Scarcity" is almost silent, a virtual non-presence (or the virtual presence of absence). She does speak one line, however, and that is a simple, automaton-like response to her mother's command to enter Lesbonicus' house and carry out her duty there, combined with a request for more exact information concerning her stay with the young man ("LUX: sequere hac me, gnata, ut munus fungaris tuom. / INOP: sequor; sed finem fore quem dicam nescio," "LUX: Follow me this way, daughter, that you may fulfill your duty. / INOP: I follow; but I do not know what I shall call our goal").[72] The nature of her duty is never explained;[73] Inopia herself is elided almost as soon as she is introduced. She functions as a pure allegory, the sign of absence that produces meaning retroactively. Scarcity is, in other words, that phenomenon or state of affairs which allows the apprehension of a foregoing debauchery, the latter being by definition an excessive expense or enjoyment tending towards depletion.[74]

It is tempting to contrast this lack already at work within expenditure, the child Inopia born of Luxuria, with the baby born off-stage to the silent character Phaedria in the *Aulularia*, a presence never recognized by Euclio, occluded as it is at first by his preoccupation with the pot of gold, then elided altogether in the actual marriage plans for Lyconides and Phaedria. Here, in the *Trinummus*, the marriage of Inopia and Lesbonicus, or at any rate the service to be performed by her for him, is sublated from the outset, transformed into the real situation of lack in which Lesbonicus finds himself. Whereas in the first play a positive presence, a prosopopoeia given life only by being addressed (the gold, and perhaps also Phaedria's child) is finally overcome or ignored in favor of the social relations it is discovered to represent or reify, in the second play these very relations are constructed by the symbolizing force of the negative presence of Inopia, embodied or personified finally in the trumped-up figure of the Sycophant, he who bears the illusory yet effective stamp of the father Charmides.

The coming and going of Charmides is what is finally represented in
the form of the Sycophant-as-money, the Sycophant as the apparent
rascal and cheat who does in fact in some sense have the guarantee of
authority: the presence behind the absence, the worthlessness of money
hiding its transitional power, the "sublime material" (in the Zizekian
language of ideology) out of which money must be imagined to be
made in order that it be socially effective.   Here we may remember the
figure of Socrates in Alcibiades' speech in the *Symposium*, in which
Socrates' *agalma*, his inner beauty and value, is masked by his outer
squalor.   Here, however, in the case of money (and indeed of the
Sycophant), that inner value too proves to be illusory, unattainable,
merely a necessary pretext so that the place-holding function of money
may take effect.

In this way the *Trinummus* represents a critique of the *Aulularia*:
whereas the *Aulularia* elides the presence of the gold (and Phaedria's
child) in a finale that tends towards the full re-establishment of
harmonious human relations, thus simply transferring the organic
illusions of Euclio's magical prosopopoeia into the social structure, the
Trinummus, by turning absence itself into an allegory, leaves open the
gap between place-holder and guarantor of presence.   The finale of the
Trinummus refuses the illusion of harmony obtained with the rapist
Lyconides' marriage to Phaedria in the *Aulularia*, and instead continues
the personification or role-playing begun with the figure of Inopia and
carried over into the Sycophant-scene.

And it is this scene to which we must now turn, having noted the
way the radical contingency of the figure of Inopia arising from the
debauchery of Lesbonicus sets the stage for an action in which the
controlling hand of a divinity will be notably absent.[75]   This action,
the decision of the two old men Callicles and Megaronides to supply
Lesbonicus with a dowry for his sister despite his slavish attitude to
public opinion and his inability to keep money, is in some sense the
point of the play, contributing as it does the title and the comedy's
humorous center-piece.[76]   Philemon's *Thesauros* seems to have stressed
the affair between Lysiteles and Lesbonicus' sister as its intrigue: in
Plautus' revamping the focus is on money.   As Muecke puts it,
"Plautus eliminated the love theme, with the result that in his play the
moral conflict of the drama appears to be based exclusively on property
transactions and a preoccupation with *res*."[77]   Indeed, love as a motive
for Lysiteles' proposal of marriage is explicitly rejected, in his anti-
encomium of Amor ("omnium primum / amoris artis eloquar," vv. 235
ff., "First of all I shall speak of the art of love") in which it is
precisely those aspects of love tending towards expense that are listed
as its disadvantages.[78]   Lysiteles champions friendship, public opinion,
and sound money-management over the blandishments of an
impoverishing passion.   The close of his entrance soliloquy features a

listing of the goals of the *boni* and the *frugi*, the (Aristotelian or Theophrastic) good and temperate: "rem, fidem, honorem, / gloriam et gratiam," vv. 272-273, "riches, credit,[79] honor, glory and favor." *Res*, property, wherewithal, money, leads the list and wins the day,[80] as Callicles and Megaronides put their plan into effect despite (or perhaps in ignorance of) Lesbonicus' resolve to sell his land to obtain the dowry. The old men reason that a dowry must be provided, in order to safe-guard both Lesbonicus' and Callicles' social standing. Money proves thus to be both genus and species in Lysiteles' classification, that which both stands in for and supplements all of the following types of social goods (credit, honor, glory and favor). This logic drives Callicles and Megaronides to their plan, the dressing-up of the hired Sycophant as bearer of the *res* supposedly sent by the absent Charmides.

The Sycophant-scene unfolds in the following manner. Callicles and Megaronides, having learnt of Lysiteles' proposal, discuss the difficulties involved in providing Lesbonicus with a dowry for his sister (vv. 729-762), including the infeasibility of borrowing money (because nobody's lending) rather than unearthing the treasure and thus apprising Lesbonicus of its existence. Megaronides hits on a plan, which he elaborates with his friend (vv. 763-819): a stranger is to be engaged to play the role of a traveler, he will then claim to have arrived from Seleucia with letters from Charmides for Lesbonicus and for Callicles and with a dowry for the sister. If Lesbonicus wonders why his father's seal is not on the letters, some excuse is to be given, to the effect that Charmides has lost his seal and has had a new one made, or that the letters were opened at the border. Meanwhile, Lesbonicus being thus distracted, Callicles is to dig up the treasure and have the stranger present it.[81]

At this juncture Charmides returns from abroad, and, alone on stage, sings a hymn of thanks to Neptune for a safe journey home (vv. 820-840). He notices the Sycophant, and is intrigued by his strange appearance (vv. 840a-842); he observes in silence as the latter approaches his house, and announces to the audience the nature of his assignment (vv. 843-870). When the Sycophant begins to demand entrance to the house Charmides accosts him, and there begins a series of interrogations and misunderstandings turning on the Sycophant's uncertain grasp of the details of his mission: he has even forgotten Charmides' name (vv. 871-970). The Sycophant proves intractable, dissembles his own name, and insists on being shown to Lesbonicus so as to hand over the money. When Charmides reveals his identity, the Sycophant refuses to believe him, then denies that he himself is in fact carrying any money at all, claiming that he has only written documents. He goes off finally, cursing Charmides (vv. 971-997).

Important in the scene are above all two details: the uncertainty of names, both Charmides' and the Sycophant's, leading to a comic stichomythy in which both men's names are deformed (vv. 883-892 for the Sycophant, 906-922 & 977 for Charmides); and the Sycophant's swift change of tune concerning the money he is bearing (at vv. 954 ff., he claims to have "mille nummum . . . Philippum," "a thousand gold coins,"[82] while at v. 982 he says the money is only scrip, "scriptum quidem"). In these ways the arbitrary character of the money function is suggested, associated as it is with aleatory naming and protean shape-changing. Significant too is the little phrase used by the Sycophant of his supposed relations with Charmides, and which links him in an unlikely but telling way with the allegorical figure of Inopia from the play's prologue.

That little phrase may serve to initiate a close examination of the Sycophant-scene's imagistic armature, coming as it does at a crucial juncture or turn in the transactions of Charmides and the mysterious stranger; it sheds light both on the problem of names and on that of the form of money carried by the Sycophant. Charmides has observed the Sycophant in silence; accosted him; asked him his name and gotten an equivocal answer; demanded the name of the man from whom he has supposedly received the money he is carrying; been obliged to supply his own name (since the Sycophant has forgotten it, despite his claim to be life-long friends with the man in question, and only recalls that he has dealt with the father of Lesbonicus); asked after his own supposed whereabouts and been given fantastically deformed information; and is now, exasperated, on the verge of revealing himself to the pretender.

CH: quid ais? tu nunc si forte eumpse Charmidem conspexeris,
    illum quem tibi istas dedisse commemoras epistulas,
    norisne hominem?
SY: ne tu me edepol arbitrare beluam,
    quiquidem non novisse possim quicum aetatem exegerim.
    an ille tam esset stultus qui mihi mille nummum crederet
    Philippum, quod me aurum deferre iussit ad gnatum suum
    atque ad amicum Calliclem, quoi rem aibat mandasse hic suam?
    mihi concrederet, ni me ille et ego illum nossem approbe?

CH: Well now, if you should by chance catch sight of
        this very Charmides,
    The one you say gave you those letters,
    Would you recognize him?
SY: By Pollux, you must take me for an idiot, if you think
    I couldn't recognize the man with whom I'd spent my life.
    And would he have been so stupid as to entrust to me a thousand
    Phillips, and to order me to hand over the gold to his son

And to his friend Callicles, whom he'd given management of his
        affairs?
Would he have trusted me, if we weren't proper friends?
(vv.950-957)

This juncture is crucial, because the naming of the exact sum carried by
the Sycophant will resolve Charmides to try and dupe him out of the
money, on the assumption that it is in fact his own money at issue;
this attempt in turn will lead to the Sycophant's explanation that the
money is only on paper after all ("scriptum quidem"), and to his angry
departure.

What is more interesting, however, is the reappearance, in the
Sycophant's indignant reply, of the phrase "quicum aetatem exegerim,"
which echoes Luxuria's explanation of her daughter Inopia's function in
the home of Lesbonicus at the play's beginning.   There the phrase
"quicum aetatem exigat," v. 15, seemed to suggest an allegorical
marriage or apprenticeship of Lesbonicus to Inopia (with various
interpretations, notably by Hertel and Waltzing, as discussed above);
here the expression refers by immediate context to the Sycophant's
fictitious friendship with Charmides. But the connection to Inopia's
imaginary cohabitation with Lesbonicus cannot fail to be noticed,
underlined as it is here by the appearance two lines later of the words
"ad gnatum suum," which echo Luxuria's apellation for her daughter
Inopia, "gnatam meam," in the formula at v. 15 used to express the
latter's assignment to Lesbonicus. Just as Lesbonicus will spend his
days figuratively with Inopia, the personification of the lack born of
his debauchery, so the Sycophant, his invention and deployment
having been necessitated by Charmides' retention of the treasure, has
already been spending his days with Lesbonicus' father: and this in the
form indeed of the hidden (or lacking) treasure, which the Sycophant
represents in an uncanny and unrecognizable fashion to the old man,
and which Charmides has been withholding from his son Lesbonicus.
The two passages, finally, are mediated by the exchange between Philto
and Lysiteles, in the scene in which the son proposes to his father his
plan of marriage without dowry.

In all three cases the dynamics are not coincidentally supplied by
parent-child relations ("gnate mi"), since it is precisely the appropriate
exchange between generations that is manifestly at issue in the
comedy. Duty, means and inheritance are debated around the economic
and social imbalance created by Lesbonicus' behavior. Charmides
finally returns, the father whose absence has weighed over the play's
action since the outset; his presence should be consonant with
amplitude, resolution, and coherence, but he is instead at first brought
face to face with the uncanny spectacle of his own money walking and
talking, as it were, dressed in suspect foreign garb, and refusing to

acknowledge him as its owner or guarantor. In this play about the proper circulation of money and morals among parents and children, there is thus an unsettling minor chord struck in the encounter of Charmides and the Sycophant before the comedy's ostensible resolution in the marriages of Lesbonicus and Lysiteles and the reconciliation of Charmides and Callicles.

In his encounter with Charmides it is of course the Sycophant whose imposture is revealed, who is foiled in his task and whose defeat reveals the strange gap between its appearance and its function necessary for money's efficacy. But it is also the father Charmides himself, the money's putative master, who is revealed as somehow unstable. He knows that he is involved in a ruse, that the Sycophant cannot possibly have received money from Charmides, *since he himself is Charmides.*[83] Nevertheless, he cannot resist entering into the game ("enim vero ego nunc sycophantae huic sycophantari volo," v. 958, "For indeed I now want to dupe this duper"[84]), although there is nothing to be gained thereby: it is as if he has been mesmerized by the apparently magical pronunciation of his own name in the correct context.[85] He is thus duped precisely by his ostensible insight into the machinations of the ruse, for the Sycophant can only interpret his sudden and apparently arbitrary taking on of the name "Charmides" ("proin tu te, itidem ut charmidatus es, rursum recharmida," "So why don't you de-Charmidate yourself the way you en-Charmidated yourself before") for what it is, an attempted counter-ruse, and is quick to perform a complementary operation with the money at issue: he declares it "not present," only written and not in coin. Just as Charmides has suddenly conjured himself into veritable presence, so the Sycophant conjures the money into virtual absence.[86]

The Sycophant's response to Charmides' asking after his name is a species of kenning, apocopated however by the Sycophant's perverse refusal to provide the right answer. His name is so long, says the Sycophant, that if Charmides were to set out at dawn from the first letter, he would not reach the last until nightfall (vv. 884-886). This arouses Charmides' interest, and he tries to join in the game with a spin on the image (one would need to bring provisions for the journey along his name, v. 887), only to be brought up short with a rude joke: "SY: est minusculum alterum quasi vexillum vinarium. / CH: quid est tibi nomen, adulescens? / SY: Pax, id est nomen mihi: / hoc cotidianumst," vv. 888-890, "SY: I've got another name, a tiny one, like a wine-label. CH: What is your name, boy? SY: Pax, that's my name: my usual one." This "name" is of course actually an insult, something like "Shut-Up" or "That's-Enough."[87] Charmides is however only half aware that he has been insulted rather than answered: he betrays his semi-consciousness by observing at this point, on the evidence of the proffered name, the Sycophant's rascally nature, comically imagining a situation in which such a name would come in handy to a sycophant: in what is of course exactly the situation in which he now finds himself (vv. 890-892).

The insult is only properly received by Charmides when it is not directly meant by the Sycophant: when the latter tries to produce for Charmides the name of the man who is supposed to have given him the money, and enrages Charmides by cursing the name he has forgotten, Charmides' own. Charmides here reveals most fully his fetishistic relation to his own name, the magical sign that lures him into the attempt to dupe his duper, an attempt that is "programmed to fail," according to Muecke (1985) 174. The Sycophant cannot immediately give Charmides the name he asks for, and tries to put him off with a descriptivist periphrasis:[88] the name of the father of Lesbonicus is . . . that of an honest man, v. 906. When Charmides demands a more precise answer, the Sycophant is trapped and must admit his ignorance, without thereby giving the game away totally. He complains that he has swallowed the name imprudently ("devoravi nomen imprudens modo," v. 908), a peculiar coining that plays in advance on the turn of phrase he is to use at v. 910, that the name was on the tip of his tongue (literally, "on the ends of my lips," "mihi in labris primoribus"). Charmides, however, in a "striking revivification of a metaphorical expression",[89] chooses to take the Sycophant at his word, and declares himself inimical to someone who keeps his friends penned in behind his teeth ("non placet qui amicos intra dentes conclusos habet," v. 909). Twice more he responds to the Sycophant's cavalier vulgarity with such offense, at vv. 923 and 926. His name is inseparable, for him, from his essence, with the result that he is pained by the Sycophant's lapses of memory and taste; for the Sycophant, meanwhile, his own name is arbitrary, "immaterial," a mere function of his job and its vicissitudes.[90] The Sycophant's name is just a garment: "In the theatre, false names are to 'parts' what disguise is to costume, both vehicles of metatheatre."[91] The "metatheatre," of course, derives in part directly from the Sycophant's drawing the audience's attention to the fact of his having been outfitted by the costume-master ("choragus," v. 858); what Charmides fails to notice is the extent to which his own role is theatrical, not to say metatheatrical, in that he is himself only representing the presence (of money) that will enable this play to end, and that his whole encounter with the Sycophant is only a short-circuit, a momentary detour on the way to this end.

The Sycophant's treatment of Charmides' name is belittling, in accordance with his own workaday regard for names and roles: he recalls only the first letter (v. 915), and must be prompted to recall the rest through Charmides' recital of a repertoire of homophonous names (vv. 916-922). This method, proposed by Charmides himself, unwittingly reveals at once the emptiness, and the absurd importance, of names (especially those of absent fathers). Charmides suggests that they try to retrieve the name through its resemblance to other names ("quod ad exemplum est? coniectura si reperire possumus," v. 921, "What's it like? If we can find it by guessing . . ."), and must finally supply his own name himself as the most perfectly like, the only name equal to his own: Charmides = Charmides, a completely tautologous and therefore meaninglessly empty equation. Nevertheless, and this is the proof of the importance of his name, he is still somehow not equal to himself: upon his earlier question as to the physical characteristics of the Sycophant's purported friend, he was told that the man in question was a foot-and-a-half taller than he (v. 903). "Something is wrong," he says to himself, "if I am taller absent than present" ("haeret haec res, siquidem ego apsens sum quam praesens longior," v. 904). His absence, his figurative death to the world of this particular drama, has rendered him *as name* all the more powerful, the lack *in whose name* all the characters have been acting, whether out of guilt and bad conscience, like Lesbonicus, or out of honor and social bonds, like Callicles, Megaronides, Philto, and Lysiteles. His dramatically inert but psychologically significant encounter with the uncanny figure of his own money, apparently animated through the personifying efforts of the Sycophant, will introduce into the ostensibly cheerful series of reunions that end the play a note of discord.

This discord is of course the submerged realization of the contingent, place-holding, personifying character of money, of names, and indeed of language. "The subject," writes the psychoanalytic critic Jeffrey Mehlman, " . . . is at the point of convergence of different(ial) lacks: absence of the mother's phallus and sexual difference; absence of the father's (imagined) potency and generational difference; absence as the motor of a language metaphoric in its essence and linguistic difference."[92] If we supplement this standard postmodern repertoire with the Lacanian observation that the father is also without the phallus, and if we paraphrase the last member of Mehlman's tricolon crescendo to render it "absence as the motor of an *economy* metaphoric in its essence," we get the approximate lines of the *Trinummus*. With this move, the fetishism of Euclio's prosopopoeia of his pot of gold is replaced, not however by any substitutive guarantee of presence that might render the illusion of money's magical body unnecessary, but rather by the uneasy truth that such a fiction is itself necessary, as fiction, for the proper functioning of society. The imaginary other body of money, whether fetishized *stricto sensu* as the unexchangeable, animate totem of Euclio's pot of gold, or dressed up in outlandish garments and rendered uncannily, inadequately human by the Sycophant, remains an unreachable supplement, a fiction that must be posited in order that the process of symbolization be kept in play. For behind the pot of gold in the *Aulularia* is the Lar, ancestral guarantor of the stability and immanence of inherited land; and yet this phantasmal figure is revealed in the *Trinummus* as a mere herm, a merely symbolic marker of land tenure.

Behind the Sycophant in the *Trinummus*, meanwhile, is a symbol even more radically destabilizing of the fiction governing the play's economy: Inopia, the spirit of lack already at work within expense. In the comic dialogue of Lucian to be discussed in the next chapter, *Timon, or the Misanthrope*, and in its distant Elizabethan heir, Shakespeare's *Timon of Athens*, the subject of my final chapter, this destabilizing of the guarantees of wealth and property is to be re-enacted, at first in a subtle shift of characters, and then finally on the level of language itself, where the figure of Wealth, so robust in Aristophanes' *Plutus* despite the ambiguities attendant upon his representation, is elided entirely, and replaced with a purely rhetorical gesture signalling the constitutive, signifying emptiness of the money form itself.

Notes

[1] Pierre Grimal, *Le siècle des Scipions* (Paris: Montaigne, 1953), 96, has pointed out the centrality of money in Roman comedy, a centrality that appeared, significantly, as this genre was seeking to distinguish itself from its Greek models: "Si nous ne connaissions l'organisation de la société romaine à cette époque [= the early second century B.C.E.], où le rang dépend d'abord de la fortune, nous devinerions, à la seule lecture de Plaute, cette tyrannie de l'argent. *Que, dans une large mesure, il en ait été de même dans les cités grecques, ne suffit pas à expliquer ce choix constant du thème.*" Emphasis supplied.

[2] See for instance W.F. Richardson, "Nummus in the Plays of Plautus," *Prudentia* 15 (1983): 27-34, and Netta Zagagi, "Amatory Gifts and Payments. A Note on munus, donum, data in Plautus," *Glotta* 65 (1987): 129-132; for the rarer recent sociological work on money in the comedies, see Eckard Lefèvre, "Plautus-Studien I: Der doppelte Geldkreislauf im Pseudolus," *Hermes* 105 (1977): 441-454, and J. M. André, "L'argent chez Plaute: Autour du Curculio," *Vichiana* 12 (1983): 15-35.

[3] Monique Crampon, *Salve lucrum, ou, L'expression de la richesse et de la pauvreté chez Plaute* (Paris: Les Belles Lettres, 1985), 7.

[4] Florence Dupont, *L'acteur-roi, ou, Le théâtre dans la Rome antique* (Paris: Les Belles Lettres, 1985), 231-248 particularly. Dupont's use of the term "mythological" in this context deserves a brief explanation: as the figures of Greek new comedy, or the *néa*, are taken over into the Roman *palliata*, they cease somehow to be living embodiments of a particular theatrical tradition and become frozen into the inevitable forms of myth, characters who belong to another time and whose stories are always already

established. I will argue below that this can hardly have been entirely true
for the figures of Roman comedy in the same sense that tragic or epic
characters followed a set, inevitable destiny: as witness the prologues
needed at the head of Plautus' texts to fill in unknown details in the lives of
the figures to be represented.

[5] Charles Mauron, *La psychocritique du genre comique* (Paris: J. Corti,
1964); on Mauron see Dupont (1985) 244-247.

[6] The salient difference between the two structuralist methods is of course
that, while Dupont follows a tradition of reading borrowed from the
Onomasticon of Pollux, Mauron is indebted to the anthropologist Claude
Lévi-Strauss.

[7] Dupont (1985) 245-246.

[8] Dupont (1985) 245.

[9] Dupont (1985) 246.

[10] Dupont (1985) 242. It may be worth pointing out that in the passage of
the *Poetics* that Dupont here paraphrases the stress is on audience reception
(ἐπὶ δὲ τῆς τραγῳδίας τῶν γενομένων ὀνομάτων ἀντέχονται. αἴτιον δ'
ὅτι πιθανόν ἐστι τὸ δυνατόν, 1451 b 15-16) as much as it is on the
relative truth-values of any given comic or tragic propositions: Aristotle
recognizes the crucial role of contemporary relevance in the construction of
dramatic verisimilitude, and of cultural recognition in the purveying of
dramatic truth.

[11] Dupont (1985) 251.

[12] "In dealing with a heroic figure, say Heracles, the tragic poet begins
with the deeds or adventures traditionally assigned to the individual
Heracles. The comic poet, on the other hand, begins with the concept of
'glutton' or 'enormously powerful individual' and develops an action or
scene which fits the concept; the action or scene will then almost certainly
be new, i.e. fictitious, and may develop in any direction the poet pleases,"
Gerald F. Else, *Aristotle's Poetics: The Argument* (Cambridge: Harvard
Univ. Press, 1963), 312. In the case of Roman *palliata*, this same
dynamics is played out on the receptive, if not on the creative, level.

[13] Dupont (1985) 249.

[14] Dupont (1985) 248.

[15] Dupont (1985) 247-248.

[16] See Dupont (1985) 19-40 on the place of spectacle in Roman
civilization.

[17] Experience shared, of course, not only by the Hellenistic Greeks and the
republican Romans, but by those peoples and the modern-day reader. On
the general topic of alleged critical 'universals' and their applicability to
ancient texts, see recently the exchange in Karl Galinsky, ed., *The
Interpretation of Roman Poetry, Studien zur klassischen Philologie* 67
(Frankfurt am Main: Peter Lang, 1992), 153 ff.

[18] Jules Michelet, *History of the Roman Republic*, trans. William Hazlitt
(London: D. Bogue, 1847), 14. The classification arises out of a discussion
of Vichian euhemerism, and is offered here as a sort of artifact.

[19] See, for instance, the central question of Plautus' political alignment as
figured in his introduction of parodic, parabasis-like monologues. Tenney

Frank, Charles Henry Buck, Jr., and Paul Shaner Dunkin all see Plautus increasingly siding with Cato against the philhellenic Scipionic party, while Eckard Lefèvre, with special reference to the *Trinummus*, would have him daringly critical of Cato (if not entirely apolitical, as Donato Gagliardi holds). On the question of Cato's actual relation to Greece and its culture, see the revision proposed by Erich Gruen in the chapter entitled "Cato and Hellenism" in his *Culture and National Identity in Republican Rome* (Ithaca: Cornell Univ. Press, 1992), where the Censor's lifetime of commentary on Greek culture is construed as a calculated campaign to raise Roman cultural prestige. See also however continuing doubts of this thesis in a review of Gruen by Gary Forsythe, *Bryn Mawr Classical Reviews* 5, no. 1 (1994): 9-14. On recent scholarly rethinking of the place of philhellenism in the social history of republican Rome, and Cato's and the Scipios' roles therein, see Gruen, "The Appeal of Hellas," in Gruen (1992) 223-271.

[20] A neologism of Droysen's invention, according to Pfeiffer, *History of Classical Scholarship from 1300 to 1850* (Oxford: Oxford Univ. Press, 1976), 189.

[21] Pfeiffer (1976) 28 neatly calls the Romans "the first translators in Europe . . . the translators κατ᾿ ἐξοχήν."

[22] On the difficulties of determining motivation and program in the Roman expansion see the historiographic remarks on the use of the word "imperialism" in Erich S. Gruen, *The Hellenistic World and the Coming of Rome* (Berkeley: Univ. of California Press, 1984), 1-8.

[23] Paul Shaner Dunkin, *Post-Aristophanic Comedy: Studies in the Social Outlook of Middle and New Comedy at Both Athens and Rome* (Urbana: Univ. of Illinois Press, 1946), 57.

[24] See notably Günther Jachmann, *Plautinisches und Attisches* (Berlin: Weidmann, 1931), and Eduard Fraenkel, *Plautinisches im Plautus* (Berlin: Weidmann, 1922).

[25] So Konrad Gaiser, "Zur Eigenart der römischen Komödie: Plautus und Terenz gegenüber ihren griechischen Vorbildern," *Aufstieg und Niedergang der römischen Welt* 1, no. 2: 1027-1028: "Sie [= die extant Roman plays] sind der Forschung wichtig als literarische Dokumente und historische Zeugnisse, zumal es sonst für diese Zeit nur spärliche Quellen in lateinischer Sprache gibt. Darüber hinaus sind diese Komödien die ersten großen Beispiele, an denen wir den bis heute in der europäischen Tradition fortdauernden Prozeß der Rezeption und Transformation der griechischen Kultur studieren können, ebenso aber auch die Kraft des Römertums, in der Auseinandersetzung mit der andersartigen griechischen Welt sich selbst zu behaupten und zu entfalten."

[26] Paul B. Harvey, Jr., "Historical Topicality in Plautus," *Classical World* 79 (1986): 297-304.

[27] Based on habits of diction, including the use of the verb *castigare* and echoes of censorial officialese dispersed throughout the two old men's interactions: see the contributions of Eckard Lefèvre and Lore Benz to *Theater und Gesellschaft im Imperium Romanum*, ed. Jürgen Blänsdorf, *Mainzer Forschungen zu Drama und Theater* vol. 4 (Tübingen: Francke,

1990), especially 50-52 and 57-64.

[28] See of course Gruen's account of the difficulties of maintaining such hard and fast political party-associations for republican Rome: Gruen (1992) 226. Nevertheless, although Gruen to some extent dismantles the strict dichotomy of a Cato righteously opposed to everything Greek and a Scipionic circle luxuriating in eastern refinement in order to argue for a generalized aristocratic policy of adoption of Hellenistic culture with an eye to aggrandizing or highlighting the emerging Roman contribution, he does in the course of his argument have to downplay much actual evidence of contemporary Roman ambivalence toward Greek culture (see again Forsythe's review), and significantly chooses Plautus as an example of a play on contemporary Roman attitudes: "Plautus is parodying Roman misapprehensions of Greeks rather than expressing hostility to Hellenism," Gruen (1992) 263. There is no doubt, in other words, that such attitudes existed to be played upon, though just what exactly their class-distribution was may have been context-specific and dictated by expediency.

[29] Marie Delcourt, "Le Prix des esclaves dans la comédie latine," *L'Antiquité classique* 17 (1948): 125. See also George Duckworth, *The Nature of Roman Comedy* (Princeton: Princeton Univ. Press, 1952), 276, on the comic exaggeration of courtesans' prices.

[30] I follow here C. H. Buck, *A Chronology of the Plays of Plautus* (Baltimore: Johns Hopkins Univ. Press, 1940), who assigns both the *Aulularia* and the *Trinummus* to Plautus' latest period, and thus to the time of the excursions against Antiochus and the disputes of Cato and the Scipios.

[31] See W. F. Richardson, "Nummus in the Plays of Plautus," *Prudentia* 15 (1983): 27-34, for a discussion of just what the denomination of the coin might be; at any rate, it is small.

[32] Compare Frances Muecke, "Names and Players: The Sycophant Scene of the 'Trinummus' (Trin. 4.2)," *Transactions of the American Philological Association* 115 (1985): 167-186, where it is noted that the title may have been given by Plautus only after the comedy's production and the success of the Sycophant-scene, or may have become associated with the play only in later didascalic details subsequently interpolated into the prologue. At any rate, what is suggested is that Plautus greatly enlarged the interest of the Sycophant scene compared to its importance in his Greek model. Lore Benz, in her "Megaronides Censorius -- Eine anticatonische Konzeption im plautinischen Trinmummus?" in Bländsdorf (1990): 55-67, notes the balance of contrasting pairs in the prologue (Luxuria-Inopia, Thensaurus-Trinummus), and traces a movement of the play towards miserliness that would bespeak Plautus' own choice of the title ("*Luxuria* weicht *Inopia*, *Trinummus* verdrängt als Titel *Thensaurus*," p. 64).

[33] Lessing, in his 1750 translation and adaptation of the *Trinummus*, restores the Philemonic designation, which he finds "einen weit anständigern Titel," and calls his play *Der Schatz*.

[34] Note that, with the exception of the *Amphitryo*, introduced by the god Hermes, who then plays a part in the action, the *Aulularia* and the *Trinummus* are the only two plays of Plautus' extant corpus with

supernatural or allegorical prologues.

[35] "Es war Sitte beim Einzug in ein Haus, sich den *Lar*, der mit der Familie das Haus wechselte, durch Gebet und Opfer (*venerari*) geneigt zu machen," J. Brix and M. Niemeyer, *Ausgewählte Komödien des T. Maccius Plautus: Trinummus* (Leipzig: Teubner, 1888), ad loc. v. 39.

[36] "Ici l'à-propos suffirait pour justifier le choix du personnage. On doit nous faire connaître le grand mystère de l'action, car les Romains n'aiment pas ou ne savent pas deviner. Si ce n'est Euclion qui vient lui-même nous révéler son secret, il faut bien que ce soit le dieu Lare, car il en est l'unique dépositaire," quoted in Ernout, *Plaute* vol.1 (Paris: Les Belles Lettres, 1932), 150. Jachmann, *Plautinisches und Attisches,* Problemata, no. 3 (Berlin: Weidmann, 1931), 133ff., is concerned to refute Krieger's likening of the Lar to a Menandrian-allegorical puller of strings, and thus stresses the god's aloofness from Euclio's psychology: "Die Dingen liegen in der Aulularia ganz einfach und in sich vollkommen klar, sie bedürfen gar keiner Aufhellung durch künstliche Klügeleien oder durch fernliegende Gesichtspunkte, die von anderwärtsher bezogen gewaltsam auf ein widerstrebendes Objekt angewendet werden. Der Lar familiaris hat zwar Euclio den Schatz, der seiner Obhut anvertraut ist, finden lassen, doch greift er in sein inneres Leben und Sein nicht ein und beeinflußt sein Tun in keiner Weise." Nevertheless, his assessment of Euclio as a character of almost Shakespearean grandeur would surely rule out even the possibility of his speaking the prologue himself, Dicaeopolis-like, and thus suggest an assignment of the Lar as *Prologgestalt* less aleatory than that imagined by the laconic Naudet.

[37] Compare with this flowing introduction the choppy end-stopped lines in which the departing figure of Luxuria introduces herself and her daughter Inopia at *Trinummus* vv. 1-11.

[38] Jachmann, as noted above, is concerned to give the *Aulularia* (and thereby its Menandrian prototype) a heroic cast, to which end he develops with fervor the absolute autonomy of Euclio's character, his inner directedness, and the probability of an ending in which the miser experiences an ethical revelation and learns the sublime value of love over and against worldly status. Although his conclusions seem in part circular, he does valuably distinguish the tone of the Plautine comedy and its forebear from the petit-bourgeois contingency otherwise to be found in Menander, and certainly at work in the play's later adaptation by Molière.

[39] Slavoj Zizek, *For They Know Not What They Do: Enjoyment as a Political Factor* (London: Verso, 1991), 134. As for mothers, or indeed, women at all, they are notably absent from the *Aulularia*, as they are from the *Trinummus*, a fact that will be seen to have different valences in the two plays, depending on the presence or absence of the fantasied object of desire in the comedies' economies.

[40] The comparison of the philosophical outlooks of Cato and Scipio Africanus in Grimal (1953) 113-116 turns significantly on Cato's disdain for Fortuna and exaltation of Fides, as against the virtual cult of Fortuna among Scipio's political partners. Burkert (1985) 186 stresses the particularly Hellenistic character of the cult of Tyche, Fortuna's Greek

version. Cato fought against the importation of the foreign goddess just as Euclio guards himself here against intrusion into his fantasied dyadic relation with the pot of gold.

[41] Note the single appearance of a Lar in the *Trinummus*: at v. 339, Callicles enters the scene from Charmides' house (which he has of course just bought), bidding his wife show "Lar noster" appropriate devotion in order that the new house be prosperous. The Lar is here reduced to its ritual role, a vestigial symbol of the family that may be moved along with the rest of the belongings (although the Pauly-Wissowa s.v. considers this line inconclusive evidence for the practice). Benz in Blänsdorf (1990) 62 notes the formulaic, ritualistic language used by Callicles here as a parody of Roman officialese.

[42] This is not to enter into the debate concerning Plautus' possible invention of these figures, which has rallied Wilamowitz, Jachmann, Abel, and Seel to the cause, against, notably, Gerhard Hertel, who admits the Roman coloring of the figures but contents himself with assigning the prologue of the *Trinummus* neither to the more Greek variety, in which the play's plot is introduced and sketched out, nor to the more Roman, a mere *captatio benevolentiae*. See Hertel (1969) 45-46. See too Elaine Fantham, "Philemon's Thesauros as a Dramatisation of Peripatetic Ethics," *Hermes* 105, no. 4 (1977): 406-421, where she contends that "it is more likely that Philemon devised the personification than that Plautus should either have borrowed or invented the conception," p. 408n10.

[43] Jean-Marie André, "L'argent chez Plaute: autour du *Curculio*," *Vichiana* 12 (1983): 15-35, citation p. 31.

[44] André (1983) 28.

[45] "L'heure est à l'abondance fondée sur l'inflation du crédit de consommation.   Plaute semble se rallier à cette conception: témoin l'hymne au Crédit du *Pseudolus*, 251 sq., dans une pièce centré sur les misères du crédit, à l'heure où Caton remet en cause ses conceptions économiques et financières antérieures. L'évolution de Caton a souvent été analysée. Le *Trinummus* permet peut-être de répondre à la question posée. La *parsimonia* est morte, le crédit est malade, sapé par la crise de *fides* (1046 sq.). Mais il est vain de prolonger le Latium primitif par des combats d'arrière-garde. L'appel au dirigisme législatif et à l'arsenal répressif est vain.   Les lois échouent dans une crise qui montre étroitement imbriquées les fragilités de l'économie antique et les mutations de la mentalité collective," André (1983) 34-35.

[46] Petersen (1939) 1-7.

[47] Lefèvre in Blänsdorf (1990) 51: "Cato sprach gegen den Wucher und wucherte selbst, er ging gegen die Wucherer vor und brachte aus Eigennutz ein Gesetz gegen die Wucherer zu Fall. Er warb für Sparsamkeit und war doch Besitzer erheblicher Güter. . . . Offenbar ging Plautus nicht der Politiker, sondern der Prediger Cato auf die Nerven."

[48] Note too Lore Benz's remarks, in Blänsdorf (1990) 63, on Cato's rhetorical style, rich as it was in "ausgesprochen plastische Metaphorik" and folksy allegory: a putatively more organic style, closer to the primitive prosopopoeia of the Lar and of Euclio's pot of gold than to the

uncanny personification of the Sycophant and Inopia.

[49] See Grimal (1953) 95-96 on the legality versus the morality of the Plautine situation: " . . . le viol d'une jeune fille libre est une peccadille aisément pardonnée, pourvu que le mariage vienne réparer et valider juridiquement la naissance qui en est la suite. Pas un mot pour évoquer le chagrin, la honte ou l'espérance de la jeune femme."

[50] Konstan, "The Social Themes in Plautus' Aulularia," *Arethusa* 10, no. 2 (1977): 307-320.

[51] Jachmann (1931) 134: "Wohl wollte er [= the Lar familiaris] ihm die Möglichkeit geben seine Tochter mit einer reichen Mitgift auszustatten, wenn Euclio wollte (27); aber der will nicht, beklagt es vielmehr als sein besonderes Unglück daß er seine mannbare Tochter mangels jeglicher Mitgift nicht verheiraten könne (191). . . . Der Kern von Euclios Wesen ist der Geiz."

[52] Regarding the "double bind" into which Euclio's character forces him I am influenced by Konstan (1977) 309.

[53] "Ridicule dictum de aula auri plena, quasi de populo *novas sedes quaerente*," Hildyard, *T. Macci Plauti Aulularia* (London: J. W. Parker, 1839), ad loc. Emphasis supplied.

[54] "Am Ende dieser Kriege wurden in ihrem Gebiete Koloniengründungen vorgenommen, so daß die Metapher v. 576 (commutet coloniam) in dieser Zeit aktuell war," Walter Stockert, *T. Maccius Plautus: Aulularia, Beilage Textedition* (Stuttgart: Teubner, 1983), 28.

[55] *The Marx-Engels Reader*, ed. Robert C. Tucker (New York: Norton, 1978; second edition), 321.

[56] Delcourt (1964) 99.

[57] Interestingly enough, Dupont (1985) 36 describes the Roman republican construction of public genealogy in just such magical-theatrical terms: "Précisons que ce spectacle [= the carrying of *imagines* in the funeral processions of magistrates] n'est pas une représentation de cette noblesse, une image, une métaphore. Car la noblesse se confond, selon sa définition juridique, avec ses masques funèbres." Euclio will prove incapable of this socially acceptable form of disavowal precisely because of his inability to claim noble extraction.

[58] The use of the term personification in the preceding paraphrase is quite deliberate, since, as we shall see, the *Trinummus* performs a kind of personification/unmasking that resembles the second of Zizek's "modes of disavowal."

[59] The entire exegesis here paraphrased may be found at Zizek (1991) 245-249.

[60] Zizek (1991) 55-56n10.

[61] Personification as enacted in the *Trinummus*, meanwhile, will be seen to operate according to the logic of the relationship between things "reflected back" into that between individuals. Recall Kurz (1982) 57: "Man kann formulieren, daß (viele) Personifikationen auf der Reifikation metaphorischer Bedeutung beruhen."

[62] Konstan (1977) 309-310 makes of exactly this paranoia and its grotesque consequences a device for isolating Euclio from the symbolic

matrix of his community: "But the elements of parody or exaggeration [in the scene with Staphyla, vv. 79-103] do not conceal the fact that Euclio, in abolishing the commerce in fire and water which define symbolically the mutual ties of community, has tried to exile the whole community from himself." We may thus see him being driven further into the logic of privileged access to the magical (or perhaps maternal) object, of an imaginary restoration of the lack left by his social position and his withheld patrimony.

[63] Of course there is also in both passages (at vv. 585 and 614) a concomitant acknowledgement of the physical fact of both the pot and the gold being consigned to the care of the temple spirit; so too we should note the fact that at vv. 614-615 Plautus plays on the sense of *fides* by using it both as a proper name and as the quality denoted by that (divine) name. Here he is clearly taking advantage of the contemporary currency of the notion of *fides* and its place in the ethical debates of the day (and setting up the more burlesque calembours to follow in Strobilus' soliloquy at vv. 616-623). On the figurative level, however, the double or sliding prosopopoiea constituted by his address of the pot and of the goddess is the occasion both of his maximal fantasmal delusion, and of the actual theft that will deprive him of his fetish and force him into human relation.

[64] "In einem umfassenden Sinne freilich ist die Sphäre der Aischrologie, der rituellen, zugleich lizensierten Rüge, mit der sich auch Obszönität verbinden kann, konstitutiv für die Alte Komödie überhaupt. Indem diese nicht zuletzt auch die führenden Persönlichkeiten, namentlich Politiker und Strategen, der Lächerlichkeit preisgab, gewährte sie temporäre Entlastung vom Druck der Autorität. Doch dieselben Zuschauer, die eben noch, im karnevalistischen Freiraum des Festes, lachend applaudiert hatten, votierten bald darauf, in die Normalität des Alltags, genauer: der Volksversammlung zurückgekehrt, wieder für jene, von deren Verspottung sie sich gerade hatten belustigen lassen," Rösler (1986) 39.

[65] "In welchem Maße das Theater zur Zeit der späteren Republik sowie der Kaiser zum Freiraum für Spöttereien und Schmähungen und -- aus der Sicht der Regierenden -- zum Beliebtheits- und Stimmungsbarometer wurde, ist bekannt," Benz in Blänsdorf (1990) 57.

[66] Zizek, *The Sublime Object of Ideology* (London: Verso, 1989), 49.

[67] The subject of plays on words in Aristophanes, notably in the *Clouds*.

[68] For the intriguing suggestion that this Socratic "myth" was actually inspired by the *Plutus*, see Perceval Frutiger, *Les Mythes de Platon* (Paris: F. Alcan, 1930). Most important to the present discussion is Frutiger's observation that both the Platonic Eros and the Aristophanic Ploutos are described as "sordid" (αὐχμηρός and αὐχμῶν respectively), a quality that connects the ideas of "wealth" and "want" as they are associated in the *Trinummus*, and describes the central point at issue here, that wealth presents itself in comedy curiously under the sign of strangeness, squalor, deficiency: just as the Sycophant will appear in our play.

[69] See vv. 169-172, 360, 406-411, 417, 424, and 753, and, in a slightly different context, v. 512. Lesbonicus has of course literally spent much of his inheritance on food, as well as on diverse other forms of entertainment,

including, notably, prostitutes (v. 412). What is important to note is the easy slide from talk of spending money to that of satisfying primal desires.

[70] Compare Wilamowitz's criticism of the prologue: "der Mangel [ist] in das Haus des Lesbonicus *schon lange eingezogen*, so daß die Luxuria sie jetzt nicht mehr schicken sollte," *Menander: Das Schiedsgericht* (Berlin: Weidmann, 1925), 148. Emphasis supplied.

[71] "Damit [= with Plautus' change of title] war das Stück von Anbeginn ausdrücklich auf das Grundmotiv einer gewissen Dürftigkeit, ja Knauserigkeit (*Trinummus!*) gestimmt," Benz in Blänsdorf (1990) 64. It cannot fail to interest us that it is precisely *this* title, Θησαυρός or Treasure, that is replaced or indeed repressed (*verdrängt*), as Benz puts it. It is of course the (missing) treasure (and the play's missing mother?) that is behind the lack filled in negatively by Inopia.

[72]Whether Luxuria means here the house belonging to Charmides and recently sold by Lesbonicus, or the little shanty into which the young man has moved, is unclear. Luxuria uses the word *aedes*, suggesting the amplitude of the main dwelling and used later, in fact, of the sold property as opposed to the *posticulum* reserved for himself by Lesbonicus (v. 194). It seems odd, however, thus to style the house now that it has been sold to the more prudent Callicles, and especially since, as we are to learn, it conceals a treasure. Muecke (1985) 171 provides a brief bibliography on the dramaturgic details of the "house problem." As we shall see, Gerhard Hertel, drawing on Karlhans Abel, imagines Inopia unproblematically moving in with Lesbonicus into his new digs. At work is no doubt the logic of comic spontaneity, or perhaps indeed the very structure of dissembled amplitude being suggested here.

[73] Hertel (1969) 45 suggests that marriage between Inopia and Lesbonicus is adumbrated by the vocabulary used at v. 15 ("dedi ei meam gnatam quicum aetatem exigat," "I have given him my daughter, that he spend his days with her"); J. P. Waltzing, *Les Trois Pièces d'Argent* (Paris: 1930), in his commentary ad loc., says simply, "Lesbonicus est mis à l'école de la Misère." We should note, too, the recurrence of the formula "munus fungari" in the same position in the line, later in the play: in the gnomic utterance with which Philto answers his son Lysiteles' caution against stinginess, vv. 353-354. There the expression is used in a punning sense, turning on the double meaning of *munus* as both "means" and "duty," since Philto needs to have the former to fulfill the latter, and he sees Lysiteles' plan to marry Lesbonicus' sister without dowry as a possible danger to the family's welfare. Significantly, too, the phrase occurs in an address by a father to his son, with the same word for "child" (*gnat-*) used in both cases. Finally, there is another significant echo of terminology, in the Sycophant-scene, v. 953, where Luxuria's phrase "quicum aetatem exigat" is repeated almost verbatim by the Sycophant. Implications will be discussed below.

[74] Waltzing (1930) 51 gives the moral equivalent of this relation: "Ici les personnages du prologue sont allégoriques: la *Débauche*, qui entre en scène richement vêtue, et la Misère, sa fille, qu'elle conduit dans la demeure du jeune dissipateur, pour montrer ainsi qu'une vie débauchée a pour

conséquence la misère." Debauchery, in other words, is that state which *will have* resulted in poverty.

[75] See, however, Pierre Grimal's observation that Lesbonicus has been "victime de la débauche," and thus somehow passive in his own undoing. Grimal wants to stress hereby the philosophical differences of Lysiteles and his father Philto, differences arising evidently from Philemon's early third-century milieu: for whereas Philto represents a certain stoical asceticism and academic or Xenocratic imperviousness to pity in the face of Lesbonicus' natural fault, his son champions the Aristotelian virtue of friendship, among other virtues, and tends to forgive Lesbonicus by thus stressing his natural goodness (v. 338). It is this last philosophical school, the peripatetic, with which Grimal holds Philemon to have sympathized, and thus he emphasizes the helpless character of Lesbonicus' taste for debauchery as manifest in the structure of the play itself. See "Analyse du Trinummus et les débuts de la philosophie à Rome?" in Grimal, *Rome: la littérature et l'histoire, Collection de l'école française de Rome* 93, no. 1 (Rome: Boccard, 1986): 283-293.

[76] See Muecke (1985) 167-168n4.

[77] Muecke (1985) 169. As noted, Grimal (1986) 292 locates the original intrigue of Philemon's comedy in the contest of philosophies between Lysiteles and his father Philto, in which it is not love but friendship that is at issue; at any rate, the fixation on money as a quasi-innovation of Plautus' does not seem endangered by this thesis. More importantly, Grimal draws a line between ancient comedy in its relative indifference to the life of the city (by which he means the speculative philosophical life of the city, although this too seems hard to credit), and new comedy, as inherited by Plautus, where "[c]'est toujours la cité et ses problèmes que l'on retrouve," because new comedy "ne se contente pas . . . de se réfugier, à la différence de la comédie ancienne, dans un monde imaginaire, romanesque, sans rien de commun avec la cité." Despite the naïvety of this direct correspondence between verisimilitude and realism, Grimal draws important conclusions from his comparison: he finds in the *Trinummus* a position-taking with regard to the debates of the Scipios and Cato that amounts to a compromise, one in which, as we shall see, the ambivalent figure of money plays a pivotal role.

[78] Muecke (1985) 169 notes the existence of a school of thought that would credit Plautus with the love motif: but only to explain *Lesbonicus'* behavior. This clearly tends to support my view that money and its appropriate uses become the over-riding concern of the Plautine comedy, and emphasizes the extent to which Lesbonicus' expenses are an attempt to satisfy an impossible infantile desire through oral and sexual gratification.

[79] Here *fides* is translated as "credit" (following Ernout and Waltzing, with Grimal opting for the more general *confiance*) to preserve its financial sense. This is the way the word appears most notably in the *Trinummus*, in the complaints of Stasimus when he is unable to retrieve his loan (v. 1048); meanwhile, as seen above, *Fides* in the *Aulularia* is more properly religious/allegorical. This realist turn is entirely in keeping with the Plautine reception of Cato's exalted notion of *fides*, as noted above.

[80] Note the frequency with which the word *res* appears in the scene (and in its staging by the two old men), in the various senses of the term, i.e. "matter," "property," "money," "cause," at vv. 733, 748, 755, 757, 773, 791, 800, 803, 842, 865, 901, 904, 956, 962, 985, and 1003.

[81] There is a slight problem in the text at this point, since Megaronides seems at vv. 754-758 to be telling Callicles to wait and use the stranger's presence as a cover for unearthing the treasure, while at vv. 798-805 he dispatches Callicles immediately to the task (from which he does indeed claim to be returning at vv. 1100-1102, before the Sycophant has even had a chance to encounter Lesbonicus, although he might reasonably be thought to have supposed that in the intervening time, while the Sycophant was being detained by Charmides, he was in fact doing his duty). Compare Muecke (1985) 170.

[82] See Waltzing (1930) ad loc.: "C'est le philippe d'or . . . frappé par Philippe II de Macédoine, père d'Alexandre le grand, et ses successeurs. Philippe II exploitait de riches mines d'or en Macédoine; lui et ses successeurs frappèrent beaucoup de ces pièces, qui avaient cours en Grèce au temps de la Comédie Nouvelle et furent introduites à Rome pendant la guerre de Macédoine [= late third century B.C.E.]."

[83] Note that he makes use of the Sycophant's own logic in the aside in which he decides to try and dupe his adversary: "enim vero ego nunc sycophantae huic sycophantari volo, / si hunc possum illo mille nummum Philippum circumducere, / quod sibi me dedisse dixit. quem ego qui sit homo nescio, / neque oculis ante hunc diem umquam vidi, eine aurum crederem? / quoi, si capitis res sit, nummum numquam credam plumbeum," vv. 958-962: "For indeed I now want to dupe this duper, if I can get those thousand philips from him that he says I gave him. I have no idea who he is, never seen him before today, and I should have trusted him with gold? Why, if the affair were really serious, I wouldn't even give him a lead coin."

[84] For the sense of *sycophantari* (a near-*hapax*) as "to dupe," cf. Ernout (1932) ad loc.; Waltzing (1930) ad loc. has "dérivé de . . . *sukofantes* . . . proprement 'dénonciateur de figues' c'est à dire dénonciateur de ceux qui violaient la loi en exportant des figues de l'Attique. Quoi qu'il en soit de cette explication . . . *sycophanta* a pris le sens de 'délateur, fourbe, imposteur, hypocrite' et *sycophantari* veut dire 'ruser'." Muecke (1985) 176 is attached to the idea that the Sycophant in our play is meant to be thought of as an out-of-work actor, and that it is thus natural for the verb formed from his name to take on the nuance of deception: "The equivocation on the roles of *sycophanta* and *histrio* [= actor] depends on the assumption, widely attested in antiquity, that the actor's business was trickery or deception."

[85] And note the possible significance of Charmides' name, "Son of Pleasure," as if to underscore the genealogy of debauch that belies the father's moralistic treatment of his wastrel son. Here again I am indebted to Richard P. Martin for an invaluable interpretation.

[86] Waltzing (1930) imagines "scriptum quidem" to mean some form of cheque, while Ernout (1932) reads a pun on the figurative meaning of written. There is some controversy over whether *scriptum* could mean anything like our paper money: "Plautus . . . refers to Greek, not Roman

money, and these bills of exchange from rich merchants seem to have been used a good deal in Greek commerce. Real paper money, that is, a currency without any intrinsic value whatever, was known to the Carthaginians alone among the states of antiquity," Freeman and Sloman, *T. Macci Plauti Trinummus* (Oxford: Oxford Univ. Press, 1890), ad loc. Just how "bills of exchange" differ from "a currency without any intrinsic value" is not clear: what is at all events obvious is the Sycophant's sleight of hand.

[87] *Pax* of course normally means "peace" in Latin; Brix and Niemeyer however ad loc. derive its use here from the Greek verb πήγνυμι, to stick, fix, or make stiff; they compare the German use of the Italian "basta." Waltzing (1930) suggests "chut!" as a French equivalent.

[88] For a useful discussion of descriptivism, the notion that names refer to objects by their meaningful attachment to clusters of descriptive properties, versus (Kripkean) antidescriptivism, the theory that names are linked to objects by means of an arbitrary "primal baptism" that still obtains despite the utter transformation of the original descriptive clusters, see Zizek (1989) 89-92.

[89] Muecke (1985) 182.

[90] Note that Ernout (1932) 12 refers to the Sycophant as "Trinummus," as if to signal the arbitrariness of the various names floating about the character and his comedy. Fraenkel (1922) 108-9 blurs the boundary by imagining that a personification of the day of the play's action itself is meant: "vielleicht spielt auch die Verstellung hinein, daß man dem Tage wie einem Menschen seinen Spitznamen gibt."

[91] Muecke (1985) 179.

[92] *A Structural Study of Autobiography* (Ithaca: Cornell Univ. Press, 1974), 91.

Chapter 3

Vicissitudes of Wealth
in Lucian's *Timon, or the Misanthrope*

Pace, pace, mio dolce tesoro:
Io conobbi la voce che adoro,
E che impressa ognor serbo nel cor.

Da Ponte (after Beaumarchais)

Prologue

The figures of Ploutos and Penia reappear in Lucian of Samosata's comic dialogue Τίμων ἡ Μισάνθρωπος (*Timon, or the Misanthrope*), composed in the second half of the second century C.E., and it is generally agreed that they owe much to Aristophanes' depiction of the allegories of Wealth and Poverty in the *Plutus*.[1] However, there are significant innovations in Lucian's fund of imagery, and in the context in which he chooses to introduce the figures, and it is difficult not to see the influence of the intervening Roman reception of the topos. In particular, there is a suggestion in Lucian's dialogue of an identification of the grotesque figure of Wealth with his human protagonist, Timon, who receives Ploutos from the gods, as was seen to be the case in the *Trinummus* in the uncanny likening of the Sycophant, bearer of wealth, and Charmides, possessor of that wealth. There is in Lucian too a special interest in the character of the miser or social misfit and his relation to the supernaturally acquired money, foreshadowed in the *Aulularia*, as if further to suggest the manichean or double nature of money's role in society: attractive and repellent, uniting and dividing, bestowing value and yet somehow integrally valueless. As well, I read in the *Timon* of Lucian a new feminizing of money's representation, which owes as much to the association of money with misogynistic social critique in the *Trinummus* of Plautus as to an uneasy reconciliation of the gendered dualism already examined in the *Peace* and the *Plutus* of Aristophanes, that between the voiceless, immanent statue of the goddess Peace and the querulous, uncanny vagabond who is Wealth. Finally, Lucian's encomium of poverty, implicit in the *Timon*'s action and explicit in Penia's own words of self-defense, takes on a new poignancy in light of its composition in a world in which a change in power structures (following the consolidation of Roman dominion over much of the Hellenic world and its satellites) is leading inexorably to the divorce of economic power and political agency among the Greek-speaking middle- and upper-classes, and tending to lend a tragic or at least fatalistic cast to the relations between money and the social whole.[2] Hence the growing interest in misanthropes and outcasts, in a solipsistic attempt at self-sufficiency in the face of an increasingly hegemonized imperial Roman power. It is this road toward tragedy that I will take up in the next and final chapter, with a reading of the tragedy Shakespeare made of the Timon legend, and the way in which the figure of Wealth finds himself finally, in the pre-modern, become a bare rhetorical allegory.

From Aristophanes to Lucian

Timon, or the Misanthrope is a late second-century C.E. portrait of legendary ingratitude, written by a Syrian schooled in Hellenistic rhetorical practices and living under Roman rule. Lucian was born around 120 C.E. in the town of Samosata in the northern Syrian province of Commagene, in what had been a client kingdom of the Romans but was then annexed finally in the first century C.E. by the Emperor Vespasian. The Hellenistic culture that had been spread to Syria four centuries earlier by Alexander the Great helped to maintain a regional resistance to Roman political domination; a tendency to archaism and nostalgia for a lost golden age of Greek imperial and cultural power, for all the material advantages brought by Roman civilization, marked the artistic production of the age.[3]

Lucian's *floruit*, then, coincided both with a period of maximal expansion of the Roman imperial borders under the Emperors Hadrian and Antoninus Pius, and with the latter stages of what is known as the "Second Sophistic," that revival of interest in the culture of classical Greece among the provincial Greek-speaking upper classes. This revival consisted, for rhetoricians, in προγυμνάσματα, or exercises, set-pieces for performance employing categories of oratory no longer practically useful, but still prized for their formal elegance.[4] That is to say, whereas the tropes and references proper to parliamentary and forensic speeches might during the period of Greek autonomy have served in the practice of politics or law, they had now been assimilated into the third Aristotelian category of public-speaking, known as the ἐπιδεικτικός, or the occasional, and used to regale audiences in artistic recitations.[5]

Lucian's particular debt to classical Greek culture, however, manifest in his specialty, the comic dialogue, is of course to old comedy. It has been noted that he must indeed have at least been reading classical tragedy, especially Euripides, but that he may have found revival performances of the great works of fifth-century Athenian theater ridiculous.[6] Tragedy does of course receive attention in his work, but only in the hybridizing form of Menippean citation, and mostly as a touch-stone of all that is high-flown and fairytale-like. Like Aristophanes, he finds his most frequent source in Euripides; he quotes from some of the same plays, extant and non-extant, as the Athenian. The conventions of old comedy, rather than those of oratory or tragedy, seem to have been most congenial to his satiric purposes; or rather, in the effort to satirize he found himself turning also on the very cultural goods with which the renaissance of the first to third centuries was to make its name.[7]

In the case of his *Timon, or the Misanthrope* it may be argued that it is the tropes and references of old comedy itself, particularly those of Aristophanes' *Plutus*, that are subjected to ridicule through the satiric prism they have themselves helped to create. As well, however, Lucian's treatment of the Misanthrope Timon, a character known in old comedy and indeed mentioned in two well-known passages in Aristophanes,[8] draws on the fourth-century middle and new comic development of the δύσκολος or μονότροπος, the disgruntled miser, and on the obsession with money that, as we have seen, was the Roman contribution to the tradition.[9] In addition to these strains must be mentioned the influence of the Cynics, a school of philosophers that began to make its name properly only in the fourth century, in the person of Diogenes.[10] That Timon in Lucian's depiction of him lives like a Cynic is of perhaps only marginal interest, given the broad range of squalid features associated with the school and with the Timon legend and bound therefore to overlap in places;[11] more important is his place in a complex of images uniting money and power, sex and social relations, a complex in whose elaboration Cynic philosophy plays a significant role. Finally, I will argue that a series of allusions to the texts of Hesiod lend Lucian's re-working of the Timon and Ploutos stories a new complexity.

A brief synopsis of *Timon, or the Misanthrope* will allow the sequence of events and main images in this less well-known work to be clearly delineated before I begin to discuss them in more detail. The dialogue opens with Timon's invocation of Zeus by every cult-title he can think of, "and any others the thunderstruck poets might call you, especially when they are stuck with their meter" (καὶ εἴ τί σε ἄλλο οἱ ἐμβρόντητοι ποιηταὶ καλοῦσι, καὶ μάλιστα ὅταν ἀπορῶσι πρὸς τὰ μέτρα). Timon reproaches Zeus for his failure to take retributive action against scoundrels in general, and against those in particular who have borrowed from Timon and now snub him in his poverty. He has been reduced to digging for a living, and wonders if Zeus might not in fact be dead and buried on Crete, as purported by the islanders, so glaring are the injustices suffered by Timon und unavenged by the god. Zeus hears Timon's plaint and summons Hermes to help him recognize the Misanthrope, so changed is he since the days of his affluence. Upon hearing the reasons for Timon's destitution (he had been overly generous, perhaps foolishly so) and in recognition of the piety Timon had shown to the gods, Zeus resolves to restore to him his lost wealth in the form of Ploutos, the god of Wealth. Hermes is to ensure that Ploutos return to Timon, that Ploutos bring along with him Treasure (Θησαυρός), and that these two remain with him no matter how hard Timon should try this time to cast them away (κἂν ὅτι μάλιστα ὑπὸ χρηστότητος αὖθις ἐκδιώκῃ αὐτοὺς τῆς οἰκίας), a reference to Timon's spendthrift tendencies; Zeus meanwhile will make plans to punish Timon's debtors, just as soon as he has had his thunderbolt repaired, damaged in a recent attempt to chastize the godless Anaxagoras (1-10).[12]

When Hermes brings Ploutos before Zeus, however, the god of Wealth complains of the careless treatment he had once received at Timon's hands and refuses to return to him; when reminded by Zeus that he has complained equally bitterly about the rich misers to whom he had been sent in the past, and who had guarded him fervently and prevented him from circulating, Ploutos agrees that he is averse to both extremes. He pleads to be sent neither to spendthrifts nor to misers, but instead to those who behave moderately with their money (μέτρον ἐπιθήσοντας τῷ πράγματι καὶ μήτε ἀφεξομένους τὸ παράπαν μήτε προησομένους τὸ ὅλον) as one might behave toward a wife, neither confining her nor letting her wander. Zeus reflects upon the punishments in store for such immoderate types, and with a reminder to Hermes to stop by the forges of the Cyclopes and see about his thunderbolt, he despatches the two (11-19).

But Ploutos is still not ready for the journey. He engages Hermes in an extended discussion of his own blindness and lameness, of the distinction between himself and Plouton, the god of the underworld, of what makes him so attractive to humans, and of his slippery powers of seduction in comparison to Poverty's grim tenaciousness. Hermes notices that they have neglected to bring Treasure along, but Ploutos explains that he has left him buried in the earth for fear of foul play; as the pair approaches Attica, Ploutos begins to fear also for his own safety: Hermes had done well to escort him, for otherwise he might have been accosted by Hyperbolos or Kleon, those (historic) bogeyman-demagogues familiar from the political landscape of Aristophanes' comedies (20-30).

Upon arrival on the rocky ground of Attica, the pair discovers Timon hard at work digging, attended by Penia and her troops, Ponos, or Toil, Karteria, or Endurance, Sophia, or Wisdom, Andreia, or Courage, and "Hunger and all his throng, much more valorous than your spear-carriers" (ὁ τοιοῦτος ὄχλος τῶν ὑπὸ τῷ Λιμῷ ταττομένων ἁπάντων. πολὺ ἀμείνους τῶν σῶν δορυφόρων). Ploutos wants to flee, but Hermes reminds him of Zeus's dictates and discourages cowardice (31). Penia, noticing the two approaching, now demands to know whither Hermes is leading Ploutos: upon hearing that he is to be returned to Timon, she begins a lament. It was she, after all, who had received him in an evil state from Tryphe, or Debauchery, and nurtured him with the help of Wisdom and Toil; is she now to give up her only possession (τὸ μόνον κτῆμα) to Ploutos again, and to the vicious clutches of Hybris, or Lust/Violence, and Typhos, or Delusion, so that they may ruin him anew? At Hermes' insistence that this is Zeus's will, she departs with her attendants, listing as she goes the qualities she has managed to instill in Timon: physical health, intellectual vigor, manliness and self-confidence (31-33).

Now Hermes and Ploutos are free to approach Timon, but he will not at first receive them. They are disturbing a working, wage-earning man (ἄνδρα ἐργάτην καὶ μισθοφόρον), he complains, and he threatens to drive them off with clods and stones. When Hermes rejoins that they are the gods Hermes and Ploutos come from Zeus to bring him prosperity and surcease from toil, Timon responds that he hates the gods just as much as human beings, and that he means especially to bash "that blind one, whoever he may be" (τουτονὶ δὲ τὸν τυφλόν. ὅστις ἂν ᾖ) with his mattock. Ploutos wants to run for it, calling Timon mad (μελαγχολᾶν γὰρ ὁ ἄνθρωπος), but Hermes invokes Zeus once more, cites Homer (τόνδε φέρω Διὶ μῦθον ἀπηνέα τε κρατερόν τε, *Iliad* 15.202), and bids him follow the gods' will, despite the specious merits of Penia, which Hermes discounts as mere puffery (τὰ ὀργίλα ταῦτα καὶ μειρακιώδη). Ploutos then lectures Timon briefly on his own advantages. He has brought Timon all sorts of boons, including luxury and esteem; if Timon has indeed suffered at the hands of his untrue friends, it is his own fault. Ploutos himself suffered by being given to such scoundrels, and was not at all eager to return to Timon and rescue him from his life of toil. In the end Timon recants, and agrees to become rich again: it is the gods' will, and he must accept the new-found gold, innocent though he is (34-39).

Hermes flies off to the forges of the Cyclopes at Mount Aetna, and Ploutos instructs Timon to begin digging for Treasure. He himself invokes Treasure, and orders him to give himself up to Timon (σέ φημι. Θησαυρὲ χρυσοῦ, ὑπάκουσον Τίμωνι τουτῳὶ καὶ παράσχες σεαυτὸν ἀνελέσθαι). Ploutos promises to stand by Timon, but is thereafter no longer heard from or mentioned throughout the rest of the dialogue (40).

Timon digs, finds gold, and greets it with an elaborate apostrophe, beginning with a citation of a line from Euripides' *Danaë*, "Oh gold, most beautiful and welcome to mortals" (ὦ χρυσέ, δεξίωμα κάλλιστον βροτοῖς, fr. 324 Nauck). He dedicates his mattock and hide to Pan, and resolves to build himself a tower over his treasure, where he will live alone. He solemnly foreswears all commerce with other humans, vowing to honor only the gods. He takes on the name of Misanthrope; his creed henceforth shall be discontent, roughness, gaucherie, pride, and anti-humanism (καὶ ὄνομα μὲν ἔστω ὁ Μισάνθρωπος ἥδιστον, τοῦ τρόπου δὲ γνωρίσματα δυσκολία καὶ τραχύτης καὶ σκαιότης καὶ ὀργὴ καὶ ἀπανθρωπία). If a man is being burnt alive and begs for water, he will respond with pitch and oil; if a man is drowning in the river, he will push him under. He proposes, seconds, and votes in the motion as law, all in his own impromptu one-man assembly (41-44).

No sooner has he made these vows, however, than he must break them, for a stream of people has begun to draw near at the first whiff of gold (ὀσφραινόμενοι τοῦ χρυσίου). He decides to meet them head on and punish them. The first to arrive is the flatterer (κόλαξ) Gnathonides, who had often drunk from Timon's jars but who has recently responded to his benefactor's request for a loan by handing him a noose; he is quickly despatched with blows from Timon's mattock, now pressed back into service after its brief dedication to Pan. The second of Timon's importuners is Philiades, whose daughter Timon had rewarded with a gift of two talents for her praise of his singing, and who had repaid this gesture by beating him when he was down; his patronizing financial advice to Timon now wins him a broken skull. The third is the orator Demeas, whom Timon had helped to fulfill his civic duty and who has in return just recently refused to recognize him as a citizen; the elaborate motion of gratitude that Demeas proposes to make to Timon at the assembly is answered with a beating. The fourth and final ἀλάζων or comic imposter to be rebuffed by Timon is the vulgarian philosopher Thrasykles. He counsels Timon to rid himself of his money as soon as possible, and offers to help him distribute it to the needy. He gets instead a headful of blows (τὴν κεφαλὴν ἐμπλήσω κονδύλων) and goes off indignantly invoking democracy and law. At the sight of a massive crowd of such imposters approaching, Timon puts down his overworked mattock (τὴν μὲν δίκελλαν ὀλίγον ἀναπαύω πάλαι πεπονηκυῖαν), climbs up on a rock, and prepares to pelt his assailants with stones. They are bloodied, and retreat (45-58).

Lucian's satirical dialogue is heavily marked by its Aristophanic heritage: it includes a skeletal agon between Wealth and Poverty and ends with a classic old comic sequence of imposters being violently driven off. Lucian's Timon is a sort of negative Aristophanic hero, a loser who does not know a Great Idea (such as the return of Ploutos and the revitalization of Zeus's vengeful justice) when it presents itself to him.[13] Unlike Dicaeopolis, Trygaeus, Pisthetaerus, or Chremylus, absurdly noble in their destitution and their will to better themselves, Timon is notable chiefly for his complaints and not for his creative energy, although even his griping attains a certain Aristophanic bombast. He is an appropriately idiosyncratic, if peculiarly unpleasant, character: querulous, oblivious to his own responsibility for his impoverishment, he is first heard, as the dialogue opens, tirelessly imprecating a Zeus grown slothful, he adjudges, in the punishment of wrongdoers. These include of course the beneficiaries of Timon's munificence, now unwilling to assist him in the penury brought on by his lavish spending. When his beseeching results in the return of Wealth, and Hermes, acting as theopomp for the occasion, praises the complaining that has won back Timon's riches, the Misanthrope greets the two divinities with hostility and further complaining (*Tim.* 34).[14] Aristophanically prodigious, thus, in his hybris,[15] Timon has about him too something of Plautus' irony as he distributes ripostes with tongue and stick to the sycophants who confront him in the last scene.

But there is in the *Timon* no equivalent to the utopian spirit of communal feasting that concludes the *Plutus*, whatever its ambivalences or strategic exclusions, or the harvest/nuptial *double entendres* that close the *Peace*; nor is there to be found the reconciliation of solitary man and society that ends the *Aulularia*, nor the re-establishment of repressive harmony and patriarchal rule over the uncanny goings-on and sexual violence that distinguish the *Trinummus*. The reason for these discrepancies is of course primarily to be sought in the formal differences among the various works. Whereas the comedies of Aristophanes were presented in theatrical performance to the free male citizenry and honored foreign visitors of Athens, a fifth-century city-state at the height of its military (and after the Peloponnesian War, at least cultural) power, and those of Plautus to the festive audiences at Rome, the burgeoning scourge of the Mediterranean, the satirical dialogues and set-pieces of Lucian were made for solo declamation in the cultural capitals (Athens, the littoral of Asia Minor) and provincial backwaters (Gaul, Macedonia, the Po Valley) on the periphery of what was by then more than a simple

Mediterranean military power. This is not to suggest that Lucian's experience was exemplary of the sophists and orators of his generation, some of whom (such as Aristides, Pollux, Polemon) achieved fame in the imperial metropolis;[16] but the sense of isolation and fragile dependence on a remote foreign overlord, reflected in Timon's railing against the indifferent and lazy Zeus, and the absolute irrelevance of his riches to his way of life when they are returned to him, is something Lucian shared with his cultural class, a nascent and economically weighty "bourgeoisie," disenfranchised by the monopoly of political power at Rome.[17] It is against this backdrop that the Lucianic conception of the apotheosis of wealth takes shape: baroque and confused, the figure as presented by Lucian is a bleak descendant of Aristophanes' Ploutos, a harbinger of a new strain of melancholic allegories of money in the modern period.

Tropes of the *Monotropos*

What first strikes the reader of *Timon, or the Misanthrope* who has come from a consideration of Aristophanic and Plautine texts is the degree to which Timon himself has taken on characteristics of the vagabond god of Wealth, sordid and repulsive as in the *Plutus*, outlandish and negative as in the *Trinummus*. This consolidation of characteristics can be seen both to create a counter-pole to the imperial hegemony of the day, whereby a lone figure absorbs the full bitterness of the Greek world's political impotence in the midst of an economic boom, and to adumbrate the turn to a non-figurative, unpersonified, tragic allegory in the version of the Timon legend to be found centuries later in Shakespeare.

Timon is first explicitly portrayed, in Lucian's version, following his diatribe directed at Zeus, by Zues himself, who in an aside to Hermes asks the identity of his haranguer and uses the word αὐχμῶν, sordid or dry, in a series of disobliging adjectives to describe the formerly wealthy Timon: "Who is this, Hermes, who croaks from the foothills of Hymettos in Attica, all shabby and sordid [αὐχμῶν] and wearing skins? I do believe he's bent over and digging; he's a garrulous and brazen fellow. He must be a philosopher, for no one else would speak of us with so little reverence." Upon hearing Timon's name from Hermes and having been reminded of his patronymic and deme, Zeus again describes him, this time using the variant αὐχμηρός: "Sordid [αὐχμηρός], wretched, a digger and a wage-laborer, from the looks of it, wielding the heavy mattock that way" (*Tim.* 7).

It will be recalled that both the Platonic Eros and the Aristophanic Ploutos are described as "sordid" in just these terms, αὐχμῶν and αὐχμηρός, at *Plut.* v. 84 and *Symp.* 203d respectively, and that

Lucian is having more than a little fun here at the expense of the sort of eccentric Socrates figure who retails stories of a "sordid" Eros, as Zeus's jibe at the philosophers helps to make clear.[18] That is to say, in two swift strokes Lucian both makes the unlikely connection of the *monotropos-* or misanthrope-figure with that of the traditional figure of Wealth, vagabond and repulsive, and sets the stage for a Timon who will introduce into the dialogue all the baggage of a marginalized and bastardized Cynic philosophy: comically understood, as Bompaire (1958) 170 makes clear, to have included Socrates in some fashion in its lineage. And Timon himself describes his activity ironically as philosophizing "with the mattock" (*Tim.* 6).

The verb αὐχμέω is also associated with labor, as in *Odyssey* 24.250, where the disguised Odysseus reproaches his father for having let himself degenerate into the sordid old age and appearance of a slave laborer, despite the fact that he is of royal blood. There too, as in the *Timon*, there is the suggestion of a sordid appearance hiding a precious or at least more valuable essence. But what seems to be particularly ignoble about the condition in which Zeus and Hermes find Timon is that he is sordid because he has been laboring for a wage, and a small one at that. At *Tim.* 7 Zeus remarks that Timon is a wage-laborer (μισθωτός), echoing Timon's own description of his plight: "I work the ground for a wage of four obols, with solitude and the mattock for company in my philosophizing" (ἐργάζομαι τὴν γῆν ὑπόμισθος ὀβολῶν τεττάρων. τῇ ἐρημίᾳ καὶ τῇ δικέλλῃ προσφιλοσοφῶν) (*Tim.* 6).[19] It should be remembered that the working poor or πένητες in fifth-century Athens suffered a popular contempt only slightly less virulent than that reserved for the newly rich;[20] Timon, who is referred to by Hermes at *Tim.* 7 as νεόπλουτος in a polysemous word suggesting both the newly rich and those who were recently but are no longer wealthy, consolidates thus traits of the vulgar Chremylus and of his tutelary deity-cum-slave Ploutos.

In Lucian's autobiography, too, at least as he presents it, the image of sordid dryness evoked by αὐχμέω is connected explicitly with working for a wage. In his *Apology for 'On Salaried Posts,'* in reference to a tract he had written condemning the employment of sophists by the wealthy, recanted now that he himself has taken a post with the Egyptian civil service, Lucian allows an imaginary accuser to harangue him for his hypocrisy by evoking the image, with a citation of the *Iliad*, of a man whose lips are wet with wisdom but whose palate is dry (αὐχμῶσαν) for the fig proffered by his patron (*Apol.* 6). Significantly, the text also contains references to wage-earning as a type of slavery, through the classical topos of enslavement to gain;[21] and to sophists performing in wealthy houses as only make-believe heroes who turn out, upon putting aside their masks, to be mere salaried tragedians (ἀποθέμενοι τὰ προσωπεῖα γίγνονται ὑπόμισθοι τραγῳδοῦντες, *Apol.* 5). This imagistic complex of masks, gain, and dramatic performance will be seen below to have resonances for my reading of Lucian's *Timon*. Here it should simply be noted that the word αὐχμέω occurs in places where an unpleasantly sordid dryness is either manifest, as in the citations from old comedy, or hidden behind an ostensibly opulent, productive exterior, as in Lucian's quotation of the Homeric verse.

Timon, then, is sordid, marginal and querulous, just like the god of Wealth when accosted by Chremylus and Karion; he has also foolishly squandered his recent wealth, and is about to be made rich once more by a ἑρμαῖον, a lucky find or (literally) Hermes-sponsored god-send, just like Chremylus. Unlike the self-sufficient Athenian or the enslaved god of Wealth, however, Timon works for a wage even in his days of destitution, thus preserving a link with the social money-economy he has ostensibly abandoned by becoming a misanthrope, and suffering a venal servitude imagistically connected with the "enslaving" patronage decried by Lucian, and with which he himself had had such an ambivalent relationship.

This note of monetary realism, however, the second-century C.E. recognition of the historic fact of money and its inescapable role in social affairs, even in those of a legendary enemy of civilization, is at first dispelled or at least repressed with the return of Ploutos to Timon. At Zeus's behest, Hermes is to go in search of the errant god and bid him return to Timon "along with Treasure" (ἀγέτω δὲ ὁ Πλοῦτος καὶ τὸν Θησαυρὸν μεθ᾽ αὑτοῦ, *Tim.* 10), who is presumably the material stuff of financial transactions.[22] But this Treasure is literally elided, as at *Tim.* 29-30 Ploutos explains that he has in fact not brought it, having preferred to leave it locked up, as usual when he goes out; when he does direct Timon to dig in search of the unspecified Treasure, apostrophized at *Tim.* 40, it is gold that Timon finds one page later, after Ploutos himself has disappeared. God of Wealth, personified Treasure and gold excavated as usual from the ground do not co-exist in this dialogue, atomized as they are into mythology and banal material reality. It is rather Timon who acts as a unifying force, reflecting into himself the various strange images of money offered in the course of the exposition, and left alone to fend for himself in the dialogue's last melancholic sequence.

"Melancholy" has in this comic tradition a special sense, since it is the word used of Chremylus by his slave Karion in the opening scene of Aristophanes' *Plutus*, and then twice more in the play, once by Chremylus to rebuff Blepsidemos' accusations that he has come by his new-found wealth illegally, and once by the Sycophant in response to the Just Man's asking him whether he is a farmer: "Do you think I'm that mad?" (μελαγχολᾶν μ' οὕτως οἴει: *Plut.* v. 903). The sense in which Karion uses the word μελαγχολᾶν or "to be mad" at *Plut.* v. 12 is directly connected with Chremylus' treatment of the as yet unrecognized god of Wealth, who seems for the moment just some blind stranger Chremylus has taken it into his head to follow and abuse, in order to force his identity from him. Chremylus' ostensibly bizarre behavior is then also linked, through this word, with hard labor, as the Sycophant's later equation of μελαγχολᾶν with the farmer's life makes clear. And it is melancholy of which Ploutos accuses Timon in their first encounter in Lucian's dialogue, as the Misanthrope singles out the blind god for expulsion by stoning at *Tim.* 34.

Here Timon's negative relation to Chremylus is made clear: whereas the Aristophanic character labors madly to extract the meaning of a supernatural allegory in order to win for himself a life of ease, the Misanthrope in his Second-Sophistic incarnation labors madly to fend off the very same allegory and to deny its identity even when it is made explicit by Hermes. He echoes Karion's words at *Tim.* 34, when he calls Ploutos "this blind man" and threatens to drive him off with his mattock (τουτονὶ δὲ τὸν τυφλόν. ὅστις ἂν ᾖ. καὶ ἐπιτρίψειν μοι δοκῶ τῇ δικέλλῃ). By the end of the dialogue, of course, Timon will have discovered the gold: significantly, however, by digging or laboring for it, and not by the more mysterious and indeed allegorical expedient of curing Ploutos' eyesight in the temple of Asklepios. He will, furthermore, have dedicated the tools of his laboring life to the statue of the rural god Pan in a symbolic gesture of the renunciation of wage-labor and the renewal of his wealthy life (*Tim.* 42).[23]

But only four sections later, Timon has taken up the mattock again, this time to chase off Gnathonides, the first in a series of toadies who have come to renew their acquaintance with the now once more wealthy Timon, the man they had snubbed during his period as a common laborer. The stream of anonymous imposters is still approaching as the dialogue ends, after Timon has driven off four named tormentors, each time with the mattock, tool of his "melancholy" laboring days. He is last seen, it is true, putting down the mattock once more, to rest it after its work-out with Gnathonides, Philiades, Demeas, and Thrasykles (ὥστε τί οὐκ ἐπὶ τὴν πέτραν ταύτην ἀνελθὼν τὴν μὲν δίκελλαν ὀλίγον ἀναπαύω πάλαι πεπονηκυῖαν, *Tim.* 58);[24] but this is merely because hand-to-hand combat is no longer the order of the day, so great is the crowd approaching: he puts down the mattock only to gather rocks to hurl at his tormentors (αὐτὸς δὲ ὅτι πλείστους λίθους ξυμφορήσας ἐπιχαλαζῶ πόρρωθεν αὐτούς, *Tim.* 58).

Timon, then, is left at the end of Lucian's dialogue entangled in the same net of agricultural toil (the mattock and the excavation of the gold) and anti-social melancholy (his vow of misanthropy, his generalized violence) in which he was first encountered by Ploutos and Hermes. Whereas Chremylus wins Ploutos for a slave and finishes the Aristophanic comedy with a feast and the establishment of that same god and/or slave in his rightful sanctuary in the opisthodomos of the Parthenon (*Plut.* vv. 768-9 and 1192-3), Timon remains within the economy of isolation, solipsistic communion with mute gold unvouched for by an allegorical deity, from which the *Aulularia* took care to recuperate Euclio. Timon is in a sense the heir of the bizarre figure of the Sycophant in the *Trinummus*, who is at once the actual bearer of wealth (Charmides' treasure, as provided by Lesbonicus' guardian Callicles) and the wage-earning actor who merely represents wealth and whose identity is inextricably linked with the pittance he is to make for his day's labor.

This quality of hybrid negativity is reinforced by the complex of images surrounding the actual figure of Ploutos in Lucian's dialogue. In a move as yet unparalleled in the comic tradition,[25] Lucian presents Ploutos under the sign of the feminine: as Danaë, imprisoned by her father, in Zeus's speech; as a young wife, subject to her husband's sexual economy, in Ploutos' own words; and again in Ploutos' speech concerning his plight, as a mother swallow, awaited anxiously by her young. Corollary images, not explicitly feminine but linked to the realm of women, are Ploutos' description of himself in Timon's reckless care as the water collected in vain by the Danaids in their broken jars; as a masked and bejewelled object of desire; and as a sort of Pandora with a retinue of troubles, dazzling her recipient so that he does not notice them. Finally there is Timon's own exaltation of the gold he digs up on Ploutos' instructions as the very gold in the form of which Zeus had managed to penetrate Danaë's chamber and rape her.

At *Tim.* 13, Zeus describes Ploutos, in the clutches of a wealthy miser, as a sort of Danaë, locked in her chamber, attended by Interest and Accounting (ἐν χαλκῷ ἢ σιδηρῷ τῷ θαλάμῳ καθάπερ τὴν Δανάην παρθενεύεσθαι ὑπ' ἀκριβέσι καὶ παμπονήροις παιδαγωγοῖς ἀνατρεφόμενον, τῷ Τόκῳ καὶ τῷ Λογισμῷ). Danaë is of course the daughter of the Argive king Akrisios, who locks her away, either in a fortified bedroom or a tower keep,[26] to prevent her from giving birth to the child fated to kill his grandfather. Zeus falls in love with her, penetrates her confines in the form of a shaft of gold, and impregnates her despite her father's precautions. Lucian's Zeus presumably means with this analogy to point out to Ploutos the undesirability of the miser's ownership of him, and by contrast to play up the virtues of Timon's freer hand; and indeed the likening of the miser's cache to the imprisoned Danaë has a parallel, at least in Lucian's corpus, at *Menippus* 2.

But the comparison, instead of simply acting as an empty cliché, serves rather to suggest to Ploutos a way of condemning the behavior of both the miser and the spendthrift, in the form of a parable about appropriate conjugal practice. Rather than praising Timon's difference from the common miser, Ploutos extolls the virtues of the moderate (τούς . . . μέτρον ἐπιθήσοντας τῷ πράγματι καὶ μήτε ἀφεξομένους τὸ παράπαν μήτε προησομένους τὸ ὅλον). He invites Zeus to consider the following hypothesis: what if someone were to marry lawfully a young and beautiful woman (εἴ τις νόμῳ γήμας γυναῖκα νέαν καὶ καλήν) and then simply let her go wherever she pleased, night and day leaving her unguarded and allowing her to associate with all comers, indeed even throwing open the doors and inviting adulterers in: could such a man be said to love his wife? And Zeus is to consider as well the opposite case. What if that same husband were on the contrary to shut up his free wife (ἐλευθέραν γυναῖκα) at home, and instead of begetting by her legitimate children (ἐπ' ἀρότῳ παίδων γνησίων) were not to touch her at all, nor to allow anyone else to look upon her, but to force her to pass her youthful nubility in sterile and childless confinement, until her skin and flesh sagged and her eyes sank into her head: would he not seem to have lost his wits (ἔσθ' ὅπως ὁ τοιοῦτος οὐ παραπαίειν δόξειεν ἄν), when instead of producing children and enjoying his marital union as he should, he allows such a good-looking (εὐπρόσωπον) and desirable (ἐπέραστον) girl to wither away, storing her up all her life long like the priestess of Demeter (καθάπερ ἱέρειαν τῇ Θεσμοφόρῳ) (*Tim.* 16-17)?

That Ploutos should produce such a strikingly sexual allegory of money-management without once using the word τόκος, that notorious sign of the metaphoric nexus of child-bearing and financial interest, suggests that the passage is not just a hackneyed rhetorical topos but an involved variation on the theme of wealth and property, both material and human, already immanent in the tradition of the comic miser and his refusal to give up either his money or his daughter (compare Menanders *Dyskolos* and Plautus' *Aulularia*) but in this passage made for the first time explicit through the equation of the possessor of wealth with the husband, and not the father, of a nubile young woman. It is of course brought to the fore here more immediately by Zeus's mention of Danaë, in which context the god does not himself shrink from a half-pun on τόκος: the imprisoned Danaë is forced to spend her virginal years (παρθενεύεσθαι) under the harsh care of her wards (παιδαγωγοῖς) Τόκος and Λογισμός, or Accounting. His comparison of Ploutos with the imprisoned Danaë, as noted above, is, on the other hand, paralleled, and seems therefore rather hackneyed; he enlivens it with the luridly synaesthetic device of introducing the two allegorical wards, proper to the comparison's tenor, into the metaphorical vehicle itself.²⁷   This composite tableau then opens the way for Ploutos to identify himself closely with the now monetarized Danaë, by producing a thoroughly sexualized allegory of economy, one that closes with an outraged rhetorical question concerning the behavior of the confining husband, as if the emotional weight of the argument had been transferred to the other scene of the simile.   Ploutos does of course follow the crescendo of this self-enclosed ethical parable with a more explicit reference to his own actual plight at the hands of the immoderate of both extremes: "I myself complain too of these things, how I am dishonorably kicked and swallowed and poured out by some, and by others shackled like a branded run-away slave" (ταῦτα καὶ αὐτὸς ἀγανακτῶ πρὸς ἐνίων μὲν ἀτίμως λακτιζόμενος καὶ λαφυσσόμενος καὶ ἐξαντλούμενος. ὑπ' ἐνίων δὲ ὥσπερ στιγματίας δραπέτης πεπεδημένος).   But this final series of images is lackluster hyperbole compared to the detailed scene of the perverse husband and his young wife, which is to be outbid in baroquery only by Ploutos' description of his powers of seduction at 27, where the themes of physical beauty and desirability introduced in the marriage-simile will be further developed to help make vivid the peculiar nature of wealth.

For the moment, however, the tone remains mock-elevated and Zeus responds to Ploutos' outrage with a second mythological simile, suggested perhaps by the use of the verbs λαφυσσόμενος, meaning to gorge on or to swallow down greedily, and ἐξαντλούμενος, with its connotations of bailing out rising water, at 17. Zeus, at 18, produces two images of the punishment reserved for such immoderate tormentors of Ploutos (διδόασι γὰρ ἄμφω καλὴν τὴν δίκην): for the profligate and the spendthrift, the punishment of the impious Tantalus, deprived of food and drink despite their mad hunger for gold (another synaesthetic simile on Zeus's part);²⁸ for the misers, the punishment of the kin-murderer Phineus, their nourishment (τὴν τροφήν) snatched away by the Harpies.

Ploutos' response to this promise of Zeus's is again to refine his opponent's rhetoric, this time by choosing an element of the imagery of the argument and twisting it to his advantage.   Playing on the motif of punishments in the underworld introduced by Zeus, and now picking up explicitly his own word ἐξαντλούμενος, or bailed out, in this new context, he recalls for Zeus the fate of the Danaids, those forty-nine daughters of King Danaos of Egypt condemned for the murder of their husbands to attempt ceaselessly the bearing of water in sieves: Ploutos in the hands of a Timon is himself, he argues, like the water borne in vain in the Danaids' vessels (ὥστε ἐς τὸν τὴν Δαναΐδων πίθον ὑδροφορήσειν μοι δοκῶ καὶ μάτην ἐπαντλήσειν), furiously bailed out by the foolishly fearful Timon.   The specter of appropriate conjugal relations and the possibly criminal comportment of a spouse has thus returned to Ploutos' self-presentation in a surprising form, with the indirect suggestion that Timon is like a particularly zealous, if strangely negative, Danaid, actively helping the money to flow out of his little basket in a preventive spending as useless as the labor of the daughters of the Egyptian king.[29]

Zeus at 19 rebuffs this last attempt on Ploutos' part to get out of returning to Timon with a typically flippant synaesthetic rejoinder: Timon will change his profligate ways if he knows what's good for him, unless he wants in short order to find his hide and his mattock waiting for him again in the lees of the jar, once Ploutos has been poured out (ἐκχυθέντος ἐν βραχεῖ σου ῥᾳδίως εὑρήσει τὴν διφθέραν αὖθις καὶ τὴν δίκελλαν ἐν τῇ τρυγὶ τοῦ πίθου). This insistence on the jar (πίθος) with which Ploutos is bailed out, or from which he is poured, is perhaps to resonate once more, at 28, where Ploutos presents himself as a version of the Hesiodic Pandora, the woman sent by the gods to Epimetheus with a πίθος full of evils.

For the moment, however, the dialogue's attention shifts to another, as yet unknown aspect of Ploutos' person: namely his apparently handicapped legs (for he is said in 20 to be χωλός, or lame, as well as blind) and his consequent slowness in arriving at the side of someone whom Zeus intends to make rich, compared with his speed in leaving that same person. The joke is of course on the perennial hardship of acquiring wealth as against the ease with which one can lose it. In the course of the ensuing discussion a comico-sophistic distinction is made between Ploutos, the god of Wealth, and Plouton, the god of the Underworld: the latter's province is said at 21 to extend to the sudden enrichment brought about by inheritance. But it is interesting to note that at least one commentator has speculated that Lucian relies here for his depiction of Ploutos as lame on a variant reading of Aristophanes *Plutus* v. 267, where Karion describes Ploutos as ψωλός, a word meaning either circumcised or erect: so that in addition to the word-play and sophistry, there is also in Lucian's otherwise Aristophanic description a de-emphasis of Ploutos' masculinity, in line with the dialogue's tendency to represent him in feminine terms.[30]

In Ploutos' response, which follows Hermes' confusion of the money god's tardy agency with that of the speedier god of the Underworld, Ploutos delivers a lengthy disquisition on the perils of inheritance, whereby there is ugly impatience on the part of the alleged mourners, and the possibility of some unworthy person's being made rich (21-23). In the course of this illumination he refers to the would-be inheritors waiting in the marketplace for the opening of the testament or δέλτον, into which he is said to have been cast and sealed up, ἐμβαλόντες με καὶ κατασημηνάμενοι (21); they are ready to pounce on him just as

soon as the testament has been opened, and in their greed they are said
to be like baby birds awaiting the approach of the female swallow with
gaping beaks, ἐμὲ δὲ οἱ ἐπελπίσαντες ἐν τῇ ἀγορᾷ περιμένουσι
κεχηνότες ὥσπερ τὴν χελιδόνα προσπετομένην τετριγότες οἱ
νεοττοί (21). The scene is that of young awaiting nourishment from
their mother, a radical imagistic shift from the literalist description of
Ploutos cast and sealed into the testament in question.[31] There does not
seem to be a parallel for the image elsewhere in Lucian's corpus,[32] and
its appearance here in the midst of a description already baroquely
ornamented (much is made of plays on proper name-changes on the part
of the newly rich, and their exotically violent behavior is vividly
described) cannot fail to impress, if only by virtue of its almost
Homeric simplicity, not to mention gender- and species-bending nature.

The whole passage ends, indeed, on an epic note, with a mock-heroic
tetracolon crescendo of comparisons with mythic figures meant to
emphasize   the   inevitability   of   the   foolish   arriviste's   self-
impoverishment: even if he is more beautiful than Nireus, says
Ploutos, nobler than Kekrops or Kodros, wilier than Odysseus and
richer than sixteen Croesuses put together, the inheritor will in no time
have given away his money to all manner of scoundrels (23).[33]   The
catalogue of heroes, including Nireus and Odysseus, two among those
present in the catalogue of the ships at *Iliad* 2, combined with the
mock genealogy of arriviste name-changing earlier in the speech, sets
the stage for the epic transformation of Ploutos which is to come,
though not with quite the effect that might be expected.

Hermes pursues his examination of Ploutos' nature: how does he
manage, although blind, to find his way to those whom Zeus wishes to
enrich? Is Zeus not perturbed to see the unjust thus made wealthy?
Why is it that Ploutos is so slow in arriving and so quick in departing
(24-25)? Finally, why do mortals desire Ploutos at all, considering
that he is blind, sallow and lame? They are prepared to hurl themselves
into the deep and off mountain-crags[34] out of despair in their terrible
desire (δυσέρωτας) for him; they are frenzied and driven mad by their
lust (κορυβαντιᾶν αὐτοὺς ἐρωμένῳ τοιούτῳ ἐπιμεμηνότας) (26).
They must all be blind, if they cannot see what Ploutos is really like
(27).

In fact, Ploutos responds, they are not blind at all, merely deceived
(οὐ τυφλοί, ὦ ἄριστε, ἀλλ᾽ ἡ ἄγνοια καὶ ἡ ἀπάτη, αἵπερ νῦν
κατέχουσι τὰ πάντα, ἐπισκιάζουσιν αὐτούς): for Ploutos is usually
careful to disguise the fact that he is so ugly (ἄμορφος) by donning a
charming mask (προσωπεῖόν τι ἐρασμιώτατον περιθέμενος), all of
gold and studded with precious stones (διάχρυσον καὶ λιθοκόλλητον),
and by putting on colorful clothes (ποικίλα ἐνδύς, for which Jacobitz
supplies ἱμάτια). The mortals to whom Ploutos then presents himself

in this form think it is his authentic appearance (αὐτοπρόσωπον) and fall in love with his evident beauty. In response to Hermes' reasonable question, as to why the rich do not realize that Ploutos' beauty is only trumpery (ὡς ἐπίχριστος ἡ εὐμορφία ἐστίν) after they have themselves been able to put on the trappings of wealth, Ploutos answers that he has not a few accomplices (οὐκ ὀλίγα . . . μοι συναγωνίζεται) in the maintenance of his ruse. Whoever should chance first to encounter Ploutos in his blind wanderings immediately throws open the door and takes him in, all unwitting as to what he is getting into the bargain: delusion (τῦφος), folly (ἄνοια), arrogance (μεγαλοψυχία), softness (μαλακία), violence (ὕβρις), deceit (ἀπάτη), "and myriad others like those" (καὶ ἄλλ᾽ ἄττα μυρία). Deluded by these bodyguards (δορυφορούμενον ὑπ᾽ αὐτῶν), the unwitting victim fails to see that Ploutos is in fact father of all these fearsome evils (τῶν φευκτῶν κἀμὲ τὸν πάντων ἐκείνων πατέρα) (28).

The whole passage, as already observed above, is reminiscent of the celebrated places in Hesiod's *Theogony* and *Works and Days* where accounts are given of Zeus's vengeful visiting of the deceitful Pandora on the world in reprisal for the trickery of Prometheus, who had duped Zeus in the apportionment of sacrificial meats and stolen fire back from the Olympian after it had been hidden from human beings.[35] In the *Theogony*, the episode is recounted only briefly (vv. 571-589), the creation and preparation of the female "fatal trap" (δόλον αἰπύν) at v. 589 segueing into a general complaint against womankind. The *Works and Days* contains a fuller telling of the myth (vv. 60-105), including Pandora's arrival at the home of Epimetheus, Prometheus' brother, escorted by Hermes at vv. 83-5; Epimetheus' failure to heed his brother's counsel never to accept a gift from Zeus; and Pandora's opening of her jar (πίθος) out of which escape "myriad woes" (μυρία λυγρά), at vv. 94-5. The two Hesiodic passages taken together offer obvious parallels to Ploutos' self-description at *Tim.* 27-28. Pandora is created to be attractive, in the form of a virgin, with a silver gown, a spangled veil, and a golden chaplet glistening with charm (χάρις) and embossed with complex representations of beasts, at *Theogony* vv. 572-82; she has a deceitful mind and lying ways, gifts of Hermes, who has also given her a voice (something refused to the evils carried in her jar), at *Works and Days* vv. 77-80 and 104. She is in both Hesiodic passages the bearer of unsuspected ills, the presence of which her receiver at first fails to notice because he has been fooled by her ostensible beauty. Both Ploutos and Pandora are disguised, the former with a mask (προσωπεῖον at *Tim.* 27), the latter with a veil (καλύπτρην at *Theogony* v. 574). Both are tricked out with ornaments made of precious materials, including of course in both

cases gold (στεφάνην χρυσέην at *Theogony* v. 578 and προσωπεῖον .
. . διάχρυσον καὶ λιθοκόλλητον at *Tim.* 27). Both inspire desire:
Ploutos' mask is said to be ἐρασμιώτατον, most lovely or desirable,
while Pandora has an εἶδος ἐπήρατον, a lovely or desirable form.
Both are escorted to their new homes (whether *chez* Epimetheus or
Timon) by Hermes, referred to with the cult-title ᾿Αργειϕόντης at
Works and Days vv. 68, 77, and 84 and at *Tim.* 32. Both, finally, are
bearing with them or are accompanied by myriad evils (μυρία at *Works
and Days* v. 100 and at *Tim.* 28).[36] The sole distinction between the
two figures seems to be that, whereas Ploutos leaves nothing to be
hoped for in his catalogue of baneful satellites, Pandora famously
replaces the lid of her jar before Hope (᾿Ελπίς) can escape.

The links between the two figures formed by the nexus of images
surrounding the jar (πίθος) and the status of being a virgin (παρθένος)
are in the case of the *Timon* a little more dispersed, yet nevertheless
also there to be seen. In the case of the jar, as noted above, it can be
observed in Ploutos' self-association with the jars of the Danaids at 18,
in Zeus's image of Timon finding his mattock and skins in the lees of
his jar if he doesn't accept back Ploutos at 19,[37] and in Timon's own
reference to the time of his prosperity as one in which he had whole
jars (πίθους ὅλους, 45) to give away. In the case of the virgin, it is
to be found in Ploutos' self-identification with the virginal Danaë
(καθάπερ τὴν Δανάην παρθενεύεσθαι) at 13, and with the
hypothetical wife (mishandled by the two examples of immoderate
husband or householder at 16-17), described in the second example as
shut away and living out her life as a virgin (ἄγονον δὲ καὶ στεῖραν
κατακλείσας παρθενεύοι, 17).[38]

What is of prime importance in the nexus of images connecting
Ploutos and Pandora in Lucian's *Timon* is first of all the novelty of
wealth's allegorical feminization, foreign to the imagistic world of
Aristophanes' *Plutus* and present in the *Aulularia* and *Trinummus* of
Plautus only in the form of extended invective linking wives and
monetary outlay. Given the interest shown by Lucian in the Cynics,
however, and the special contemporary association of the figure of
Timon with the stereotype of the anti-social Cynic philosopher
Diogenes (as explained by Bompaire), there is added force in the
Hesiodic scene-painting because of the mythological role played by
Prometheus in the visiting of Pandora and her attendant woes on the
earth. That is to say, in both the *Theogony* and the *Works and Days*
Zeus has Pandora created and sent to earth expressly in retribution for
the Titan's crimes against the Olympian's order. In the *Theogony*, at
vv. 535-60, it is Prometheus' deceitful apportionment of the sacrificial
meats, whereby Zeus receives only the bones while the mortal
sacrificers get the delicious flesh, that causes Zeus to punish mortals

thus; in the *Works and Days*, at vv. 42-58, Prometheus steals back from Zeus the fire hidden from mortals because of unspecified prior deceit on Prometheus' part (ὅττι μιν ἐξαπάτησε Προμηθεὺς ἀγκυλόμητις, v. 48). In both cases Prometheus hoodwinks Zeus for the good of human life and progress, whether in ritual proceedings or in basic housekeeping. In both cases the result is a qualitative set-back for those same humans, who have to suffer the depredations of an ambiguous creature, appealing yet destructive (αἰπύν), whose deceit and guile answer that of Prometheus, and who brings with her woe and grief, albeit mingled with hope. And it is of course just this sort of Stoic *chiaroscuro* that was rejected by the Cynics, whose rugged moral individualism led them to refuse the amenities of "civilized" life, including both money and fire.[39] Ploutos is himself associated with Prometheus already in Aristophanes, in the suggestion at *Plut.* vv. 87 ff. that the god of Wealth's blindness came about as a result of an act of rebellion committed against Zeus: to wit, Ploutos' daring to distribute wealth to the just and the wise despite Zeus's "envy of mortals" (ἀνθρώποις φθονῶν, v. 87).[40]

The shade of the Titan haunting this dialogue comes once more onto the scene in the person of Thrasykles, the pompous, hypocritical moralist philosopher who is the last of the individual imposters to be chased off by Timon.[41] Before giving him a headful of blows in return for his generous offer of help in getting rid of his dangerous new-found wealth, the Misanthrope describes the philosopher's ways in a mordant soliloquy (54). Thrasykles is said to be glaring like a Titan (τιτανῶδες βλέπων) as he comes on, thrusting out his chin and swaggering;[42] despite his ostensible devotion to the virtues of moderation, which he preaches from morning on in numberless discourses (ἔωθεν μυρία ὅσα περὶ ἀρετῆς διεξιών), and his Stoic, anhedonic severity with pleasure-seekers, he reveals himself in private to be a glutton (" he's always complaining about his portion, even when he's eaten the whole cake or the pig," μεμψίμοιρος ἀεί, κᾶν τὸν πλακοῦντα ὅλον ἢ τὸν σῦν . . . λάβῃ, 55) and a lying, arrogant money-grubber ("even when he's sober he yields to none in falsehood or arrogance or love of money," καὶ νήφων οὐδενὶ τῶν πρωτείων παραχωρήσειεν ἂν ψεύσματος ἕνεκα ἢ θρασύτητος ἢ φιλαργυρίας, 55). All in all, he is a completely cunning creature, super-subtle and perfect in his complexity (καὶ ὅλως πάνσοφόν τι χρῆμα καὶ πανταχόθεν ἀκριβὲς καὶ ποικίλως ἐντελές, 55).

Thrasykles comes to Timon with the stated purpose of helping him get rid of his wealth, since it is corrupting (ὡς μὴ διαφθείρῃ σε τὸ κάκιστον τοῦτο, 56), and suggests that he throw it into the ocean, though not into the deeps: better just to wade out up to his hips and leave it in the surf, with only Thrasykles as witness. Or better still, why not distribute it among the needy according to their merits, making sure of course to give the most to any philosophers he should chance to meet? When Timon eventually sends him packing, Thrasykles goes off invoking democracy, laws, and the free city in which this outrage is taking place.

It is not hard to discern behind all of this buffoonery the lineaments of the Titan Prometheus, the people's hero whose gluttonous rebellion against Zeus (in the sacrificial meats-trickery) is punished by the advent of Pandora, the deceitful vision of bounty who turns out to be in fact a trap. Thrasykles is said by Lucian to be πάνσοφος and ποικίλος like the punishment for Prometheus' infraction, and his bogus "share-the-wealth" program hides a hurtful, self-serving motive, just as Prometheus' very philanthropy leads to disasters for the human beings whom he putatively champions. And true to his freshly pledged creed, Timon answers fire with fire, responding to the insult latent in Thrasykles' smarmy suggestions with patent injury meted out by the business end of his mattock (57).

That Lucian was thoroughly familiar with the figure of Prometheus, and indeed with his presentation in the works of Hesiod, is borne out by the dialogue *Prometheus, or the Caucasus* (Προμηθεὺς ἢ Καύκασος). There a brief scene assembles Prometheus, Hermes, and Hephaestus in the ranges of the Caucasus, where the two Olympians are in the process of carrying out Zeus's order that Prometheus be pinned to a rock (ἀνεσταυρῶσθαι, 1) and have his liver eaten out by an eagle in punishment for his two principle infractions of the new order, the sacrificial meats-trickery and the theft of fire. In the course of his exposition of those infractions, Hermes indeed mentions Hesiod by name, and in reference to the sacrificial-meats infraction, actually cites part of *Theogony* v. 541, in which Prometheus is seen "concealing with glistening fat" (καλύψας ἄργετι δήμῳ, 3) the bones and gristle he means to pass off on Zeus. At *Prometheus* 4 the Titan defends himself against Hermes' charges of wrong-doing not by denying them, but by calling instead for a reward for services rendered: honorary meals in the prytaneion, the very recompense suggested ironically by Socrates in Plato's *Apology*, as counter-proposal to the punishment ordained for his alleged corruption of the youth of Athens. At *Prom.* 5 Prometheus refers to Zeus as "father." At 11 he defends his education of humankind, his gift of culture (πλαστική), as ultimately beneficial to the gods themselves: or perhaps they would have preferred a world empty and bereft of humans (ἐρήμην καὶ ἀπάνθρωπον), without altars or temples to the divinities, without offerings or effigies or anything else (οὔτε δὲ βωμοὶ θεῶν ἢ ναοί, -- πόθεν δέ; -- ἢ ἀγάλματα ἢ ξόανα ἤ τι ἄλλο τοιοῦτον). At 14 he amplifies these observations with a more vivid picture of his boons, an earth now covered with cities and agriculture and no longer sordid (αὐχμηράν) and uncultivated. Finally, at 18, he justifies his theft of fire with the truism that that element, after all, does not diminish as often as it is shared: besides, who would begrudge it to those who need it (τοῖς δεομένοις)? He might just as well have taken all the fire, for that matter, and buried it underground, for all the gods have need of it (ὅπου γε καὶ εἰ τὸ πᾶν τοῦτο πῦρ ὑφελόμενος κατεκόμισα ἐς τὴν γῆν μήδ᾽ ὅλως τι αὐτοῦ καταλιπών. οὐ μεγαλὰ ὑμᾶς ἠδίκουν, 18).

The *Prometheus* thus contains some of the main strands of imagery being examined here in regard to the Timon: the malevolent father Zeus, withholder of goods (fire, wealth); the association of Prometheus with civilization and its disadvantages, as well as with classical philosophy as embodied in Socrates or in the pompous hypocrite Thrasykles, whose program of distribution of Timon's new-found gold is as false and self-serving as Prometheus' theft of fire is ultimately harmful to the mortals he means to help, inasmuch as it visits upon them Pandora and her evils; and the use of the word αὐχμηρά to describe the uncultivated earth, the very property shared by both Ploutos and Timon. Much of the ambivalence of the Lucianic figure of Wealth is here also legible: a seeming boon that turns out to be a bane and should never have been accepted; a divinity who enriches the sordid earth while remaining himself sordid and unenriched (note that at 15 Prometheus complains that he has grown no richer as a result of his education of mortals); a tricky and deceitful bringer of mixed blessings (Prometheus' ruses with the sacrificial meats and the theft of fire at *Prom.* 2-3; Ploutos' changeful form, now halt and blind, now sharp-sighted and sure-footed at *Tim.* 25). At the end of the *Prometheus*, the Olympians Hermes and Hephaestus leave the Titan Prometheus to his grisly fate, having at the outset pinned him not so high above the ground that he will fail to be seen by mortals, nor so low that those same mortals will be able to tend to him (1). His crucifixion and torture are to be both a warning and a punishment to mortals, an apt reflection of the mixture of boons and banes he himself represents.[43]

Timon, or the Misanthrope ends with the ambivalent figure of Ploutos both driven away and retained, and Timon himself glowering down from on high at a throng of would-be parasites. Recall of course that Hermes had already, early on in the dialogue, implicitly connected Timon with the chastened, if not the culture-bringing, Prometheus, when in conversation with Zeus he remarks that it was ignorance that drove Timon to give away his wealth to his seeming friends, not realizing that they were in fact just a pack of beasts, vultures waiting to eat out his liver (ὃς οὐ συνίει κόραξι καὶ λύκοις χαριζόμενος. ἀλλ᾽ ὑπὸ γυπῶν τοσούτων ὁ κακοδαίμων κειρόμενος τὸ ἧπαρ φίλους εἶναι αὐτοὺς καὶ ἑταίρους ᾤετο, *Tim.* 8). Timon then is last seen in the attitude of a sort of Prometheus already punished, albeit in possession of wealth, which has itself been figured in the course of the dialogue as both the Promethean gift of self-sufficiency wrested from the gods by force of Timon's persistent complaint, and, in the associations with Pandora, as the unwanted scourge sent by those same gods as punishment for mortal over-reaching.[44]   The ambiguous gendering of the images used to describe wealth and its proper connection with its possessor tend finally to a condensing of social relations in the figure of Timon, who has already accrued to himself the status of lone assembly-man and is now to be thought of as somehow sexually self-sufficient as well.   Like the miser Euclio of Plautus' *Aulularia*, who wants to give up his daughter no more than he does his treasure, Timon short-circuits the economy of exchange: only Timon manages also to keep everything, wealth, "children" (τόκος, child or interest), the appropriately chaste "wife" he has found in Ploutos, and visitation by the ravishing, gold-bringing father Zeus (41).

As in the *Trinummus*, the figure of wealth in the *Timon* is unmasked as a kind of fraud (as the Sycophant in the former, as a painted lady with a jar full of baneful troubles in the latter) even as it is made clear that the ostensible fraud is in fact the real thing.   For the Sycophant of the *Trinummus* is in truth the bearer of Charmides' wealth, or could at least be exchanged against such wealth, which is in reality in safe-keeping with Lesbonicus' guardian Callicles; and the Ploutos of the *Timon*, for all his attendant disadvantages and deceitful make-up, does finally make good his promise of Treasure, of "gold, gift most beautiful to mortals" (χρυσέ. δεξίωμα κάλλιστον βροτοῖς, *Tim.* 41; compare Euripides, *Dan.* fr. 324 Nauck). In fact, in the last-mentioned incarnation, in Timon's figuring of the mineral wealth he has found as the golden shaft in the form of which Zeus is said to have visited and impregnated Danaë, Timon seems decisively to have closed the gap introduced at the dialogue's beginning with his plaintive cries to a Zeus who may after all be nothing more than his name (see *Tim.* 1, where the Misanthrope wonders if Zeus is not simply an illusory smoke-and-mirrors effect *of his appearance in poetry*).   Here, in the form of the golden Treasure caused to appear by Ploutos acting on Zeus's behest, the father has apparently made himself present in the most relevant form, in the precious object that had been lost, just as Charmides at the close of the *Trinummus* heals up the rift consequent upon his absence and his insistence that the treasure hidden in his house not be handed over to Lesbonicus.

But the stakes in the Timon are different.   Whereas in the *Trinummus* the return of Charmides and the freeing up of the family fortune unleashes a veritable spate of reconciliations, including two marriages and the re-integration into society of Lesbonicus, previously dogged by debts in the allegorical form of Inopia, the *Timon* closes with the definitive exclusion of the Misanthrope from society: or rather, with his constitution of a new, idiosyncratic society of one. He lives out thus Euclio's dream of private usufruct of his money; but of course even in the *Aulularia* the burgeoning misanthrope Euclio is made to see the impossibility of his monetary (and marital) autarky.

Timon's self-positioning in regard to his newly refound gold is significantly different: whereas Euclio was content to treat his pot of treasure as a sort of confidant, Timon refigures the relation, in keeping with the themes of feminization of Ploutos and of Timon's assimilation to Ploutos, as that of a virgin, Danaë, to the seductive power of Zeus, who brooks no resistance, neither on the part of the prison in which the girl is kept, nor on the part of the girl herself. "Come," says Timon at 41 after he has discovered the gold by digging for it with his mattock on Ploutos' instructions, "oh most lovely and most desirable. Now I believe that even Zeus once became gold: for what virgin would not have accepted with open arms such a beautiful lover flowing down through the roof" (ἐλθέ, ὦ φίλτατε καὶ ἐρασμιώτατε. νῦν πείθομαί γε καὶ Δία ποτὲ γενέσθαι χρυσόν· τίς γὰρ οὐκ ἂν παρθένος ἀναπεπταμένοις τοῖς κόλποις ὑπεδέξατο οὕτω καλὸν ἐραστὴν διὰ τοῦ τέγους καταρρέοντα"). So in the general economy of the dialogue's imagery, Timon has now become the virgin Ploutos had once complained of being, imprisoned by the jealous male authority; the seductive gold is represented now by the figure of the ravishing Zeus; and Ploutos has entirely disappeared, elided between his misanthropic *semblable* and the Treasure he has delegated to him.[45]

Or has Ploutos in fact disappeared? The dialogue begins with a complaint to a "father," the father of gods and men, Zeus, that he has become lazy, absent, inconsequential, Zeus only in name (ἅπαντα γὰρ ταῦτα λῆρος ἤδη ἀναπέφηνε καὶ καπνὸς ἀτεχνῶς ποιητικὸς ἔξω τοῦ πατάγου τῶν ὀνομάτων, 1). He no longer punishes those guilty of hybris the way he used to (πόσοι Φαέθοντες ἢ Δευκαλίωνες ἱκανοὶ πρὸς οὕτως ὑπέραντλον ὕβριν τοῦ βίου; 4): perhaps the rumors of his death are true (6). In the course of the dialogue, however, the only "father" who actually presents himself to Timon is Ploutos, beneath whose ravishing form mortals are fatally incapable of discerning the father of all their troubles (κἀμὲ τὸν πάντων ἐκείνων πατέρα τῶν εἰσεληλυθότων κακῶν, 28); he is in fact himself the bringer of myriad woes, which include notably hybris, or violence (*Tim.* 28), in whose firm grip Timon is to be seen as the dialogue draws to a close. The *Timon*'s indictment of the money-system is then incomparably bleaker than that conveyed by the *Trinummus*, in which the father also withholds wealth and is absent while his son discovers the scarcity at the heart of debauch. In the *Trinummus* Lesbonicus responds by attempting to transform his ancestral land into a dowry so as to maintain control over his sister; this valiant short-circuiting of the property-maintaining point of the patriarchally arranged marriage is then presumptively forestalled by the men who stand to Lesbonicus *in loco parentis*, and who have recourse only to the ruse of representing the absent father by a grotesque facsimile, the Sycophant.

In the Plautine comedy, all is righted by the actual encounter of the returned benevolent father with his fraudulent if adequate representative, the physical dismissal of the latter, and the consequent normalization of patriarchal economy. In the *Timon* such an economy cannot be normalized, since it has never properly existed: Timon cannot be re-integrated into a society that was already from the outset devoted exclusively to fleecing him, in which the death of the transcendental father has been announced, and in which his emissary turns out indeed to be a grotesquely camouflaged bringer of debility. Therefore Timon resolves to make a virtue of this necessity, and closes the gap by forming his own society of one, in which he will play all the parts at once.

Timon will, however, have some company, at least allegorically speaking: note that at *Tim.* 32 Poverty complains that her Timon is now being delivered back into the hands of Τρυφή, or Debauchery, of whose abuses she had previously healed him (Ploutos too, at 38, uses the term τρυφή non-figuratively, to refer collectively to the luxurious boons he has offered Timon). Recall that τρυφή is the name of the figure in Philemon's *Treasure* of whom Luxuria, the allegorical figure who delivers the prologue of the *Trinummus* and who introduces her daughter Inopia into Lesbonicus' house, is the Latin counterpart. In the *Timon*, then, the situation of the *Trinummus* is reversed: whereas in the Plautine comedy the prolix figure of Debauchery ushers in that of Scarcity, who speaks only one line, in the Lucianic dialogue the garrulous figure of Wealth, attended at least metaphorically by Debauchery, drives out the figure of Poverty, who makes only three interventions.

And yet Ploutos too, as noted, soon disappears from the scene, leaving in his place a Treasure that is destined to be neither squandered on debauches nor guarded sensibly against scarcities, but hoarded in such a fashion as to render altogether null and empty its social significance. In this fashion the *Timon* goes the *Trinummus* one better in its social critique, pointing out the relations of subjugation condensed in money (wage-slavery, control of sexuality and reproduction) while refusing to promise any recuperation of these imbalances in a potentially well-ordered society, and instead throws the possessor of wealth back onto himself and the misfit consolations of a violent, anti-human hermeticism.

Notes

[1] Jacques Bompaire, *Lucien écrivain* (Paris: Boccard, 1958) is the standard work on Lucian's sources, and indeed on Lucian (Bompaire is also responsible for the important Budé edition of Lucian). See also, for particular study, Hertel (1969) 48-62, where Lucian's concordances and divergences are well documented and a case is made for the pervasive "Aristophanism" of the dialogue. The chronology of Lucian's writings is extremely sketchy: see the short essay on dating that appears as an appendix to Graham Anderson, *Lucian: Theme and Variation in the Second Sophistic* (Leiden: Brill, 1976), 177-181.

[2] I am indebted here and in the discussion that follows to E.L. Bowie, "Greeks and Their Past in the Second Sophistic," *Past and Present* 46 (1970): 3-41.

[3] See Christopher Robinson, *Lucian and His Influence in Europe* (London: Duckworth, 1979), 3: "Roman occupation of Commagene has left few traces. It was a policing exercise conducted for the benefit of Rome, not part of a process of cultural proselytization. The principal social institutions remained Greco-Iranian even where Roman material alterations -- bridges, roads, public monuments -- were made." See also G. W. Bowersock, *Hellenism in Late Antiquity* (Ann Arbor: Univ. of Michigan Press, 1990), particularly the chapter entitled "The Syrian Tradition" at pp. 29-40. Bompaire (1958) 102 explicitly links the Hellenism of the period with the middle east: "En tout cas, sans porter de jugement de valeur, on ne peut nier, après les enquêtes minutieuses de Wilamowitz et de M. Boulanger, le rôle de premier plan joué par l'Asie dans l'élaboration de la IIe Sophistique."

[4] The cultural revivalism known as the Second Sophistic included of course much more than just rhetoric, affecting also historiography, travel writing, anthropological investigations, and so-called foundation verse, among other forms; the emphasis is here placed on rhetoric because of Lucian's loose adherence to the genre, and because of the rhetorician's (and the sophist's) special prestige: see Bowie (1970) 4-6.

[5] Robinson (1979) 6.

[6] Gustav Adolf Seeck, "Lukian und die griechische Tragödie," in Blänsdorf (1990) 233-241. Seeck notes in particular reference to Lucian's *Anacharsis* the anachronistic view of tragedy as moral education or philosophical consolation, and infers from this that Lucian meant tragedy as a text to be privately read: "Aber Trost ist wohl doch mehr eine Privatangelegenheit, und Liebe zur Tragödie kann man nicht öffentlich anordnen. . . . Da Lukian das Erscheinungsbild der Tragödie auf der Bühne seiner Zeit unerträglich findet, er aber andererseits auch nirgendwo davon spricht, daß im alten Athen die Aufführungen anders ausgesehen hätten, kann er nur die Tragödie als Text, als Literatur, meinen," Seeck in Blänsdorf (1990) 239. Seeck goes on to note similarities between Lucian's and Aristophanes' use of tragedy as ethical object lesson. On the subject of the changing aesthetics

of tragedy's reception, it is worth remembering that Vernant, in Vernant and Vidal-Naquet (1990) 29, maintains that for Aristotle in the fourth century B.C.E. "tragic man" had already "become a stranger:".

[7] Lucian makes farcical reference to his indebtedness to Aristophanes and old comedy in the mouth of the character "Dialogue" at *Bis Accusatus* 33.

[8] *Birds* vv. 1547 ff. and *Lysistrata* vv. 805 ff.: in the first he is merely proverbial as a scorner of the gods, while in the second, for the sake of a ribald jest, his misanthropy is said not to have extended to women.

[9] The character of the μονότροπος or misanthropic hermit has at least one of its origins, of course, in the fifth-century play of that name by Phrynichus, but it is not until the fourth century and new comedy that it becomes a stock role.

[10] Bompaire notes the close association of the Timon legend with the figure of Diogenes, and the presence of Cynic clichés in the dialogue, even as he discounts the probability of individual Cynic sources for various episodes: Bompaire (1958) 169-170. As in the case of the μονότροπος, of course, Cynic philosophy has its roots in the fifth century, in the teachings of Antisthenes; but (at least for Lucian, as for Diogenes Laertius) Diogenes of Sinope was the emblematic figure.

[11] Bompaire remarks, in connection with the Timon of Plutarch's account and his association there with a Cynic figure, on the contemporary diffusion of Cynic characteristics among marginal figures in general: "D'autres indices d'une élaboration rhétorique du personnage sont son association avec une abstraction, Apémantos (innoxius), son manque d'individualité qui le rend interchangeable avec Myson, Diogène, Ménédème, Héraclite, Socrate même, comme Solon avec tel autre Sage. . . :" Bompaire (1958) 170. Plutarch's account will, of course, be further discussed below, in connection with the treatment of Timon by Shakespeare.

[12] References are to the standard manuscript pagination: that is, since the dialogue is composed in prose and not in verse, unlike the comedies studied above, to a page and not to a discrete line-unit.

[13] See Whitman (1964) passim on the Great Idea and its function in Aristophanic comedy. See too Anderson (1976) 92: "Aristophanes' hero Chremylus starts poor and becomes rich: Timon starts rich, becomes poor, then has a second windfall; and their two characters are completely opposite."

[14] See Hertel (1969) 50 and Bompaire (1958) 170 on the inconsistencies of Timon's loyalty to Wealth and/or Poverty; it should be noted, however, that the hostility towards Hermes and the as yet unacknowledged Wealth is to some extent compulsory behavior for a Timon whose literary pedigree includes the reference to him at *Birds* v. 1548 as a proverbial "god-hater" (θεομίσης).

[15] Ὕβρις, above translated Lust or Violence, is of course explicitly mentioned by Penia as one of Ploutos' sometime allies, at *Tim.* 32; the notion of hybris being the means to a speedy enrichment, as is the case with Timon here despite Ploutos' quibbles on inheritance as the only quick route to wealth, can be traced at least back to Bacchylides *Dithyramb* 1, vv.

59 ff., which was itself in turn influenced by Solon and thus inaugurates a celebrated fifth-century tragic topos of hybris' place in the progression from abundance through delusion to doom.

[16] See Robinson (1979) 3-4.

[17] Bowie (1970) 37-41 well sums up the contrast of Greek middle- and upper-class wealth with diminished political power, beyond the immediately local sphere, under the late principate. Note that Engels in his *Zur Geschichte des Urchristentums* calls Lucian "der Voltaire des klassischen Altertums," thus claiming him implicitly for the genealogy of enlightened bourgeois revolution. An opposite assessment is offered by the British-born Houston Stewart Chamberlain, Richard Wagner's son-in-law and a convert to German-nationalist theory, in his *Die Grundlagen des 19. Jahrhunderts*, where in a piece of transparent anti-Semitism he links Aristophanes and Voltaire as constructively satirical folk-poets as against the corrupt and significantly "homeless" griping of Lucian and Heine. Chamberlain is cited (with approval) by Curt Hille, *Die deutsche Komödie unter der Einwirkung des Aristophanes* (Leipzig: Quelle & Meyer, 1907), 81. See too the interesting discussion in C. P. Jones, *Culture and Society in Lucian* (Cambridge: Harvard Univ. Press, 1986), 1-4 on the debate surrounding nineteenth-century German reception of Lucian, and Heine's place in it as a common reference point for defenders and attackers alike. For analogous discussion of Heine's role in the nineteenth-century reception of Aristophanes, see my "Heine's Aristophanes: Compromise Formations and the Ambivalence of Carnival," *Comparative Literature* 49, no. 3 (summer 1997): 227-40.

[18] Αὐχμέω and αὐχμηρός are associated also with agricultural conditions, as in the quality of a field that has become dry or sordid without rain: this is the sense given by Hesychius s.v., and in Theophrastus *Historia Plantarum*. (This connection is interesting given the archaic association of Ploutos with the ploughed field, and the Aristophanic separation between agricultural prosperity and monetary wealth sketched in Chapter 1 above.) Note, however, that in the *Clouds* Strepsiades uses the word in conjunction with images of fasting and exposure to describe the treatment he is willing to undergo at the Phrontisterion in order to be rid of his debts (vv. 437 ff.), a catalog of humiliations that includes being thought an imposter and being eaten as a sausage!

[19] Four obols is indeed a pittance, but not absurd. If the dialogue is meant to be set in or after 429 B.C.E., the terminus ante quem for the events described at *Tim.* 10, on which see Hertel (1969) 55, then Timon is earning between the average for a laborer in the mid-century, two obols, and that produced by inflation in the last decade of the fifth, one drachma (= 6 obols). Such a wage would have kept him on a modest diet of cereals and figs. For estimates see Frank J. Frost, *Greek Society* (Lexington: D.C. Heath & Co., 1971), 55-59.

[20] See Ehrenberg (1951) 242-243.

[21] The line ὅπου τὸ κέρδος, παρὰ φύσιν δουλευτέον, "where there is gain, there is unnatural slavery," is cited at *Apol.* 3 as τὸ ἀγεννέστατον ἐκεῖνο ἰαμβεῖον, "that most ignoble iambic verse."

[22] This treasure is of course a reference to the tradition of middle and new comedies with titles like *Thesauros* or *Hydria*, a common container for treasure. The *Trinummus* itself, of course, was based on the *Thesauros* of Philemon. Bompaire (1958) 170-173 cautions against looking for a Cynic source for the episode of the gold's discovery, and emphasizes the comic character of sudden enrichment through treasure. The comic lineage of the topos is not here in dispute. What should be remarked is merely the fact that Lucian's dialogue straddles the line between social realism and fairy-tale allegory in its treatment of the money form and of the god of Wealth.

[23] "Es war Sitte bei den Alten, daß, wenn jemand seine frühere Beschäftigung änderte, er die Abzeichen derselben dem Gotte weihte, der derselben vorstand," Jacobitz, *Ausgewählte Schriften des Lucian* (Leipzig: Teubner, 1862), ad loc. Compare Horace's dedication of his drenched clothing to the god of the sea after surviving a (metaphorical) ship-wreck, at *Odes* 1.5.

[24] Note the verb πονέω, which refers classically to toil and wage-labor, and which is related to the word πενία, or (working-)poverty, used here to describe the mattock's wear through employment for digging and beating.

[25] Hertel (1969) 55 mentions this novelty briefly: "Der Vergleich zwischen dem Geld und einer jungen Frau war bei Aristophanes noch nicht vorgeformt."

[26] Fortified bedroom, Sophocles *Antigone* vv. 945 ff.; tower keep, Horace *Odes* 3.16. The argument to the lost *Danaë* of Euripides seems to confuse the cask or κιβώτιον, into which Akrisios is conventionally said to have cast Danaë and her infant son after the latter's birth, with the room in which she is initially confined, and which Zeus manages to penetrate.

[27] The terminology is of course that of I. A. Richards in *The Philosophy of Rhetoric* (Oxford: Oxford Univ. Press, 1936).

[28] Here I differ from the reading of Oskar Schmidt, *Metapher und Gleichnis in den Schriften Lukians* (Winterthur: Ziegler, 1897), 45, who assigns the Tantalus-punishment to the misers, despite the suggestion of Zeus's οἱ μέν-οἱ δέ construction in answer to Ploutos' listing of the two sorts of immoderates, the profligate and the miserly. The punishments of Tantalus and of Phineus should rather be assigned respectively, in accordance with the more typical use of the οἱ μέν-οἱ δέ construction, and not chiastically, which latter usage is only sparsely attested. The nature of the two punishments, too, makes better sense in this distribution: the sensuous enjoyers (the profligate, Tantalus) are frankly denied the object of their desire, while the ascetic fetishists (the misers, Phineus) must have their fantasy of being robbed repeatedly enacted with the snatching away of their τροφή by the Harpies.

[29] Note that the expression "to pour into a perforated jar" (εἰς τὸν τετρημένον πίθον ἀντλεῖν) is attested in other places (Xenophon *Oec.* 7.40, Lucian *Herm.* 61 and *Dial. Mort.* 11.4) as proverbial for useless toil; here what is interesting is the piling up of means of representing Ploutos that associate him with the feminine and with marital relations.

[30] The commentator is Wilhelm Süss, "Scheinbare und wirkliche Inkongruenzen in den Dramen des Aristophanes," *Rheinisches Museum* 97

(1954): 115-59, see pp. 143 ff. Recall that the passage in the *Plutus* in which Karion describes the god of Wealth as ψωλός or erect (that is, with foreskin retracted) is emended by Herwerden to read ψωρός or mangy; van Leeuwen notes Lucian's use of χωλός but rejects it as not likely to have required Karion to qualify his observation with the verb οἶμαι or "I think," since Ploutos' lameness would have been immediately obvious. This same objection, it may be noted, could be raised against the emendation to ψωρός, or mangy; the point in Aristophanes seems to be that the old god is ugly, sordid, and comically libidinous: see Dover (1980) 129 ff. for evidence that retraction of the foreskin, especially in an old man, was a typical marker of comic squalor. The marked avoidance of the term in Lucian may then also be explained by a general tendency in his dialogue to resist the frankly sexual humor of Aristophanes.

[31] The choice of the swallow as the particular species of (mother-)bird is also interesting, because the swallow is associated elsewhere with strange noises and foreign tongues: this thus lends a further dimension to the simile, whereby Ploutos' outlandishness may be emphasized. The Kleiner-Pauly, s.v. "Schwalbe," cites Aeschylus *Agamemnon* v. 1050 and Aristophanes *Birds* v. 1681 as evidence that "[i]hren Gesang . . . empfand man als Geschwätz in Barbarensprache. . . ." Interestingly, sources like the *Palatine Anthology* and Moschos are reported to have associated the swallow with melancholy.

[32] There is in *Dial. Mort.* 6.4 the image of a miser croaking at the expectant would-be inheritors gathered around him "like a young bird not yet out of the egg" (καθάπερ ἐξ ᾠοῦ νεοττὸς ἀτελὴς ὑποκρώζων). Schmidt (1897) 115 compares Juvenal *Sat.* 10 vv. 230 ff.

[33] One could, of course, just as easily refer the tone of the passage's coda to that of the Sapphic priamel (or indeed of the parodos of the *Iphigeneia at Aulis*, where Nireus' beauty is also stressed); at any rate, an archaic note.

[34] Another archaic note: Jacobitz compares Theognis vv. 175 ff., where the identical behavior is described as appropriate in the flight from poverty.

[35] These two escapades of Prometheus are not both, of course, recounted in each poem: the sacrificial meats-trickery belongs to the *Theogony*, the stealing of fire to the *Works and Days*.

[36] Note that Timon himself, at 36, before he has agreed to take back Ploutos, complains that the god of Wealth has been the cause of myriad woes (ὅτι καὶ πάλαι μυρίων μοι κακῶν αἴτιος οὗτος); he goes on to praise Penia for all that she has taught him, including the wherewithal to pin his hopes (τὰς ἐλπίδας) only on himself.

[37] Here the sense of the image seems to go against the grain of the likeness to Pandora, since the baneful mattock and skins are to be found by Timon in the lees of his jar precisely if he *fails* to accept Ploutos back, and not if he prudently refuses him, as Epimetheus should presumably have done with Pandora in accordance with his brother's cautions. It is worth noting, however, that Zeus's threat is of course perversely prophetic, for by the end of the dialogue Timon will in fact have taken up his mattock again. Besides, Zeus's pleasantry serves as well to keep the image of the πίθος to

the fore despite the immediate logical inconcinnities: note Zeus's generally perverse attitude in the dialogue, and his vested interest in making Timon accept back Ploutos (Zeus's own prestige is after all at stake).

[38] Finally it may be worth noting that Hermes at 37 manages to overcome Timon's resistance to accepting back Ploutos with the Homeric apothegm, "The gifts of Zeus are not to be rejected" (οὔτοι ἀπόβλητά ἐστι τὰ δῶρα τὰ παρὰ τοῦ Διός, cf. *Iliad* 3.65), which brings into play the important notion of the gift and its place in Pandora's name.

[39] See Diogenes Laertius 6.20, 21, and 75; see too Michel Onfray, *Cynismes* (Paris: Grasset, 1990), 43-52 and 108-117 for a Nietzschean development of the transvaluation of values implied by the Cynics' refusal of "progress."

[40] The scholia to *Plut.* vv. 87 ff. actually cite *Works and Days* v. 42 on Zeus's hiding of the wellsprings of life from mortals, an act that in turn leads to Prometheus' theft of fire. R.G.A. Buxton, in "Blindness and Limits: Sophocles and the Logic of Myth," *Journal of Hellenic Studies* 100 (1980): 22-37, describes Ploutos' act as a "'quasi-Promethean' transgression," p. 31n48.

[41] Note, in connection with this spoof of a modern philosopher, that Prometheus is said to have been honored, along with Athene, at the Academy: see *Fragmente der griechischen Historiker* 224 F 147.

[42] Note however the other occurrences of this expression in Lucian: at *Ikaromenippus* 23, where the phrase τιτανῶδες . . . ἀπίδων is used of Zeus (!), and at *Philopatris* 22, where τιτανῶδες ἐνίδων is used simply of an angry participant in an argument. (The authenticity of the *Philopatris* is in dispute. Robinson [1979] 241 calls it "indubitably spurious;" see for an opposing view Jones [1986] 167-171.) Schmidt (1897) 41 maintains that Prometheus in particular does not stand behind such turns of phrase, because "*Prometheus* ist in der Metapher der Alten selten." Whatever the case, despite the fact that "glaring like a Titan" may have no more than ossified, hackneyed status in Lucian's writing, it does occur here in this description of the hypocritical philosopher Thrasykles, in a dialogue already full, as has been shown, of references to the Hesiodic account. On the general question of Lucian's repetitiveness and self-quotation see Anderson (1976) 1-22, where a good case is made for treating Lucian as more than just a hack. See Jones (1986) passim for a defense of Lucian as an observer of contemporary society and not simply a sort of literary recluse.

[43] Ambivalence in Lucian's own relation to the cultural boons represented by Prometheus is beyond the scope of the present discussion. It should be noted that he was himself associated with the Titan for his prodigious eloquence, apparently referred to by his contemporaries as a "Prometheus in words," on which see Schmidt (1897) 41; note too that in the portrait of the artist as a young man given in the *Dream*, Lucian depicts himself failing at the sculptor's trade and then choosing in a dream the allegorical figure of Παιδεία or Education, associated with wealth and renown, over that of Τέχνη or Craft, associated with poverty and barbarism. See the discussion in Jones (1986) 9.

[44] Note however that of course Timon is much more the refuser of Prometheus' gifts than a sort of instantiation of the Titan in any way other than in Prometheus' martyr-aspect: as remarked above, he is a Prometheus only insofar as he is alone and has in time past had his liver figuratively eaten out by ungrateful parasites. Indeed, at *Tim.* 43 the Misanthrope foreswears even the likenesses of men in his anti-human frenzy: the word he uses, ἀνδριάντων, is ambiguous, meaning both sculptures of human beings and, as Vernant has shown, a cult representation on a continuum with the ξόανα, the effigies Prometheus claims at *Prom.* 12 to have invented for the gods. Timon thus rejects Promethean representational culture in favor of the thing itself. In this sense the departure of Ploutos is apposite, since, following Vernant, ἀνδριάς can be used in contexts where the name of the god represented alone would suffice: Ploutos then is effaced along with all other anthropomorphic representation. See Vernant, "Figuration et image," *Mètis* 5 (1990): 225-38.

[45] The "complete" fragment of the *Danaë* of Euripides from which Timon's address to the new-found gold is quoted, as recorded by Nauck from the *Florilegium* of Stobaeus, has interesting ramifications for the present train of interpretation. Nauck fr. 324 runs in its entirety ὦ χρυσέ, δεξίωμα κάλλιστον βροτοῖς. / ὡς οὔτε μήτηρ ἡδονὰς τοίας ἔχει, / οὐ παῖδες ἀνθρώποισιν. οὐ φίλος πατήρ. / οἵας σὺ χοἰ σὲ δώμασιν κεκτημένοι. / εἰ δ' ἡ Κύπρις τοιοῦτον ὀφθαλμοῖς ὁρᾷ, / οὐ θαῦμ' ἔρωτας μυρίους αὐτὴν τρέφειν." "oh gold, gift most beautiful to mortals, / no mother holds out hope of such pleasures, / nor any mortals' children, nor a dear father, / such as you and those who have you in their homes do. / If Aphrodite were to look thus with her eyes, / it would be no wonder that she nourished myriad desires." Both the notion of gold concentrating kin relationships and that of its being somehow seductive and desirable (not to say ultimately also productive of "myriad" items, whether desires or banes) are obviously germane to my analysis and might perhaps be thought to have influenced Lucian's composition beyond what he actually quotes.

Chapter 4

Everything Becomes Allegory: The Instrumentalization of Wealth in Shakespeare's *Timon of Athens*

Thus history, with all its concrete force, remains forever a figure, cloaked and needful of interpretation.

Erich Auerbach

Prologue

The figure of the Misanthrope, of the hermit, of the anti-humanist, anti-social, miserly μονότροπος, is of course not original with Lucian. As noted above, the early fifth-century poet Phrynichus had written a *Monotropos*; there is known to have existed, although it is not extant, a comedy by the name of *Timon* by the old comic playwright Antiphanes; and the fifth and fourth centuries were productive of comedies with references, at very least, to such a stock character.[1] Lucian's innovation seems rather to have been the grafting onto the misanthrope-theme of the allegorical figures Ploutos and Penia, clearly borrowed from the *Plutus* of Aristophanes, and enlivened, as shown in my last chapter, with typically new comic meta-theatrical burlesque. The conjuring up of Wealth in this form, however complicated by bizarre new imagery, is still comprehensible within Lucian's Second-Sophistic attachment to the figures and usages of classical Athens. Ploutos' summary dismissal from the scene of the dialogue, however, on which he leaves behind only the mute (though still veiled) object of desire, glittering, seductive gold, whose uselessness is then signalled with its insertion into an absurd society of

one, bereft of exchange: all this derives from a more modern, more
Cynic sensibility than had given rise to the fables of old comedy and
the family dramas of Roman new comedy, dependent as they were on
divine presence and mostly harmonious conclusions.

And indeed, Lucian's dialogue is not, properly speaking, comedy at
all, but a rarefied amusement designed to be performed as a dramatic
reading to a learned audience of Greek cultural *revanchistes*. This group
was very much on the fringes of imperial power and was politically
decentered in such a way as to make of their preferred literary genres,
those of classical Athens, both an invaluable bridge to a former
potency and a continuous reminder of the impossibility of
reconstituting the identity they seemed to promise, since that identity
had been rooted in forms of social organization now irretrievably
shattered, overextended and impotent against the superior Roman
might. Against such a backdrop it must have been tempting to
construct a performance around the figure of a man so disappointed by
the ingratitude of those whom his munificence had benefited that he
begs Zeus for retribution and vengeance, only to condemn the deceitful
form in which such retribution comes. Ambivalence about the
effectiveness of god-sent money, which tends only toward debauch and
abuse, leads to Timon's significant policy of economic isolation,
which is itself figured as a perfect containment of the forces (both
sexual and technological) that threaten local order. The additional cruel
fact that the gift of Wealth must be applied for from a distant,
ineffectual, uncaring Zeus reflects too the contemporary fact of the
displacement of power from the local city-state or principate to the
remote Roman capital. This also helps to explain why the function of
the god Ploutos is absorbed into the golden Treasure he instructs
Timon to dig up, why he does not linger to fill a role, even as a slave,
in Timon's new isolationist economy: for the replacement of the
carping Ploutos with his inanimate token, gold, is then a means of
perpetuating the fantasy of divestment of both the Olympian overlord
and his various henchmen.

It must of course be recalled that Lucian was not simply a Hellenist,
nor indeed a Greek at all, but that he was in fact originally a Syrian
speaker of Aramaic, one who had assimilated to the Hellenistic culture
of the Greco-Roman period and made himself thoroughly at home in
that culture's language and mythology. It is worth remembering too
that he does not seem to have been born a Roman citizen:[2] but this is
also not reason enough to assume that his motives in writing his
critical tracts were strictly social-progressive, or forever based on any
putative outrage at the split between the cultural capital at Athens and
the political capital at Rome. Certainly his most patent excoriation of
the dependence of Hellenistic intellectuals on Roman money, *On*

Salaried Posts, was sufficient to win him an admiring notice from Marx and Engels in *The German Ideology*;[3] but he was of course to reverse his position, in the *Apology for 'On Salaried Posts,'* following his own acceptance of a post in the Egyptian bureaucracy. As C. P. Jones points out, just because Lucian decries Greek intellectual dependence on Roman capital, "[i]t does not follow . . . that in Lucian's view all Greeks are oppressed, still less that his cultivated Greek is a proletarian."[4] Furthermore, provincial territories were not hampered by Rome from pursuing their local business, especially in matters of trade, even though "[e]conomic independence was not a complete counterbalance to political dependence."[5]

Hence precisely, however, the fantasy of the *Timon*: that of hoarding up goods, relations, and cultural products against the encroaching throng of preposterous hypocrites and ingrates. Lucian's curious mixture of Aristophanic allegory, new comic or Plautine character, and Cynic commonplaces at once celebrates the power of wealth concentrated in the self-sufficient individual and at the same time indicts the illusory nature of wealth itself. With the subsumption of the allegorical figure Ploutos into the squalid Timon and his prosopopoeisized cache of gold, the Lucianic dialogue effects a kind of suture in the tradition of Ploutos' representation, abstracting the actual god from the scene and concentrating attention instead on his mortal proprietor, himself become now a sort of grotesque allegory in the more strictly literary sense.

Money, Melancholy, and Misanthropy: Shakespeare's Timon

That this process of abstraction of the god Ploutos from the fantasy of an isolationist economy signals both a form of aspiration to freedom from imperial constraint as well as the reinscription of that constraint into the very means by which it is evaded; that it signals the recontainment, in other words, of the very liberationist energies put into play by the fantasy; that this concentration of the attributes of the personified allegory of Wealth into the person of the wealth-hoarder leads to a melancholy and a violence no longer assimilable by the economy of comedy at all, is demonstrated aptly by the reception of Lucian's imagery in Shakespeare's late tragedy, the *Timon of Athens*. In that Elizabethan revenge-drama, in keeping with the period's para-realist conventions of tragic representation, the god of Wealth is of course nowhere visible; but there is everywhere to be read that pagan deity's negative presence, in the extreme despair and melancholy of the images used by Shakespeare's Misanthrope to manage his own private economy, an economy imagined now against the backdrop of the modern capitalism already nascent in the last days of English medieval feudalism, as opposed to the transition from city-state to imperial economy that had marked Lucian's day.[6] Shakespeare's Timon does not jealous hoard up his god-sent gold, as Lucian's Timon does, nor does he fetishize it, as Plautus' Euclio does, nor does he put it back into social play, as Plautus' Charmides does, nor indeed does he revel unabashedly in it, as Aristophanes' Chremylus does: instead, Shakespeare's Timon distributes the gold freely but morosely, hoping to do as much harm with it as he can, and then retreats into his grave, entirely indifferent to the new wealth he has been deploying.[7]   In Shakespeare's *Timon of Athens* an entirely new tragic-allegorical tradition is initiated, building on the characters, situations, and tropes of ancient comedy.

Walter Benjamin, in his study of the German baroque tragic drama form known as the *Trauerspiel*, comments thus on the diffuse but rich allegorical strain in Shakespeare:

> for all Shakespearian 'tragedies', the theory of the *Trauerspiel* is predestined to contain the prolegomena of interpretation.   For in Shakespeare allegory reaches much deeper than the metaphorical forms where Goethe noticed it: 'Shakespeare is rich in wonderful figures of speech, which arise from personified concepts and which would not be at all suitable nowadays, but which are entirely in place in his work because in his day all art was dominated by allegory.'[8]

In fact, Benjamin contends, Shakespeare's brand of allegory is at once more modern than a simple parade of personifications and represents at the same time a transitional stage between the medieval Christian allegories and their more sophisticated seventeenth-century descendants. Shakespeare's allegorical style was in fact to find an echo in the succeeding generation of baroque poets,[9] where it served to heighten dramatic effect by rendering visually powerful the language in which characters revealed their pathology.

> The tendency to achieve a balance, so to speak, between the atmosphere of the dramatic character's visionary perception -- a theatrical gamble which even Shakespeare seldom risks -- can be seen all the more clearly, the more unsuccessful these lesser masters [of the baroque *Trauerspiel*] were.   The visionary description of the *tableau vivant* is one of the triumphs of baroque vigour and baroque antitheticism.[10]

In Benjamin's formulation, direct allegorical personification, such as is found in baroque drama but only rarely in Shakespeare, constitutes not a sort of primitivism but an advance in the techniques of figuration, for "[a]llegorical personification has always concealed the fact that its function is not the personification of things, but rather to give the concrete a more imposing form by getting it up as a person."[11] In this pursuit, then, Shakespeare's ornate verbal allegories may be seen as a stage in the development of just such a figuring of the concrete, one that arose in a later age as the pantomimic legend-bearing processions of allegorical figures central to baroque drama, but which worked its way too on the language of such productions. Those productions were thereby able to attain a higher order of concrete metaphoric imagery.[12]

But Shakespeare's language is not only innovative in the representation of the wealth-and-poverty scenario: his Timon is a radically new and different character, for all that his conception is indebted in different and uncertain ratios to the main sources discussed here.[13] This difference is due not least to the fact that, as is generally thought, Shakespeare's principal source the account given of the Misanthrope in North's *Lives of the Noble Grecians and Romanes*, and thus came from outside the comic tradition.[14] Shakespeare's protagonist shows some stylistic connection to Lucian's Timon, but more than anything, *Timon of Athens* is the tragic extension of the same general tradition of the character from which Lucian draws, but which the Hellenist's own historical milieu prevents him from presenting other than grotesquely or satirically.

Shakespeare's *Timon of Athens* differs most importantly from Lucian's comic dialogue in its dramatic scope. Whereas Lucian treats the Misanthrope only after his reckless self-impoverishment, and leaves him still railing away at mortals from the safety of his newly wealthy retreat, Shakespeare devotes all of his act I to scenes of Timon's original generosity; he leaves him at the tragedy's end in his grave, having passed on his loathing of humankind in two different epitaphs.[15] And throughout Shakespeare's treatment of the betrayal of Timon by his erstwhile friends, there runs a gravity and brutality of tone quite unlike Lucian's.[16]

The basic lines of Shakespeare's plot may be briefly summarized. In act I Timon is seen generously aiding the noble lords of Athens, who are his clients, and bestowing lavish gifts on them; he is courted and flattered by various tradesmen, and gives a banquet for his courtiers. The only characters to express reservations about his profligacy are his faithful Steward, out of concern for his master's estate, and the "churlish philosopher" Apemantus, who disdains Timon's worldliness.[17] In act II the cracks begin to appear in Timon's citadel, as his creditors call in his loans and he is revealed to be bankrupt. He is amazed to learn from his Steward the true state of his resources, but resolves simply to make good again by borrowing from the friends he has been so generous with in the past. In act III his servants, despatched to several of the lords who have benefited from his munificence, are turned down for loans on various hypocritical pretexts. Timon hears of the betrayal and resolves to be revenged. Meanwhile Alcibiades, the Athenian general and associate of Timon, is seen begging the senate for clemency in the case of an unnamed friend of his who has been found guilty of murder and sentenced to die. When his petition is refused and he still persists in his entreaties, he is banished from Athens for insubordination. He too now plots revenge, and against the entire city. Timon's banquet for his perfidious friends, finally, ends with his dousing them with water and stoning them; with imprecations of the traitors he flees Athens, swearing general enmity against humankind. In act IV he retreats to the woods, finds gold while digging for roots, and is visited by various people, including Alcibiades, Apemantus, two Thieves, and his Steward, all of whom he rebuffs with contemptuous gifts of gold or harsh words. In act V (not so marked in the Folio but conventionally so set off by later editors) he continues to abuse his visitors, notable among whom are two Senators come to invite him back to Athens to assist them in their battle with Alcibiades, who has now laid siege to the city. Timon spurns all and goes to his grave; his epitaphs are discovered and reported to Alcibiades by a soldier in the rebel general's host. Alcibiades has meanwhile decided to put to the sword only those Athenians most implicated in his and Timon's betrayal.

The single reference to the ancient god of Wealth in the entire play is emblematic of the negative place of the traditional comic allegory in Shakespeare's version.[18] In act I, scene i two Lords of Athens are making ready to go in to Timon's feast; in response to the First Lord's comments on their host's "bounty," the Second Lord elaborates on Timon's fortune. "He pours it out. Plutus the god of gold / Is but his steward. No meed but he repays / Seven-fold above itself: no gift to him / But breeds the giver a return exceeding / All use of quittance" (I.i.275 ff.). And indeed, in the very next scene, Timon's actual Steward (also referred to as Flavius) is summoned onstage to distribute just such fabulous bounty. His appearance is the banal reification of the Second Lord's elaborate allegory, but he does nonetheless bring with him at Timon's bidding just such excessive wealth and gifts as might represent a seven-fold return on an investment. In this sense he is a sort of figurative "Plutus, the god of gold;" but his response to Timon's request for favors to give his guests is telling. In an aside as he leaves the stage to fetch the "little casket" in which Timon stores his jewels, he remarks: "More jewels yet! / There is no crossing him in's humour, / Else I should tell him well, i' faith, I should, / When all's spent, he'd be cross'd then, and he could" (I.ii.155-158). This "Plutus," in other words, is more akin to the "Luxuria" of Plautus'

Trinummus, already ushering in, as the comedy begins, the "Inopia" or Scarcity who is her daughter.

And yet of course the Steward is no god or allegory at all, but only a sublunar stand-in for the ancient divine provider, and one who is only too aware of the scarcity that precedes and follows abundance. It is the Steward who keeps Timon's books, and who is conscious of the rate at which his disbursements have outstripped his debts. For it is upon debts that Timon has based his economy of expense, that reverse usury described by the Second Lord, whereby so far from charging interest on loans, he instead multiplies potlatch-style the gifts made to him.[19] This ruinous policy is, to be sure, welcomed by Timon's debtors, but mocked by his creditors. As act II opens, the first of these appears, an Athenian Senator, determined to call in his loan; he marvels at Timon's folly, drawing an ironic picture of the gift-giving, a fantastical hyperbole that is subtended by a significantly bestial image of generation: "If I want gold, steal but a beggar's dog / And give it Timon -- why, the dog coins gold; / If I would sell my horse and buy twenty moe / Better than he -- why, give my horse to Timon; / Ask nothing, give it him, it foals me straight / And able horses" (II.i.5-10). This counter-posing of Timon's demand-side economics with effortless animal procreation serves to reinforce the totally human quality of money in Shakespeare's play.[20] Its management and valuation is in fact *unlike* the instinctive generation of the animal kingdom, for it requires the deliberate intervention and circulation of human agents.[21] Gold will furthermore be associated with humanity by Timon, and reviled along with it, when he hands out the new-dug treasure to his visitors later in the play, in the hopes that it will do them ill.

The absence of a deus ex machina, too, from the upper register of this pessimistic, all too human society, even one in the rhetorical form of a divine allegory, has indeed been signaled since the very beginning of the play. The *Timon*'s first scene, as often in Shakespeare, features an assembly of minor characters whose ruminations constitute an oblique comment on the main action to come.[22] Here, in the prologue-like conversation of four toadies awaiting their chance to flatter Timon, the trope of allegorical personification is well and truly consigned to the dust-bin of *Timon of Athens'* aesthetics. What it is to be replaced with is unclear; perhaps it is meant only to be dismantled as yet another idle product of human culture in this play that, as has been suggested, sank and failed in production under the weight of its own misanthropy.[23]

The opening scene of the *Timon* is in fact more than just a prologue or a bit of stage-painting: it is quite extensive and involved, giving its characters a chance to elaborate a sort of phenomenological manifesto for the play to follow. "At several doors" enter a Poet, a Painter, a

Jeweller and a Merchant, to meet before Timon's house. The first three
have prepared something for their patron, and they take some care to
display their gifts (with false modesty) to the others, who are equally
careful to admire them (with false enthusiasm).[24] The mood of venality
tempered by hypocrisy is thus not only an overture to the two-
facedness Timon is to encounter as the play progresses, it is also a
radical destabilizing of the efficacy of symbolic representation.[25]

The scene opens with greetings and a quibble. To the Poet's "How
goes the world?" the Painter replies, "It wears, sir, as it grows;" the
Poet responds with recognition of the hackneyed sentiment, but is
quick to supply a meliorist interpretation and so raise the tone of the
exchange from the world-weary to the inflatedly self-congratulatory.
Turning to the rest of the company, he invokes his colleagues as if
they were emanations of Timon's fortune: "See, / Magic of bounty, all
these spirits thy power / Hath conjur'd to attend" (I.i.5-7). The world
is not deteriorating, he seems to say, for the power of wealth manifest
in the patron can call up the demiurges of creation and have them do
his bidding, thus staying the world's degradation in its course.[26] This
exultant fantasy is as soon marred, however, with the Poet's aside to
the Painter as the Jeweller vaunts the stone he will offer Timon
(against a sufficient price, it is understood): "When we for recompense
have prais'd the vild, / It stains the glory in that happy verse / Which
aptly sings the good" (I.i.15-17). Already the "magic" relationship
between patron and client is subject to the warping effects of hypocrisy
and bought praise.

The Poet will nevertheless present his offering in apparent sincerity,
after the Painter has displayed his portrait of Timon: which the Poet
admires effusively, noting particularly the temptation the beholder feels
to imagine the likeness of Timon speaking, such a verisimilitude has
the Painter achieved. The Poet thus supplements the portrait with his
own craft, underhandedly pointing out its failings. But the Painter will
not be outdone, and seizes the next opportunity to extol the
supplementary virtues of his craft; the result is at first a vision of the
arts' powers complementing each other, followed by their withering
away altogether under the evidence of their failure to communicate.

A crowd of Senators passes, on the way to Timon's feast; this vision
prompts the Poet to describe his dedicatory in particularly visual terms,
in what might be called a sort of ecphrasis. Andrzej Jankowski, in
Shakespeare's Idea of Art, comments on the peculiar fact that the Poet
describes his poem as if it were a painting. "As there was allegorical
poetry, so was there also allegorical painting," Jankowski writes, and
notes that the Horatian tag "ut pictura poesis" was a Renaissance
commonplace.[27] Jankowski observes too that Shakespeare might have
included sculpture in his generalized conception of mimesis,

encompassing as it did both painting and poetry.[28]   The Poet will indeed describe his own composition of the piece glyptically, as a carving in wax: "My free drift / Halts not particularly, but moves itself / In a wide sea of wax" (I.i.45-47). The hyperbole obscures the image of the simple wax tablet and lends a grandiose plasticity to the overblown creation. What is thus created in the Poet's description of his verse and the Painter's reception of it is a synaesthetic art-form, poetry, painting, and sculpture all in one, a super-mimesis that will actually cause its central allegorical figure, Lady Fortune, to recede into the aesthetic distance.[29]

"You see this confluence, this great flood of visitors," the Poet begins at I.i.42; "I have in this rough work shap'd out a man, / Whom this beneath world doth embrace and hug / With amplest entertainment." He explains that this is Timon, courted by all, generous to everyone. "Sir," he continues to the Painter,

I have upon a high and pleasant hill
Feign'd Fortune to be thron'd. The base o' th' mount
Is rank'd with all deserts, all kind of natures
That labour on the bosom of this sphere
To propagate their states. Amongst them all,
Whose eyes are on this sovereign lady fix'd,
One do I personate of Lord Timon's frame,
Whom Fortune with her ivory hand wafts to her,
Whose present grace to present slaves and servants
Translates his rivals. (I.i.65-74)

The stage is very literally set, as Timon is beckoned to from the ruck of humanity by Fortune enthroned on a hill. The Painter expresses his admiration for the justness of the Poet's conception, feigning actually to see the image the other has so vividly described: "'Tis conceiv'd to scope. / This throne, this Fortune, and this hill, methinks, / With one man beckon'd from the rest below, / Bowing his head against the steepy mount / To climb his happiness, would be well express'd / In our condition" (I.i.74-79). The deictic adjectives ("this throne, this Fortune"), the interjection of the observer ("methinks"), the suggestion that the group would make a fitting subject for a painting, all add to the impression of a piling up of representational media around the central theme of the allegorical Fortune.

But the coda is still to come. The Poet has not yet completely presented his hybrid masterpiece, which, being literary, has after all the necessary attribute of temporal extension, unlike a painted tableau, which can be taken in at a glance. "Nay, sir, but hear me," he continues, with a vision of Timon's train of courtiers and lobbyists, "on: -- all those which were his fellows but of late," abandoning their

erstwhile benefactor "when Fortune in her shift and change of mood /
Spurns down her late beloved;" then those false friends will let Timon
drop in unhappiness, "not one accompanying his declining foot"
(I.i.79-90). The play's subsequent action is thus adumbrated. The train
of courtiers actually entering Timon's house as the two converse has
been included in the lyric landscape, and the at first stable and
championing allegory at the center of the scene has been shown to be
in fact dynamic and fickle.

It remains only for the Painter to add the final visual touch to the
disembodied work, at once stressing one last time the super-mimetic
nature of Fortune's representation in the prologue and making a final
pitch for his own particular field of art. "'Tis common. / A thousand
moral paintings I can show / That shall demonstrate these quick blows
of Fortune's / More pregnantly than words. Yet you do well / To show
Lord Timon that mean eyes have seen / The foot above the head"
(I.i.91-96). His grudging praise ("yet you do well") is both
professional one-upmanship and recognition of the meta-aesthetic use
to which allegory is, in this opening scene, finally put: that of secret
communication. The Painter can think of "a thousand moral
paintings," which Oliver glosses ad loc. as "paintings pointing a
moral" or "allegorical wall-hangings;" each would be more aesthetically
efficient than mere verse (for here the artistic saturation of the image
has begun to disintegrate). Yet the Poet is given his due, albeit in
entirely visual diction ("to show Lord Timon that mean eyes have
seen"). The allegorical confection of the two artists is revealed to have
been in fact nothing more than a code: no Fortune, no Plutus will in
fact enliven the action, nor even be present much at the level of the
play's language. Though there will be talk of "fortune" in a non-
specific sense, that deity's single further appearance as a personification
of destiny and vicissitudes is significant: in Timon's revilement of
Apemantus, the "churlish philosopher" who has come to visit him in
the woods after the Misanthrope's flight from civilization, he invokes
the allegorical figure negatively. "Thou art a slave, whom Fortune's
tender arm/ With favour never clasp'd, but bred a dog" (IV.iii.252-253).

Nor will the Poet's message to Timon even be heard. When later on
(I.i.155 ff.) the two artists obtain an audience with their patron, after
Timon has distributed favors to others of his clientel, the Poet's suit
("Vouchsafe my labour, and long live your lordship!") is summarily
dealt with: "I thank you; you shall hear from me anon," answers
Timon, and turns with fuller attention to the Painter. The fascination
that artist's product holds for him is evident: "Painting is welcome. /
The painting is almost the natural man: / For since dishonour traffics
with man's nature, / He is but out-side; these pencill'd figures are /
Even such as they give out. I like your work, / And you shall find I

like it" (I.i.159-164). The portrait of himself seems to Timon to be a true representation of his nature, not the show required by "dishonour" and "traffic," or trade. Representation will indeed turn in this play around the figure of Timon himself and his "nature," around the way he appears and just how much of him may be apprehended, seized, or consumed, and not around the actual forces at play shaping his vicissitudes. When the Poet and the Painter come to find Timon in his forest retreat much later in the play, after the peripety that has cast him out of society, the Poet will have significantly altered his project, turning from the allegorical poem of his first appearance to a sort of portrait of Timon all his own. "I am thinking what I shall say I have provided for him. It must be a personating of himself; a satire against the softness of prosperity, with a discovery of the infinite flatteries that follow youth and opulency" (V.i.32-35). But it is too late for such a mirror to be held up to nature: the Painter's work is all "counterfeit," however "lively," and the Poet's "fiction" is full of "stuff so fine and smooth / That thou art even natural in thine art" (V.i.79-84). Their artifacts have been discovered to be mere masks, faithful to "reality" only insofar as they are as deceitful.

Timon is confirmed in his misanthropy, and will have nothing more to do with his own image, having been shown it painfully enough already. Instead he ironically urges the two artists to investigate their own natures, bidding them in a sort of kenning ("There's never a one of you but trusts a knave, / That mightily deceives you," V.i.92-92) to find out the villain within each of them, and to kill him. Timon himself will shortly do the same. The last use to which the Poet's "wide sea of wax" will be put is in the wax squeeze made by Alcibiades' soldier of Timon's two incomprehensible epitaphs at V.iii.6, a final desperate vulgarization of the literary medium found so wanting in its poetic representative, and so incapable of revealing to Timon the truth of his destiny.[30] The unreadability of Timon's lesson provides the linguistic equivalent of the play's economic pessimism: just as there is no other-worldly guarantor of wealth, no original or ultimate source of bounty but rather just an unending circulation of objects among mortals all equally motivated by lack, so is the medium of language itself destabilized, unguaranteed, reduced to two contradictory epitaphs on a violently misanthropic "hero's" tomb. The nature of the contradiction of the two epitaphs, too, is in itself significant for the play's nihilism. "Here lies a wretched corse, of wretched soul bereft: / Seek not my name. A plague consume you, wicked caitiffs left," reads the first. The second runs, "Here lie I, Timon, who, alive, all living men did hate. / Pass by and curse thy fill, but pass and stay not here thy gait."[31] Timon's very name is subject to the vagaries of speech: it had earlier proved insufficient to raise him credit;[32] here it lies at the center of a sardonic game of hide-and-seek, in which the name is casually supplied to the same passers-by to whom it has just been scornfully denied.

For Timon's nature has already been sounded, by himself in his solitude: he is revealed to be the debased conduit of money,[33] which both feeds and poisons. Not changeful Fortune, but the mute earth, which yields both roots and gold,[34] is the indifferent mother/whore of contingencies, and Timon is her procurer.[35] It is on this disillusioned culmination of the Timon-legend that Shakespeare's play will expend its imagistic powers, on the truth that the earth brings forth mineral and vegetable substance capable of human valuation, but otherwise absolutely unmediated by any divine or supernatural intercession. "The world is but a word," sighs the Steward, as Timon inquires in mounting panic after his land holdings, having just discovered that his money supply has dried up. "Were it all yours, to give it in a breath, / How quickly were it gone" (II.ii.156-158). Timon's land, which once stretched "to Lacedaimon," is "all engag'd, some forfeited and gone, / And what remains will hardly stop the mouth / Of present dues" (II.ii.150-152). The world is, however, precisely not a word, but an assemblage of tracts of land, gift-objects, and moneys, to be bought, sold, and given away. The trouble is that Timon cannot conjure up, with all his prayers and entreaties, any metaphysical aid the way his Lucianic forebear could, that Timon who surrounded himself with alternating cohorts of allegorical body-guards. Shakespeare's Timon is alone, and it is his own substance that is quite literally eaten up.

The Steward's figure of speech, "to stop the mouth / of present dues," is entirely apt, for Timon has been consumed by his false friends from the outset, and he will continue to "feed" them, in a gesture unparalleled by Lucian's Misanthrope, with the gold that he laments he himself is unable to eat, even after he has retreated into the forest. This is nevertheless an important legacy, however transmuted, of the Hellenistic *Timon*: the image of the "friends" picking Timon clean. In the *Timon* of Lucian, it will be remembered, Hermes' image was of vultures eating Timon's liver, in an explicit allusion to the fate of Prometheus (ἀλλ' ὑπὸ γυπῶν τοσούτων ὁ κακοδαίμων κειρόμενος τὸ ἧπαρ, *Tim.* 8); in the *Timon of Athens* the image is generalized and spread throughout the play.[36] At I.i.204 Apemantus, invited to join Timon's feast, refuses on the grounds that "I eat not lords;" at I.ii.38 ff., being present at the feast but at a separate, more humble table, he observes that "a number of men eats Timon, and he sees 'em not! It grieves me to see so many dip their meat in one man's blood." At II.ii.169 ff. the Steward invokes Timon's past magnanimity with a transferred epithet: "How many prodigal bits have slaves and peasants / This night englutted;" he calls the courtiers "flies," who feed on Timon but disappear at the first signs of winter.[37] At III.iv.89-98 Timon responds to his creditors' demands for payment with the pathetic invitation to "[c]ut my heart in sums" and "[t]ell out my blood;" finally, at IV.iii.283-284, he imagines his revenge in the form of a counter-consumption, praying as he bites into a root "[t]hat the whole of Athens were in this! / Thus would I eat it." An exchange between Timon and Alcibiades in the early banquet scene at I.ii.73-81, there commented upon by Apemantus, has set the stage for this fantasy turn-about: the rich man and the general are quibbling over niceties, Timon insisting that Alcibiades would rather be at a "breakfast of enemies than a dinner of friends," Alcibiades answering that in fact "there's no meat like 'em; I could wish my best friend at such a feast."[38] Apemantus draws the image to its grotesque conclusion: "Would all those flatterers were thine enemies then, that then thou mightst kill 'em -- and bid me to 'em." But Apemantus will provide the clearest evocation of the fact that Timon's false friends see in him nothing but his resources, in a trope drawn from outside the complex of eating and bleeding images. "Thou giv'st so long, Timon, I fear me thou wilt give away thyself in paper shortly" (I.ii.242-243), he says, and his extended financial metaphor is ruthless: Timon's very substance will shortly run out, and like a bankrupt state he will be forced to start issuing notes to cover debts he cannot possibly meet, since his "capital" is mortal, and not to be had back at any available lending rate.[39]

So Timon's false friends have been gorging themselves on his substance, a cannibalism the vengeance for which can at first be imagined as only retributive. But in fact the form Timon's vengeance will finally take is rather more round-about. He will distribute the gold he finds in the earth, in the hopes that it will continue to poison Athens. This is most clearly, if not most directly, expressed in his plea to Alcibiades: "Here's gold. Go on. / Be as a planetary plague, when Jove / Will o'er some high-vic'd city hang his poison / In the sick air" (IV.iii.109-112). Alcibiades has brought two of his "Mistresses" with him, and Timon offers them gold as well, to make of them also instruments of Athens' poisoning: "Plague all, / That your activity may defeat and quell / The source of all erection" (IV.iii.164-166).

Thus Timon has gone from being Athens' familiar provider (providing the city, unwittingly of course, with his very substance) to being its procurer, the object of whose pimping is the earth, that "common mother," and her mineral by-products. Timon the familiar provider had been evoked at III.ii.68-70, where the first of two Strangers laments the Athenians' general perfidy with a particular example of treachery: "For in my knowing / Timon has been this lord's father, / And kept his credit with his purse."[40] His passage to "bawd," or procurer, is prepared at II.ii.63-63, where Apemantus calls the servants who have come to call in Timon's debts "[p]oor rogues, and usurers' men, bawds between gold and want!" By IV.iii Timon is playing this bawd's role himself, supplying Alcibiades and his Mistresses, Phrynia and Timandra, with gold, and promising to make bawds of the Mistresses too: in response to the women's inquiring after his stock of gold, he replies that he has "[e]nough to make a whore forswear her trade, / And to make whores a bawd." That he means Phrynia and Timandra becomes clear in his next words: "Hold up, you sluts, / Your aprons mountant" (IV.iii.135-137). But Timon's own past as a kind of a whore, used as he was to suit the pleasures of the false friends who saw nothing more in him than his money, is also evoked in these scornful words.

Timon's relational status in Athens has by this point entirely changed. No longer the rich man who keeps a wholly figurative, unpersonified Plutus as a steward, he has realized the unaccomodated hollowness of the world by taking up a position at the simple mid-point of a banal convection system: "the earth's a thief," he explains to the Two Thieves who visit him in the forest, "that feeds and breeds by a composture stol'n / From gen'ral excrement" (IV.iii.443-445). This is the filthy truth of the circular economy earlier evoked by his servants at III.iv.18-25, whereby debts and loans merely circulate, and the Lord who wears Timon's jewel sends for money owed a third for that very gift.

Gold, however, which is the object of these relationships, and which is the material co-relative of the signifying systems taken over by Shakespeare from the Timon-tradition, is represented in the Timon of Athens, despite that play's demystifying bent, not wholly materially, but within a symbolic frame that yetlies on a continuum with the history of the classical Ploutus-figure. Gold is the subject of two famous monologues, spoken by Timon, in the first of which he addresses "the gods" and "earth," and in the second of which, in the form of a prosopopoiea, he addresses gold itself. Sections of both monologues have already been quoted above; it is worth, however, giving them again in full, as they constitute a certain rhetorical culmination both of Shakespeare's play and of my argument here.

The first address comes at the end of Timon's second monologue in act IV, after he has cursed his false friends at the banquet of stones and water, and fled to the forest. Having abjured "[a]ll feasts, societies, and throngs of men" (IV.iii.21), Timon sets about digging for a meal of roots, in an echo of the humble repast enjoyed by Apemantus in act I. Instead of roots, however, he finds

Gold? Yellow, glittering, precious gold?

No, gods, I am no idle votarist.
Roots, you clear heavens! Thus much of this will make
Black, white; foul, fair; wrong, right;
Base, noble; old, young; coward, valiant.
Ha, you gods! Why this? What this, you gods? Why, this
Will lug your priests and servants from your sides,
Pluck stout men's pillows from below their heads.
This yellow slave
Will knit and break religions, bless th'accurs'd,
Make the hoar leprosy ador'd, place thieves,
And give them title, knee and approbation
With senators on the bench. This is it
That makes the wappen'd widow wed again:
She whom the spital-house and ulcerous sores
Would cast the gorge at, this embalms and spices
To th' April day again. Come, damn'd earth,
Thou common whore of mankind, that puts odds
Among the rout of nations, I will make thee
Do thy right nature. (IV.iii.26-45)

The second address follows Apemantus' abusive visit and Timon's
resolution to prepare his own grave.

[*Looking on the gold.*] O thou sweet king-killer, and dear divorce
'Twixt natural son and sire, thou bright defiler
Of Hymen's purest bed, thou valiant Mars,
Thou ever young, fresh, loved and delicate wooer,
Whose blush doth thaw the consecrated snow
That lies on Dian's lap! Thou visible god,
That sold'rest close impossibilities,
And mak'st them kiss; that speak'st with every tongue,
To every purpose! O thou touch of hearts,
Think thy slave Man rebels, and by thy virtue
Set them into confounding odds, that beasts
May have the world in empire! (IV.iii.384-395)

Two distinct pictures of gold emerge from these apostrophes. In the
first, gold is figured as the transvaluator of values, the changer of
stations, the cosmetic seducer by proxy.[41] In the second, a flood of
classical allusions comes close to performing the apotheosis of gold,
only to climax in a vision of unclassical, godless, "natural" mayhem.
Common to both passages is a certain rhetorical personification of the
metal, albeit diffuse and overblown, and an emphasis on lasciviousness
and violence as gold's effects on the world. Echoes in however indirect
a fashion of Lucian's imagery include the grotesquery of changes of
class wrought by wealth (the *arriviste* inheritors at *Tim.* 22 and
Shakespeare's "place thieves, / And give them title"); the powerfully

seductive properties of gold (the account of Ploutos' Pandora-like disguise at *Tim.* 27 and Shakespeare's "She whom the spital-house . . . / Would cast the gorge at, this embalms and spices"); the image of gold as actively ravishing (the *Danaë*-citation at *Tim.* 41 and Shakespeare's "Thou ever young . . . wooer, / Whose blush doth thaw the consecrated snow / That lies on Dian's lap");[42] and gold's tricky virtuosity (Hermes' admiring comparison of slippery Ploutos with sticky Penia at *Tim.* 29 and Shakespeare's "that speak'st with every tongue, / To every purpose"). Missing is the analogy of fiscal and marital economy, so striking at *Tim.* 16-17, and the concomitant image of wealth as a chaste virgin needing supervision. A signature "innovation" of Shakespeare's is the particular violence of his gold's depradations: "lug your priests and servants," "Pluck stout men's pillows," "knit and break religions," "king-killer," "dear divorce / 'Twixt natural son and sire," "bright defiler / Of Hymen's purest bed," "valiant Mars," "thy slave Man rebels," and "Set them into confounding odds, that beasts / May have the world in empire." The cosmic instability wrought by gold is reflected in the rhetorical instability of its representation: Shakespeare's Timon calls gold a "visible god," yet the pastiche of regicidal, Hymen-raping, Diana-seducing, Protean, Bacchanal-leading Mars effectively obscures this visibility in a layering of images reminiscent of the super-mimetic laying on of artistic media in the play's prologue-scene.

Shakespeare's Timon has an apocalyptic vision of gold's place in the order of things, one that will remain essentially unreconciled, since Alcibiades' merciful justice at the gates of Athens comes only after Timon's death. He is avenged posthumously by the general, his fellow exile, who makes clear the common bond of resentment: "Those enemies of Timon's and mine own / Whom you yourselves shall set out for reproof / Fall, and no more" (V.iv.56-58);[43] but Timon is survived by his Cynic double, Apemantus, whose diet of roots the Misanthrope had adopted, and whose last words are an encouragement to continue in his policy of social rejection. "Moe things like men! Eat, Timon, and abhor them," he urges, as yet more visitors are seen approaching Timon's forest hideaway (IV.iii.400). Despite the reconciliation effected by the Fortinbras-like Alcibiades at the end of the play,[44] Timon's Cynic critique of money, and his view of human life as contingent, lingers.

This is due in large part to the representation of gold sketched above, whereby the mineral stuff is sapped of its numinous guarantee and powerful aura through a judicious blend of violently mundane imagery and a saturation with figurative godhead. But perhaps Timon's most succinct personification of gold comes, significantly, in an aside made during his encounter with the Poet and the Painter, those purveyors of deceitful mimesis. Timon overhears the two artists as they plan their suit: they have heard that their former patron has been distributing largesse once more, and have resolved to make him new offerings in hope of gain. The Poet has been describing the new work he projects for Timon, "a personating of himself; a satire against the softness of prosperity, with a discovery of the infinite flatteries that follow youth and opulency" (V.i.33-35); Timon mocks him in an aside for proposing a critique of the very flattery his ode would represent. As the two set off to find him, Timon damns them with a final unheard prayer. "What a god's gold, / That he is worshipp'd in a baser temple / Than where swine feed? / 'Tis thou that rigg'st the bark and plough'st the foam, / Settlest admired reverence in a slave: / To thee be worship; and thy saints for aye / Be crown'd with plagues, that thee alone obey!" This ultimate apotheosis of gold locates it firmly in a mundane human economy, among the "baser temple" that is the debased possessor of wealth himself; the "bark," the classic metonymy of human industry and genius, reduced to a bottomry loan;[45] the "reverence in a slave," the venal obsequiousness of the bondsman; and the "saints . . . crown'd with plagues" the heroes of a corrupted church.

Timon himself will be such a damned hero/saint, his holy body, gold drawn from the mute storehouse of the earth and distributed with curses in a reverse eucharist, consumed in the form of the money he offers up in his "temple."[46] The Shakespearean rendering of the Timon theme is tragic, without a supernatural allegorical scapegoat ororiginal guarantor onto which to project the workings of money. Instead, the contemplation of gold turns in on its contemplator, making of him both a Ploutos, grotesque in his squalor and melancholy violence, and a Prometheus, proto-messianic in his lonely sacrifice. Behind these two, finally, is the figure of Pandora, alluring creature of earth who reveals herself to be deceitful and destructive: "damn'd earth, / Thou common whore of mankind." The earth produces the "yellow, glittering, precious gold," which "embalms and spices / To th' April day again" the "wappen'd widow," in a masquerade akin to that of Ploutos at *Tim.* 27-28.[47] In Shakespeare's text, however, the ravages of such a delusion are literal, in the form of the syphilis left behind by the Mistresses of Alcibiades, paid by Timon to spread their diseases in the guise of seduction, and in the form of Alcibiades himself, the darling of Athenian society whom Timon would pay to be its destroyer. Wealth in Shakespeare's *Timon of Athens* has indeed become merely verbal allegory, while the world continues in its degraded path, unaccomodated and untriumphalist.

The Merchant of Venice and the Return of Ploutos?

Timon of Athens was written sometime between 1604 and 1607, not published until the first Folio of 1623, and first produced only in 1761, one hundred and forty-five years after Shakespeare's death.[48]   Many places in the text suggest that it is far from being a fair copy; indeed, it is today prized chiefly for its presumed merits as an example of Shakespeare's composition methods in action.[49] Whether the play was abandoned because it did not turn out to provide the stuff of grand tragedy,[50] or whether its putative contemporary target, the evils of usury,[51] was not after all well served by the dramatic material, Shakespeare's essay on money never received the final polish. Perhaps, however, those who find the play altogether too full of invective[52] have understood the problem: Shakespeare had seized on a character and a theme borrowed, as we have seen, from a tradition of comedy and satire; the excessively dark colors needed to counter-balance the otherwise risible nature of Timon's dilemma may effectively have capsized the play.

But perhaps it may be ventured that the Timon-material, which proved ultimately intractable, had in fact already found its place, some years earlier, in another play. Sometime before 1598, Shakespeare had drawn on disparate classical, medieval, and renaissance sources to write *The Merchant of Venice*.[53] That comedy concerns: a respected citizen of a great city who is generous with his friends; a squalid and foreign supplier of wealth who is critical of imprudent money-management; and the suggestion of an equivalence between money and human substance.   These themes effectively recuperate those of the Aristophanic *Plutus*, the *Timon* of Lucian, and the Shakespearean *Timon*; they have the advantage of being presented in a comic frame, which allows them to stage their problem with the promise of greater immediate pleasure for the audience, and thus to avoid simply inundating the spectators with jeremiads; and they are grouped around a grand villain, onto whom the venom of the problem can be projected, and who can be either expelled or assimilated at the play's end. It is as if the figure of Ploutos had been resuscitated and presented in the form of Shylock, drawing on the Christian-Jewish dialectic in such a way as to resolve the ancient contradiction of money as an ambiguous boon, descended from the divine ranks of justice and prosperity yet blind, morally aimless, and repulsive. In the guignolesque shape of Shylock the god of Wealth has truly been diabolized. In his name, the principle of sound money-management, based on a traditional husbandry paradigm[54] but here demonized with the appellation "usury," is unambiguously juxtaposed to the courtly virtue of magnanimity; the base alien is discovered plotting against the noble citizen;[55] and justice must cede to mercy.[56]   When Antonio's ships sink on their trading voyages and the bond of flesh on his loan from the money-lender becomes forfeit, the Merchant offers his breast martyr-like to Shylock, in an adumbration of Timon's scene of pathos with his creditors.[57] The proto-Christian shadings of Timon's betrayal by his friends, his offering himself up bodily to his creditors, and his final mystic disappearance into the grave,[58] are in *The Merchant of Venice* brought to the fore, with the explicit counterpointing of diabolized Jew ("The devil can cite Scripture for his purpose," I.iii.93) and generous Christian, prepared to die a martyr's death for the love of his fellow. By situating his characters in the landscape of Christian chauvinism, familiar to his Elizabethan audience, Shakespeare manages to evoke both the Pandoric evil necessity of the money economy, and the Promethean nobility of its heroic sufferers. In the form of Shylock, the foreign grotesque who is in the end both converted to Christianity, and thus domesticated, and also dispossessed and threatened with death, and thus expelled, Eagleton's reconciliation by magic of the world of feudal, landed gentility and that of unstable, profit-oriented capitalism has at last been achieved.

In the chapter of his study of Shakespeare devoted to *The Merchant of Venice*, René Girard suggests that Shakespeare may have been playing on the contemporary anti-Semitism of his audience in order to smuggle in a mordant comment on the hypocrisies of Christian Venice.[59] If this is indeed the case, then it is an example of Jameson's double hermeneutic, whereby a progressive reading of an ostensibly conservative text can be produced by paying attention to the ways in which the text subverts the structures that make it intelligible to its historical audience. The progressive energies released by Aristophanes, Plautus, and Lucian are recontained by their own final status as grotesque fantasy, as family drama, or as Cynic tract.   By discerning the figure of Ploutos underneath that of Shylock, it may be possible to glimpse the lineaments of another narrative there too, whether its energies are eventually recontained or not: a narrative in which the society with ostensibly legitimate, organic right to its land and property has been forced to recognize the entirely mediated and contingent nature of its claims. Through the uncanny personification of money, base and discomfiting as he is, the roots of present wealth in original poverty have been made uncomfortably clear: as has been the ever-present possibility of returning to that poverty, for despite the best efforts to reify it in an allegory and expel it from the comfortable system of present guarantees of land and native heritage, it will always return, since it was always already at the very roots of that system.

Epilogue

What I have discovered in my reading of allegorical tropes in selected ancient comic texts, and in my consideration of their surprising issuance in an early modern tragedy of impoverishment and social isolation, is the persistent association in wealth's dramatic depiction of diverse and occasionally opposed complexes of images: fixity and mobility, country and town, female and male, mute and speaking, interior and exterior, hoarded and shared. These polarities have been by no means stable: whereas for example the Aristophanic counterpointing of the female figure of Peace in a male countryside with the male figure of Wealth co-opted into the female space of the home tends to establish and subvert categories in one particular direction, the Plautine juxtaposition of a female allegory of Debauch with an unmasked male pretender to the role of Wealth suggests the susceptibility of these categories to a differently oriented critique.   Lucian's Timon, meanwhile, learns to treat his wealth like a wife, in keeping with a rhetoric of thesaurization that moves from the daughterly, built on allusions to Danaë, to the wifely, in the figure of Pandora, whereas for Plautus' Euclio his pregnant daughter and her instantiation in his non-circulating pot of gold is the focus of interest; Shakespeare's Timon, finally, sees in money the literally defamiliarized reflection of venal sexuality.

One constant in all of the cases I have examined, however, has been the representation of money as mutable, shape-shifting, polyvalent: as allegory, in other words, requiring reading and interpretation to discern the history condensed within its sometimes deceptively facile or on occasion simply offputting form.   This has been the case, of course, most provocatively for money as such, whether understood as token of exchange, precipitate of labor, and sign of power relations (in the Marxian formulation), or as fantasy object, curious distillate of the self to be celebrated or flushed away, and mask of subjection to an order not of one's choosing (in the Freudian).   The goddess Peace, the Lar familiaris, Euclio's pot of gold, Timon's discovered hoard of precious metals not to be shared (in Lucian's account): all of these non-monetary (yet similarly thesaurized) goods seem to render themselves up to inspection and intellection with relative ease; on the other hand, the blind and sordid god of Wealth, Luxuria, her spawn Inopia and the uncanny Sycophant, and the Timon of Lucian's dialogue, already shading into an association with the sordid Ploutos himself and unknown to Zeus until Hermes interprets him, all of these figures of the transient money form must be read and decoded in order to be put into play.   Although it is a manifestation of the "visible god," in Shakespeare's words, still money's ability to force the conjunction of

paradoxical things and to speak beguilingly in multiple registers sets it
somehow above the trusty realm of the visually rationalized, out of
control of the gaze, beyond the certain horizon of money's early
begetting in field or treasure-house.

In the sense that it depends for its social efficacy upon being
circulated, money is homologous, perhaps, with other discourses: with
the sharing of food and property in ritualized procedures, with the
exogenous reproduction of children, or with the securing of kin bonds
by means of exogamy. All of these forms of interaction may be said
to produce meaning, as well, and to require interpretation; yet none
makes of a stubbornly material substance an ethereal abstraction in the
way that money does, literally "soldering close impossibilities" by
connecting the economic and the psychic to embed speaking structural
value in a mute token.

In reference to Priam's gift of a gold and silver grapevine to his sister
in order to obtain her aid in the defense of Troy, Louis Gernet makes
what might stand as a paradigmatic comment on the paradoxical nature
of money:

> The object created by labour that *represents* a thing endowed with
> magical properties, and which we have seen to have acted as a talisman,
> is here the same as the object in which economic value inheres. We
> have to do with a sort of projection of the ideal notion in the other
> world on to the plane of human life: treasure is real enough socially --
> an institution indeed; but it is also real enough in myth. It is both a
> social reality and a mythic reality.[60]

Hence the dilemma of money's dramatic representation, hence the odd
overlap of reification and personification. For money is at once a vast
complex of discursive practices and magically meaningful ceremonial
treasures, and at the same time an irrelevant object arbitrarily invested
with high significance: the one must be reified and materialized so as to
be controlled, the other must be personified and pressed into a speaking
part so as to render up an account of its uncanny power over human
affairs.

Money in its corporate aspect, in other words, demands to be split
off and separated from the social body, which then in turn attempts to
reabsorb or re-incorporate its straying member. This play of forces and
subjects is archetypally dramatic, for it orchestrates the human and the
mechanical, the will and fate, the self and other, in a primal dynamic
running through both the pretext (economic relations) and the text
(psychic allegory) of human life. Money is not a convenient symbol
for loss and recovery, property and alienation, it *is* those contradictory
phenomena, in extremest condensation; and the dramatic stage, with its
uncanny mandate to represent social and mythic structures by means of

actual participants in those structures, is the ideal place to put such a
doubling of reality into play.

Notes

[1] See the useful repertory in Hertel (1969) 50-51.
[2] Jones (1986) 8.
[3] "Um die wirkliche Bedeutung der letzten antiken Philosophen während
der Auflösung des Altertums zu würdigen, hätte Jacques le bonhomme nur die
wirkliche Lebensstellung ihrer Jünger unter der römischen Weltherrschaft
zu betrachten brauchen. Er konnte u. a. bei Lukian ausführlich beschrieben
finden, wie sie vom Volk als öffentliche Possenreißer betrachtet und von
den römischen Kapitalisten, Prokonsuln etc. als Hofnarren zur
Unterhaltung gedungen wurden, um, nachdem sie sich über der Tafel mit den
Sklaven um ein paar Knochen und Brotkrummeln gezankt und einen aparten
sauren Wein vorgesetzt bekommen hatten, den großen Herrn und seine
Gäste mit den ergötzlichen Phrasen Ataraxie, Aphasie, Hedone usw. zu
amüsieren," Marx and Engels, *Gesammelte Werke* vol. 3 (Berlin: Dietz,
1960-1969), 126. The sentence that follows in the original manuscript
version makes explicit, however, the use to which Lucian is being put by
the two social theorists: "gerade wie die französischen Aristokraten nach
der Revolution die Tanzmeister von ganz Europa wurden, und wie die
englischen Lords bald als die Stallknechte und Hundefütterer der
zivilisierten Welt ihre rechte Stelle finden werden."
[4] Jones (1986) 82, in which see also the whole discussion of *On Salaried
Posts* at pp. 78-84. It is worth noting, nevertheless, that the analogy
implied by Marx and Engels in the stricken passage referred to above, that
connecting the Roman Empire, Republican France, and the new order to be
ushered in by the revolution awaited in England, is at very least
challenging to Jones's sense of the representation of the Romans in "the
fountainhead of modern socialism" as one that was resolutely pejorative.
[5] Robinson (1979) 2.
[6] Terry Eagleton, *William Shakespeare* (Oxford: Basil Blackwell, 1986),
98-99, discusses *Timon of Athens*, among others of Shakespeare's works,
as a staging of the conflict between the "feudal body," stable, controlling,
and attached to use-values, and "capitalist language," which is protean,
expanding, and mindful of exchange-value. This conflict, Eagleton notes,
is often resolved in the Shakespearean text through the intervention of
magic or of an ideology of nature. We shall have cause to see that this is
not the case in the *Timon*. On Shakespeare's characters as "bourgeois
individualists," caught between feudalism and capitalism, see also Margot
Heinemann, "How Brecht read Shakespeare," in *Political Shakespeare: New
Essays in Cultural Materialism,* ed. Jonathan Dollimore and Alan Sinfield
(Manchester: Manchester Univ. Press, 1985), 202-230, esp. pp. 207 ff.
[7] See Oliver in Deighton (1963) xliv for a useful repertory of the critics
who have confined their interpretation of the *Timon of Athens* to the stock

argument that it is an attack on the part played by usury in the downfall of the medieval nobility; these commentators seem principally to have missed the radical and tragic critique of money in general represented by the play. Others have not been so misled: see most famously Marx (1988) 218 ff.

[8] Walter Benjamin, *The Origin of German Tragic Drama*, trans. John Osborne (London: New Left Books, 1977), 228.

[9] It is unclear just how much direct access to Shakespeare's texts the poets of the German baroque age had: the first translations of Shakespeare into German only began appearing in the middle of the eighteenth century, but Andreas Gryphius' *Peter Squentz* may have been based on an episode from *A Midsummer Night's Dream*, and English players of Shakespeare seem to have been visiting Germany as early as the first years of the seventeenth century. See Hermann Uhde-Bernays, *Der Mannheimer Shakespeare. Ein Beitrag zur Geschichte der ersten deutschen Shakespeare-Übersetzungen* (Berlin: E. Felber, 1902), and Hugh Powell, ed., *Andreas Gryphius' Herr Peter Squentz* (Bath: Leicester Univ. Press, 1957).

[10] Benjamin (1977) 192-3.

[11] Benjamin (1977) 187.

[12] See too Benjamin's formulation in the final section of *German Tragic Drama* on the special relationship of allegory and melancholy: "Allegories are, in the realm of thoughts, what ruins are in the realm of things," p. 178. That is to say, allegories are the mournful reconfiguration of antique elements into a modern pageant. This rhetorical alchemy is particularly in evidence in Shakespeare's use of ancient comic stuff to fashion a mourning-play about money. His use of verbal allegory in this endeavor aptly follows the pattern elaborated by Michael Murrin, *The Veil Of Allegory* (Chicago: Univ. Of Chicago Press, 1969), 55: "in a wider sense allegory depends upon the wealth of language as well as upon its poverty. Language has many words for one thing as well as things for which it has no word." Imagistic bounty substitutes in just such a way for the elusive god of Wealth in Shakespeare's mourning play on poverty.

[13] See for discussions of the possible sources for Shakespeare's *Timon of Athens:* Geoffrey Bullough, *Narrative and Dramatic Sources of Shakespeare* vol. 6 (London: Routledge and Kegan Paul, 1966); H. J. Oliver's introduction to *Timon of Athens*, ed. K. Deighton (London: Methuen, 1963); R. Warwick Bond, "Lucian and Boiardo in 'Timon of Athens'," *Modern Language Review* 26 (1931): 52-68; and W. H. Clemons, "The Sources of Timon of Athens," *Princeton College Bulletin* 15, no. 4 (1904): 208-223. Bond discusses notably the influence of Plautus, and particularly of his *Trinummus*, on Boiardo's *Timone* (1500), which it is that study's purpose to show may have been one of Shakespeare's sources; Bullough (1966) 234 mentions the probable influence of Plautus on the "academic Timon," an anonymous embellished treatment of the Timon story written around 1600 and probably never seen by Shakespeare. For general treatment of Plautus' influence on Shakespeare see T. W. Baldwin, *William Shakspere's Small Latine and Lesse Greeke* 2 vols. (Urbana: Univ. of Illinois Press, 1944), 1: passim. While 2: 611 lists the only traces of a

direct link between a Shakespearean play and the *Trinummus*, the Shakespearean play in question, however, is *Hamlet*.

[14] Thomas North, *The Lives of the Noble Grecians and Romanes*, a sixteenth-century English version of Amyot's French translation of Plutarch, itself already considered a sort of classic or standard work: see Pfeiffer (1976) 113. The passage from Plutarch in which Timon's history is related falls in North's rendering of the 69th and 70th chapters of Plutarch's *Life of Marc Antony*. Antony, in retreat after the rout of his forces at Actium, is said to have emulated Timon, in that he shunned human company in response to humanity's general ingratitude. This is the occasion for Plutarch to deliver a summary of the legendary Misanthrope's experience, in which the details do not entirely accord with those of Lucian's dialogue: Timon is said to have forsaken human company as the result of an unspecified slight, and henceforth to have consorted only with Alcibiades, because the young man was the future scourge of his hated Athens, and Apemantus, since that Cynic's lifestyle conformed so well to that now adopted by Timon. Plutarch's Timon is recalled to have wished even Apemantus absent, so as to enjoy his solitude more perfectly; to have invited all the citizenry of Athens to hang themselves on his fig-tree; and to have composed his own epitaph, a curse to be inscribed on his remote tomb without naming the man buried there. Callimachus is also said by Plutarch to have composed an epitaph for him, urging passers-by to continue expeditiously on their way.

[15] The two epitaphs are from Plutarch, rendered accurately by North through Amyot, where however they are given not as concurrent messages on Timon's gravestone but rather as his own and Callimachus' separate compositions. The double epitaph seems to be among the pieces of evidence that Shakespeare left revisions undone on the *Timon*, which was never produced in his lifetime. See Oliver's comments in Deighton (1963) ad loc. on *Timon of Athens* V.iv.70-73 (references are to act, scene, and line).

[16] Critics have seen fit to emphasize this. See Oliver in Deighton (1963) xxxviii: "Lucian may be cynical but behind the cynicism is a kind of joviality that neither Shakespeare nor any of his characters display;" and see Bullough (1966) 250: "Unlike previous Timons he is not tempted by riches, but prefers roots to 'yellow, glittering, precious gold', and expatiates on its power of corrupting men. He will use his treasure in accordance with its evil nature. This savage twist is peculiarly Shakespeare's."

[17] The Steward is once in the Folio referred to as "Flavius," and some editions attribute the Steward's lines to a character so named; in keeping with the rough-draft confusion of the text, however, the name is also elsewhere given to another servant of Timon's. Apemantus is the associate named in Plutarch's *Life of Marc Antony* 69, a sort of composite Cynic: Bompaire (1958) 170 calls him "une abstraction" and draws attention, by way of demonstrating his fabricated nature, to Apemantus' signifying name, which might mean "free from misery" or "untroubled."

[18] Caroline F. E. Spurgeon, *Shakespeare's Imagery and What It Tells Us*

(Cambridge: Cambridge Univ. Press, 1958), appendix chart VI, graphs the number of "personifications" in each of the plays in the Shakespearean corpus. *Timon of Athens* is indeed relatively poor in such tropes: with only five "personifications" among its store of images, it falls into the bottom quarter of the plays classed thus, well outstripped by such personification-rich plays as *King John* (with 40), *Romeo and Juliet* (with 23), and *Richard II* (with 21). Elsewhere in the same study (p. 345), in a fuller discussion of our play, and in response to Wilson Knight's contention that the *Timon* is persistent in its "gold-symbolism," she notes that there may be many different images *for* gold in the text but that I.i.275 is the only "image *from* gold" (emphasis supplied). This strikes one perhaps as hair-splitting; but if the single "personification" of the god of Wealth does indeed thus co-exist with the single vivid "picture" of gold, then such a concentration manifests exactly the tension between wealth-as-material substance and wealth-as-divine allegory that it is this play's mandate to exploit. (It should be noted, however, that the conclusion Spurgeon draws from her statistics is that the *Timon* is not about gold at all, but about falseness and flattery.)

[19] Ted Hughes, *Shakespeare and the Goddess of Complete Being* (London: Faber & Faber, 1992), 284, is more generous to Timon's "business friends," as he calls them: "the system of gifts and borrowings is a system of commerce, or barter. The system works in the play as a metaphor for institutionalized brotherly love -- a prudent, basically selfish, but necessary and interesting arrangement, on which society depends." Eagleton (1986) 84 finds that Timon invalidates others' gifts by over-giving, oblivious as he is to use-value.

[20] And see the exchange of the various servants and creditors' men at III.iv.18 ff., where the closed circle of lending and borrowing is ironically remarked: Timon owes money to men who wear the jewels he gave them as gifts, and which were bought with money he borrowed from other men.

[21] But see on I.i.279 Derek Traversi, *An Approach to Shakespeare* 2 vols. (London: Hollis & Carter, 1969), 2: 173: "It is, of course, 'gold' that so 'breeds' in an unnatural parody of life, and the product will soon be shown to be, like the society which hangs upon it, finally sterile."

[22] Compare *Romeo and Juliet* (after a brief choral prologue), *Julius Caesar*, and *Hamlet*.

[23] Hughes (1992) 284 speculates that Shakespeare might have been moved to take up such a "refractory" theme as the Timon-story either in response to his father's bankruptcy, the foundational trauma of his young life, or out of a need simply to disburden himself of spleen against city life. The latter motive, he argues, would account for the unmanageable torrents of abuse filling the second half of the play.

[24] R. H. Fletcher, ed., *Timon of Athens* (London: 1913), 113 calls the craftsmen's language "pretentiously affected;" Oliver in Deighton (1963) 5 maintains that "after the fashion of bad artists, [each] is hypocritical in his lavish praise of the other's work."

[25] W. I. D. Scott, *Shakespeare's Melancholics* (London: Mills & Boon, 1962), 108, notes in his clinical study of the plays the presage of

melancholy also given by the appearance of the Poet and the Painter at the play's head. For given Robert Burton's observation, in his *Anatomy of Melancholy*, that poets and painters are particularly apt to represent strange and fearful things, "[t]he use by Shakespeare of these two characters representing the most imaginative of the arts to introduce his play foretokens the bizarre nature of the events which we are to witness."

[26] Traversi (1969) 171 calls the Poet's image of magic "clearly a reflection of the world," an equation that is not entirely clear; further on, however, Traversi qualifies this world as one in which the Poet and the Painter, who are "creatures dedicated to the pursuit of self-advancement through flattery, are thoroughly at home." Recall Eagleton (1986) 98-99, where it is suggested that "magic" may help to reconcile the contradictions between Shakespeare's "feudal body" and "capitalist language." This particular magic, however, will certainly not do it.

[27] Jankowski, *Shakespeare's Idea of Art* (Poznan: Adam Mickiewicz Univ. Press, 1988), 114.

[28] Jankowski (1988) 115.

[29] I propose the term "super-mimesis" on a parallel with the neologism "hyperviewing," developed by Froma I. Zeitlin with regard to the Euripidean ecphrasis, in her "The Artful Eye: Vision, Ecphrasis and Spectacle in Euripidean Theater," in *Art and Text in Ancient Greek Culture,* eds. Simon Goldhill and Robin Osborne (Cambridge: Cambridge Univ. Press, 1994), 138-196: on "hyperviewing" see there p. 145. Whereas, however, Zeitlin's term is apt to describe a more positive moment of verbally-constructed spectatorship, if I understand it correctly, I mean by super-mimesis (with its deliberate nuances of "super-nova") to suggest a saturation of the theatrical moment through several levels of artistic representation, leading to an implosion of aesthetic effect and the ensuing destabilization of the meaning thus produced.

[30] Note the final nod, too, to the synaesthetic art-form or super-mimesis discussed above: the soldier says to Alcibiades, presenting him with the squeeze, "My noble general, Timon is dead, / Entomb'd upon the very hem o' th' sea; / And on his grave-stone this insculpture which / With wax I brought away, whose soft impression / Interprets for my poor ignorance" (V.iv.65-69).

[31] The two epitaphs, given distinctly as separate and differently authored in North's *Plutarch*, are in fact printed continuously in Shakespeare's text; as noted above, this is typically taken as a sign that Shakespeare had intended to come back to this passage and choose between them for his fair copy. But it is worth noting that Alcibiades, having read out the four lines, then refers to them as "these," as if the recognition that Shakespeare's Timon had left two mutually incompatible epitaphs had already infiltrated the surrounding text.

[32] At II.ii.203-207 the Steward, in response to Timon's bidding him ask the senators for money, answers, "I have been bold, / For that I knew it the most general way, / To them to use your signet and your name; / But they do shake their heads, and I am here / No richer in return."

[33] "*Apem.* Art thou proud yet? / *Tim.* Ay, that I am not thee. / *Apem.* I,

that I was / No prodigal. / *Tim.* I, that I am one now. / Were all the wealth I have shut up in thee, / I'ld give thee leave to hang it" (IV.iii.279-282).

³⁴ "Earth, yield me roots. [*Digging*] / Who seeks for better of thee, sauce his palate / With thy most operant poison. What is here? / Gold" (IV.iii.23-25).

³⁵ "[*Digging*] Common mother, thou / Whose womb unmeasurable and infinite breast / Teems and feeds all," and "Come, damn'd earth, / Thou common whore of mankind, that puts odds / Among the rout of nations, I will make thee / Do thy right nature" (IV.iii.179-181 and IV.iii.42-45).

³⁶ The Prometheus-imagery in the *Timon of Athens* has been noted before, albeit with diffidence as to source: "However, structural arguments alone are always insufficient to prove direct influence. . . . To give a Shakespearean example, the last two acts of *Timon*, where a stationary Timon is approached by a number of visitors, bear a striking resemblance to the structure of Aeschylus' *Prometheus Vinctus* . . . which we have no reason to believe Shakespeare knew," Charles and Michelle Martindale, *Shakespeare and the Uses of Antiquity: An Introductory Essay* (London: Routledge, 1990), 43.

³⁷ Traversi (1969) 175-176 seems to draw the Promethean comparison in reference to this passage: "As the creditors, like so many vultures, gather round their declining patron, the faithful Flavius expresses in realistic terms the excess and indulgence which have constituted the reverse side of his master's generosity."

³⁸ Shakespeare is possibly drawing here on one of the anecdotes recounted in North's *Plutarch*, in the "Life of Alcibiades," concerning the young Alcibiades' ferocious biting of a wrestling partner. See Bullough (1966) 253.

³⁹ This image obviously depends on a contemporary Elizabethan economy rather than on any possible interpretation of the ancient Greek (on which see among others Finley [1982] 185-186). Devaluation of the coinage had already led to at least one financial crisis in the England of Shakespeare's day: "'inflation' for Shakespeare was by no means just a metaphor. Prices in England rose five times between 1530 and 1640; by the 1550's after a century or more of relative price stability, agricultural prices were 95% above those of the 1530's," Eagleton (1986) 103.

⁴⁰ Richard P. Wheeler, "'Since first we were dissevered: Trust and Autonomy in Shakespearean Tragedy and Romance," in *Representing Shakespeare,* eds. Murray M. Schwartz and Coppélia Kahn (Baltimore: Johns Hopkins Univ. Press, 1982), 150-168, reads the *Timon* with the insights of Mahlerian ego-psychology, and speaks of "Timon's bizarre attempt to appropriate for himself the role of nurturant mother to all of Athens," p. 152. In fact the idea of Timon's "mothering" Athens is nowhere present in the text; Timon as "father" in the citation above is the construction of an observer, while Timon himself fantasizes the relationship with his false friends, in happier times, as that among brothers: "O what a precious comfort 'tis to have so many like brothers commanding one another's fortunes" (I.ii.101-103). At any rate the fantasy is of free and mutual aid among kin, in which Timon exhuberantly

172   *The Visible God*

over-shares his good fortune.

[41] In Shakespeare's train of images the stress is definitely on gold as pimp, but not as prostitute. This is not the case in Marx's *Economic and Philosophic Manuscripts*, where these two passages are also famously cited: "Shakespeare hebt an dem Geld besonders 2 Eigenschaften heraus. . . . 2) Es ist die allgemeine Hure, der allgemeine Kuppler der Menschen und Völker." The imprecision is perhaps caused by the fact that Marx is quoting from the Tieck-Schlegel translation of the *Timon*, which unaccountably renders "damn'd *earth*, / Thou common whore of mankind" at IV.iii.42-43 as "verdammt *Metall*, / Gemeine Hure du der Menschen" (emphasis supplied). The drift of the Shakespearean passage is better given by Marx earlier in this same explication, where (in what is perhaps an echo of Apemantus' "bawds between gold and want") he calls money "der *Kuppler* zwischen dem Bedürfnis und dem Gegenstand." For the whole discussion see Marx, *Ökonomisch-philosophische Manuskripte vom Jahre 1844*, ed. Joachim Höppner (Leipzig: Reclam, 1988), 218-220.

[42] Both this passage and IV.iii.136-137, "Hold up, you sluts, / Your aprons mountant," vaguely reminiscent as they are of the Danaë iconography, have on occasion been cited as evidence of Shakespeare's direct indebtedness to the Lucianic text: see Oliver in Deighton (1963) xxxvi-xxxvii and Bullough (1966) 240. No such claim seems supportable, nor indeed necessary, since what is at issue is the sexually violent image of gold as seducer or ravisher, available with or without the stylized Danaë vocabulary.

[43] At least one critic has seen in Alcibiades a doublet of Timon: E. K. Chambers, *Shakespeare: A Survey* (London: Sidgwick & Jackson, 1925), 269.

[44] See E. H. Wright, *The Authorship of "Timon of Athens"* (New York: Columbia Univ. Press, 1910), 17.

[45] The locus classicus is of course Sophocles *Antigone* vv. 332-341, where agriculture is mentioned after seafaring as emblematic of the human triumph over nature: and see Baldwin (1944) 1: 457 and 2: 648 for accounts of the likelihood that Shakespeare knew Sophocles' corpus. See Finley (1982) 186 for significant comment on naval lending in ancient Greece, the only form of loan in antiquity remotely like the modern credit instrument: "Only the bottomry loan was in any sense productive, and it was invariably restricted in amount and usurious in rate, as much an insurance measure spreading the high risks of seaborne traffic as a proper credit instrument."

[46] Note that in both the *Plutus* of Aristophanes and the *Timon* of Lucian, the accusation is leveled against the suddenly wealthy protagonist that he has acquired his riches by robbing a temple: at *Plutus* vv. 356-358, Blepsidemus suggests that Chremylus has stolen "silver or gold" from Delphi during his recent visit; at *Tim.* 53, Demeas protests between blows from the Misanthrope's mattock that Timon must have broken into the opisthodomos, the treasure-house attached to the Parthenon. In the imagistic world of the *Timon of Athens*, exactly the reverse is the case: Shakespeare's Timon has become the high-priest of a new temple, one that

his forest acolytes would plunder.

[47] Oliver in Deighton (1963) 92 notes the suggestion that "wappen'd" in Elizabethan parlance meant "worn out" or "stale" in addition to its more frankly sexual meanings of "exhausted" or "effete." The former sense would then connect it intriguingly with the words αὐχμῶν and αὐχμηρός, already seen to be connected with the figure of Ploutos, and meaning both "sordid" and also "dry" (like a fallow field).

[48] On dating see Oliver in Deighton (1963) xl and Bullough (1966) 235.

[49] Bullough (1966) 250; see too Oliver in Deighton (1963) xxviii: "it could not have been handed to the acting company in this state."

[50] Oliver in Deighton (1963) li.

[51] E. C. Pettet, "*Timon of Athens*: the Disruption of Feudal Morality," *The Review of English Studies* 23 (1947): 321-336.

[52] See for instance Hughes (1992) 283.

[53] Brown (1961) xxvii-xxxii.

[54] See *The Merchant of Venice* I.iii.66-85, Shylock's account of Jacob and Laban's sheep.

[55] *The Merchant of Venice* IV.i.343 ff.

[56] See of course Portia's celebrated oration at IV.i.180 ff.

[57] *Timon of Athens* III.iv.89-98. With regard to the sinking of Antonio's ships as the cause of his sudden inability to repay the loan, note the intriguing fact that in the "old" or "academic" *Timon*, the anonymous Cambridge play produced around 1600, which it is however unlikely Shakespeare knew, Timon is in fact brought low by just such a naval mishap; significantly, in his reconstruction of Shakespeare's composition of the *Timon of Athens*, H. J. Oliver notes the possibility of having Timon suffer such a loss, as if it had nevertheless been available to Shakespeare, as the cause for Timon's misanthropy: "It would not do to have some arbitrary cause, such as the loss of Timon's ships; the shock must come from a situation for which Timon himself was partly responsible, in however worthy a way, namely the gradual dissipation of his estate," Oliver in Deighton (1963) xlvii. With the (re-)introduction of the "arbitrary cause" into the vicissitudes of Antonio's fortune, tragic responsibility is replaced with comic contingency, at least in the case of Wealth's possessor, and the full force of recrimination may fall on Shylock, "Wealth," himself. Note too the fact that the passage of Plutarch's *Life of Marc Antony* from which Shakespeare drew his primary portrait of Timon, and in which Antony is explicitly likened to the unlucky Misanthrope, follows of course the rendering of Antony's defeat in the naval battle at Actium.

[58] See Hughes (1992) 284: "Timon's generosity, so 'total and unconditional', bears the same relationship to this judicious, rational system as Christ's love bears to the common or garden social bond."

[59] René Girard, *Shakespeare: les feux de l'envie*, trans. Bernard Vincent (Paris: Grasset, 1990), 299-310. In the section of the same book devoted to the Timon of Athens, Girard makes the following lapidary but intriguing observation: "Le processus comique/tragique par excellence n'est autre que ce cercle vicieux de la 'déstructuration' ou de la 'désymbolisation' qui

toujours coincide avec la perte de l'ordre différentiel," p. 217. Is it possible to read here an oblique comment on the less properly allegorizing powers of tragedy, its tendency to produce pessimistically realist texts, while comedy puts allegory into play to mask the destructuring of society brought about by the revelation of injustice and iniquity?

[60] Gernet in Gordon (1981) 139.

Bibliography

Note
Sections 1-4 list, in alphabetical order by editor, editions of works by the four principal authors studied above. Section 5 lists, in alphabetical order by author, editions of works by other ancient authors mentioned above. Section 6 is a general listing of mostly critical and literary-historical works consulted.

1: Aristophanes

Coulon, Victor and Hilaire van Daele, eds. *Aristophane.* 5 vols. Paris: Les Belles Lettres, 1985.

Dover, K. J., ed. *Aristophanes' Clouds.* Oxford: Oxford Univ. Press, 1968.

Droysen, Johann Gustav, ed. *Des Aristophanes Werke.* Leipzig, 1835-8 and 1881.

Frischlin, Nicodemus, ed. *Aristophanes, veteris comoediae princeps.* 1586. Reprint, Hildesheim: Georg Olm, 1982.

Hall, F. W. and W. M. Geldart, eds. *Aristophanis comoediae.* 2d ed. 2 vols. Oxford: Oxford Univ. Press, 1906-7.

Leeuwen, J. van, ed. *Aristophanis Plutus cum prolegomenis et commentariis.* Leiden: Sijthoff, 1904.

Platnauer, Maurice, ed. *Aristophanes: Peace.* Oxford: Oxford Univ. Press, 1964.

Rogers, Benjamin Bickley, ed. *Aristophanes' Plutus.* London: Heinemann, 1907.

Sommerstein, Alan H., ed. *Clouds.* Warminster: Aris and Philips, 1982.

---. *Aristophanis Pax cum prolegomenis et commentariis.* Leiden: Sijthoff, 1906.

2: Plautus

Brix, J. and M. Niemeyer, eds. *Ausgewählte Komödien des T. Maccius Plautus.* Leipzig, 1888.

Ernout, Alfred, ed. *Plaute.* 7 vols. Paris: Les Belles Lettres, 1932-52.

Freeman, C. E. and Rev. A. Sloman, eds. *T. Macci Plauti Trinummus.* Oxford: Oxford Univ. Press, 1890.

Hildyard, Jacob, ed. *T. Macci Plauti Aulularia.* London: J. W. Parker, 1839.

Waltzing, J. P., ed. *T. Macci Plauti Trinummus.* Louvain: Peeters, 1913.

3: Lucian

Bekker, Immanuel, ed. *Lucianus.* 2 vols. Leipzig: Brockhaus, 1853.

Jacobitz, Karl, ed. *Ausgewählte Schriften des Lucian.* Leipzig: Teubner, 1862.

Levy, Harry L., ed. *Lucian: Seventy Dialogues.* [Norman]: Univ. of Oklahoma Press, 1976.

4: Shakespeare

Brown, John Russell, ed. *The Merchant of Venice.* Reprint, London: Methuen, 1961.

Fletcher, R. H., ed. *Timon of Athens.* London, 1913.

Deighton, K., ed. *Timon of Athens*. Introduction and notes by H. J. Oliver. Reprint, London: Methuen, 1963.

5: Various Ancient Authors

Apuleius: Verteidigungsrede, Blütenlese. Edited by Rudolf Helm. *Schriften und Quellen der alten Welt* 36. Berlin: Akademie Verlag, 1977.

Aristote: Économique. Edited by B. A. van Groningen and André Wartelle. Paris: Les Belles Lettres, 1968.

Aristote: Politique. Edited by Jean Aubonnet. Vol. 1. Paris: Les Belles Lettres, 1960.

Aristotle: The Poetics. Edited by D. W. Lucas. Oxford: Oxford Univ. Press, 1968.

Euripide. Edited by Henri Grégoire, Louis Méridier and Fernand Chapouthier. Vol. 5. Paris: Les Belles Lettres, 1950.

Fragments of Attic Comedy, The. Edited by J. M. Edmonds. 2 vols. Leiden: Brill, 1959.

Hésiode: Théogonie -- Les travaux et les jours -- Le bouclier. Edited by Paul Mazon. Paris: Les Belles Lettres, 1928.

Homeri Opera. Edited by David B. Monro and Thomas W. Allen. 3d ed. 5 vols. Reprint, Oxford: Clarendon Press, 1969.

Iambi et Elegi Graeci ante Alexandrum Cantati. Edited by M. L. West. 2 vols. Oxford: Oxford Univ. Press, 1971-2.

Menander: Das Schiedsgericht. Edited by Ulrich von Wilamowitz-Moellendorf. Berlin, 1925.

Platon: Oeuvres complètes. Edited by Édouard Des Places. Vol. 11, *Les Lois.* Paris: Les Belles Lettres, 1968.

Plutarque: Vies. Edited by Robert Flacelière and Émile Chambry. Vol. 13, *Démétrios -- Antoine.* Paris: Les Belles Lettres, 1977.

Poetae Melici Graeci. Edited by D. L. Page. Oxford: Oxford Univ. Press, 1962.

Politique d'Aristote. Edited by J. Barthélemy-St.-Hilaire. Vol. 1. Paris: Imprimerie royale, 1837.

Sophoclis Fabulae. Edited by H. Lloyd-Jones and N. G. Wilson. Reprint, New York: Oxford Univ. Press, 1992.

Théognis: Poèmes élégiaques. Edited by Jean Carrière. Paris: Les Belles Lettres, 1975.

Tragicorum Graecorum Fragmenta. Edited by August Nauck. Leipzig: Teubner, 1856.

[Johannis] Tzetzae commentarii in Aristophanem. Edited by Lydia Massa Positano, D. Holwerda and W. J. W. Koster. Groningen: J. B. Wolters, 1960.

Xenophon, Oeconomicus: A Social and Historical Commentary. Edited with notes by Sarah B. Pomeroy. New York: Oxford Univ. Press, 1994.

6: General Works Cited

Agnew, Jean-Christophe. *Worlds Apart: The Market and the Theatre in Anglo-American Thought 1550-1750.* Cambridge: Cambridge Univ. Press, 1986.

Anderson, Graham. *Lucian: Theme and Variation in the Second Sophistic.* Mnemosyne, supp. 41. Leiden: Brill, 1976.

André, J. M. "L'Argent chez Plaute: autour du *Curculio*." *Vichiana* 12 (1983): 15-35.

Arendt, Hannah. *The Human Condition.* Chicago: Univ. of Chicago Press, 1958.

Arnould, Dominique. "Ploutos et Pénia dans la poésie lyrique, élégiaque et iambique archaïque." In *L'univers épique,* edited by Michel Woronoff, 157-71. Paris: Les Belles Lettres, 1992.

Auerbach, Erich. *Scenes from the Drama of European Literature: Six Essays.* Reprint, Gloucester: Peter Smith, 1973.

Austin, M. M. and Pierre Vidal-Naquet. *Economic and Social History of Ancient Greece: An Introduction.* Translated and revised by M. M. Austin. London: B. T. Batsford, 1977.

Baldwin, T. W. *William Shakspere's Small Latine and Lesse Greeke.* 2 vols. Urbana: Univ. of Illinois Press, 1944.

Bamber, Linda. *Comic Women, Tragic Men: A Study of Gender and Genre in Shakespeare.* Stanford: Stanford Univ. Press, 1982.

Benjamin, Walter. *The Origin of German Tragic Drama.* Translated by John Osborne. London: New Left Books, 1977.

Benz, Lore. "Megaronides Censorius -- Eine anticatonische Konzeption im plautinischen Trinummus?" In *Theater und Gesellschaft im Imperium Romanum,* edited by Jürgen von Blänsdorf, 55-67. Tübingen: Francke, 1990.

Bernays, Jacob. *Lucian und die Kyniker: mit einer Übersetzung der Schrift Lucians Über das Lebensende des Peregrinus.* Berlin: Wilhelm Hertz, 1879.

Blänsdorf, Jürgen von, ed. *Theater und Gesellschaft im Imperium Romanum.* Mainzer Forschungen zu Drama und Theater, no. 4. Tübingen: Francke, 1990.

Bompaire, Jacques. *Lucien écrivain: imitation et création.* Bibliothèque des écoles françaises d'Athènes et de Rome, no. 190. Paris: Boccard, 1958.

Bond, R. Warwick. "Lucian and Boiardo in 'Timon of Athens'." *Modern Language Review* 26 (1931): 52-68.

Bowersock, G. W. *Hellenism in Late Antiquity.* Ann Arbor: Univ. of Michigan Press, 1990.

Bowie, E.L. "Greeks and Their Past in the Second Sophistic." *Past and Present: A Journal of Historical Studies* 46 (1970): 3-41.

Brown, Norman O. *Hermes the Thief: The Evolution of a Myth.* New York: Vintage Books, 1947.

Bubel, Frank. *Bibliographie zu Plautus 1976-1989*. Bonn: Dr. Rudolf Habelt GmbH, 1992.

Buck, Charles Henry, Jr. *A Chronology of the Plays of Plautus*. Baltimore: Johns Hopkins Univ. Press, 1940.

Bullough, Geoffrey. *Narrative and Dramatic Sources of Shakespeare*. 8 vols. London: Routledge and Kegan Paul, 1961-75.

Burkert, Walter. *Greek Religion*. Translated by John Ruffan. Cambridge: Harvard Univ. Press, 1985.

Buxton, R. G. A. "Blindness and Limits: Sophocles and the Logic of Myth." *Journal of Hellenic Studies* 100 (1980): 22-37.

Carrière, Jean-Claude. *Le Carnaval et la politique: une introduction à la comédie grecque -- suivie d'un choix de fragments*. Paris: Les Belles Lettres, 1979.

Chambers, E. K. *Shakespeare: A Survey*. London: Sidgwick & Jackson, 1925.

Chantraine, Pierre. *Dictionnaire étymologique de la langue grecque: Histoire des mots*. Paris: Klincksieck, 1980.

Clemons, W. H. "The Sources of Timon of Athens." *Princeton College Bulletin* 15, no. 4 (1904): 208-223.

Conacher, D. J. *Aeschylus' Prometheus Bound: A Literary Commentary*. Toronto: Univ. of Toronto Press, 1980.

Crampon, Monique. *Salve Lucrum, ou, L'expression de la richesse et de la pauvreté chez Plaute*. Annales littéraires de l'Université de Besançon, no. 319. Paris: Les Belles Lettres, 1985.

David, E. *Aristophanes and Athenian Society of the Early Fourth Century B.C.* Leiden: Brill, 1984.

Delcourt, Marie. "Le Prix des esclaves dans les comédies latines." *L'Antiquité classique* 17 (1948): 123-32.

---. *Plaute et l'impartialité comique*. Brussels: La Renaissance du livre, 1964.

Dollimore, Jonathan. "Introduction: Shakespeare, Cultural Materialism and the New Historicism." In *Political Shakespeare: New Essays in Cultural Materialism,* edited by Jonathan Dollimore and Alan Sinfield, 2-17. Manchester: Manchester Univ. Press, 1985.

--- and Alan Sinfield, eds. *Political Shakespeare: New Essays in Cultural Materialism.* Manchester: Manchester Univ. Press, 1985.

Donlan, Walter. "Pistos Philos Hetairos." In *Theognis of Megara: Poetry and the Polis,* edited by Thomas J. Figueira and Gregory Nagy, 223-44. Baltimore: Johns Hopkins Univ. Press, 1985.

Dougherty, Carol. *The Poetics of Colonization: From City to Text in Archaic Greece.* Oxford: Oxford Univ. Press, 1993.

Dover, K.J. *Aristophanic Comedy.* Berkeley and Los Angeles: Univ. of California Press, 1972.

---. *Greek Homosexuality.* Cambridge: Harvard Univ. Press, 1978.

DuBois, Page. *Sowing the Body: Psychoanalysis and Ancient Representations of Women.* Chicago: Univ. of Chicago Press, 1988.

Duckworth, George. *The Nature of Roman Comedy.* Princeton: Princeton Univ. Press, 1952.

Dunkin, Paul Shaner. *Post-Aristophanic Comedy: Studies in the Social Otlook of Middle and New Comedy at Both Athens and Rome.* Urbana: Univ. of Illinois Press, 1946.

Dupont. Florence. *L'acteur-roi, ou, Le théâtre dans la Rome antique.* Paris: Les Belles Lettres, 1985.

Eagleton, Terry. *William Shakespeare.* Reprint, Oxford: Basil Blackwell, 1986.

---. *The Ideology of the Aesthetic.* Oxford: Basil Blackwell, 1990.

Edmunds, Lowell.   *Cleon, Knights and Aristophanes' Politics.*
     Lanham: Univ. Press of America, 1987.

Ehrenberg, Victor.   *The People of Aristophanes: A Sociology of Old
     Attic Comedy.* Reprint, Oxford: Basil Blackwell, 1951.

Else, Gerald F.   *Aristotle's Poetics: The Argument.*   Cambridge:
     Harvard Univ. Press, 1963.

Fantham, Elaine.   "Philemon's Thesauros as a Dramatisation of
     Peripatetic Ethics." *Hermes* 105, no. 4 (1977): 406-21.

Figueira, Thomas J. and Gregory Nagy, eds.   *Theognis of Megara:
     Poetry and the Polis.* Baltimore: Johns Hopkins Univ. Press,
     1985.

Finley, M. I.   *The Ancient Economy.* Sather Classical Lectures, no.
     43.   Berkeley and Los Angeles: Univ. of California Press,
     1973.

---. *The Use and Abuse of History.* London: Chatto & Windus, 1975.

---. *Economy and Society in Ancient Greece.* Edited by Brent D. Shaw
     and Richard P. Saller. New York: Viking Press, 1982.

Fletcher, Angus. *Allegory: The Theory of a Symbolic Mode.* Reprint,
     Ithaca: Cornell Univ. Press, 1975.

Foley, Helene, ed.   *Reflections of Women in Antiquity.*   London:
     Gordon & Breach, 1981.

Forsythe, Gary.   Review of *Culture and National Identity in Republican
     Rome*, by Erich S. Gruen. *Bryn Mawr Classical Reviews* 5,
     no. 1 (1994): 9-14.

Fraenkel, Eduard. *Plautinisches im Plautus.* Berlin: Weidmann, 1922.

---. *Beobachtungen zu Aristophanes.*   Rome: Edizioni di Storia e
     Letteratura, 1962.

Frisk, Hjalmar.   *Griechisches etymologisches Wörterbuch.*   2 vols.
     Heidelberg: Carl Winter, 1970.

Frost, Frank J. *Greek Society.* Lexington: D. C. Heath and Co., 1971.

Frutiger, Perceval. *Les Mythes de Platon.* Paris: F. Alcan, 1930.

Gabrielsen, Vincent. "Φανερά and Ἀφανὴς Οὐσία in Classical Athens." *Classica et Mediaevalia* 37 (1986): 99-114.

Gaiser, Konrad. "Zur Eigenart der römischen Komödie: Plautus und Terenz gegenüber ihren griechischen Vorbildern." *Aufstieg und Niedergang der römischen Welt* 1, no. 2: 1027-1028.

Galinsky, Karl, ed. *The Interpretation of Roman Poetry: Empiricism or Hermeneutics?* Studien zur klassischen Philologie, no. 67. Frankfurt am Main: Peter Lang, 1992.

Gelzer, Thomas. *Der epirrhematische Agon bei Aristophanes.* Munich: C. H. Beck, 1960.

Gernet, Louis. "'Value' in Greek Myth," tranlated by R. L. Gordon. In *Myth, Religion and Society: Structuralist Essays by M. Détienne, L. Gernet, J.-P. Vernant and P. Vidal-Naquet,* edited by R. L. Gordon, 111-46. Cambridge: Cambridge Univ. Press, 1981.

Girard, René. *Shakespeare: les feux de l'envie.* Translated by Bernard Vincent. Paris: Grasset, 1990.

Goldhill, Simon and Robin Osborne, eds. *Art and Text in Ancient Greek Culture.* Cambridge: Cambridge Univ. Press, 1994.

Gordon, R. L., ed. *Myth, Religion and Society: Structuralist Essays by M. Détienne, L. Gernet, J.-P. Vernant and P. Vidal-Naquet.* Translated by R. L. Gordon and others. With an introduction by R. G. A. Buxton. Cambridge: Cambridge Univ. Press, 1981.

Greenblatt, Stephen. *Shakespearean Negotiations.* Berkeley and Los Angeles: Univ. of California Press, 1988.

Grimal, Pierre. *Le Siècle des Scipions: Rome et l'hellénisme au temps des guerres puniques.* Paris: Montaigne, 1953.

---. *Rome: la littérature et l'histoire.* Collection de l'école française de Rome, 93, no.1. Rome: Boccard, 1986.

Gruen, Erich S. *The Hellenistic World and the Coming of Rome.* 2 vols. Ithaca: Cornell Univ. Press, 1984.

---. *Culture and National Identity in Republican Rome.* Ithaca: Cornell Univ. Press, 1992.

Harvey, Paul B., Jr.   "Historical Topicality in Plautus." *Classical World* 79 (1986): 297-304.

Heath, Malcolm.   *Political Comedy in Aristophanes.*   Göttingen: Vandenhoeck & Ruprecht, 1987.

Heinemann, Margot.   "How Brecht Read Shakespeare." In *Political Shakespeare: New Essays in Cultural Materialism,* edited by Jonathan Dollimore and Alan Sinfield, 202-30.   Manchester: Manchester Univ. Press, 1985.

Heinsohn, Gunnar. *Privateigentum, Patriarchat, Geldwirtschaft: Eine sozialtheoretische Rekonstruktion zur Antike.* Frankfurt am Main: Suhrkamp, 1984.

--- and Otto Steiger.   "Private Ownership and the Foundations of Monetary Theory." *Économies et Sociétés* 9 (1987): 229-243.

--- and ---. "The Veil of Barter: The Solution to 'The Task of Obtaining Representations of an Economy in which Money is Essential'." Kregel, J.A. In *Inflation and Income Distribution in Capitalist Crisis: Essays in Memory of Sidney Weintraub,* edited by J. A. Kregel, 175-201. London: Macmillan, 1988.

--- and ---. "A Private Property Theory of Credit, Interest and Money." *Économies et Sociétés* 26 (1994): 9-24.

Hemelrijk, Jacob.   *Penia en Ploutos.*   Amsterdam: Blikman & Sartorius, 1925.

Henderson, Jeffrey. *The Maculate Muse: Obscene Language in Attic Comedy.* New Haven: Yale Univ. Press, 1975.

Hertel, Gerhard. *Die Allegorie von Reichtum und Armut: Ein aristophanisches Motiv und seine Abwandlungen in der abendländischen Literatur.* Nürnberg: Hans Carl, 1969.

Hille, Curt. *Die deutsche Komödie unter der Einwirkung des Aristophanes.* Leipzig: Quelle & Meyer, 1907.

Holzinger, Karl. *Aristophanes' Plutos.* Reprint, New York: Arno Press, 1979.

Hubbard, Thomas K. *The Mask of Comedy: Aristophanes and the Intertextual Parabasis.* Ithaca: Cornell Univ. Press, 1991.

Hughes, Ted. *Shakespeare and the Goddess of Complete Being.* London: Faber & Faber, 1992.

Jachmann, Günther. *Plautinisches und Attisches.* Problemata, no. 3. Berlin: Weidmann, 1931.

Jameson, Fredric. *Marxism and Form.* Princeton: Princeton Univ. Press, 1971.

---. "Reification and Utopia in Mass Culture." *Social Text* 1, no.1 (1979): 130-148.

---. *The Political Unconscious: Narrative as a Socially Symbolic Act.* Ithaca: Cornell Univ. Press, 1981.

Jankowski, Andrzej. *Shakespeare's Idea of Art.* Poznan: Adam Mickiewicz Univ. Press, 1988.

Jones, C. P. *Culture and Society in Lucian.* Cambridge: Harvard Univ. Press, 1986.

Kahn, Laurence. *Hermès passe: ou les ambiguités de la communication.* Paris: François Maspero, 1978.

Kerényi, Karl. *Hermes der Seelenführer.* Zurich, 1944.

Konstan, David. "The Social Themes in Plautus' *Aulularia.*" *Arethusa* 10, no. 2 (1977): 307-20.

---. *Roman Comedy.* Ithaca: Cornell Univ. Press, 1983.

--- and Matthew Dillon. "The Ideology of Aristophanes' *Wealth*." *American Journal of Philology* 102 (1981): 371-394.

Koster, W. J. W. and D. Holwerda, eds. *Scholia in Aristophanem*. Groningen: Bouma's Boekhuis B. V., 1960.

Kregel, J. A. *Inflation and Income Distribution in Capitalist Crisis: Essays in Memory of Sidney Weintraub*. London: Macmillan, 1988.

Kurke, Leslie. *The Traffic in Praise: Pindar and the Poetics of Social Economy*. Ithaca: Cornell Univ. Press, 1991.

Kurz, Gerhard. *Metapher, Allegorie, Symbol*. Göttingen: Vandenhoeck & Ruprecht, 1982.

Lacan, Jacques. *Écrits*. Paris: Seuil, 1966.

Lefèvre, Eckard. "Politik und Gesellschaft in Plautus' Trinummus." In *Theater und Gesellschaft im Imperium Romanum*, edited by Jürgen von Blänsdorf, 45-54. Tübingen: Francke, 1990.

Lever, Katherine. "Poetic Metaphor and Dramatic Allegory in Aristophanes." *The Classical Weekly* 46 (1953): 220-223.

Loraux, Nicole. "Préface: Un secret bien gardé." In *Le corps virginal: La virginité féminine en Grèce ancienne,* edited by Giulia Sissa, 7-16. Paris: Librairie philosophique J. Vrin, 1982.

---. "Aristophane, les femmes d'Athènes et le théâtre." In *Aristophane*, edited by Olivier Reverdin and Bernard Grange, 203-44. Geneva: Fondation Hardt, 1993.

Martindale, Charles and Michelle. *Shakespeare and the Uses of Antiquity: An Introductory Essay*. London: Routledge, 1990.

Marx, Karl. *The Economic and Philosophic Manuscripts of 1844*. Translated by Martin Milligan, edited by Dirk J. Struik. New York: International Publishers, 1964.

---. *Grundrisse: Foundations of the Critique of Political Economy (Rough Draft)*. Translated by Martin Nicolaus. London: 1973.

---. *Capital: a Critique of Political Economy.* Translated by Ben Fowkes and D. Fernbach. New York: Vintage Books, 1977.

---. *Ökonomisch-philosophische Manuskripte vom Jahre 1844.* Annotated by Joachim Höppner. Leipzig: Reclam, 1988.

--- and Friedrich Engels. *Gesammelte Werke.* 43 vols. Berlin: Dietz, 1960-9.

---. *The Marx-Engels Reader.* Edited by Robert C. Tucker. New York: Norton, 1978.

Mauron, Charles. *La psychocritique du genre comique.* Paris: J. Corti, 1964.

Mehlman, Jeffrey. *A Structural Study of Autobiography.* Ithaca: Cornell Univ. Press, 1974.

Michelet, Jules. *History of the Roman Republic.* Translated by William Hazlitt. London: D. Bogue, 1847.

Muecke, Frances. "Names and Players: The Sycophant Scene of the Trinummus." *Transactions of the American Philological Association* 115 (1985): 167-186.

Murrin, Michael. *The Veil of Allegory: Some Notes Toward a Theory of Allegorical Rhetoric in the English Renaissance.* Chicago: Univ. of Chicago Press, 1969.

Nagy, Gregory. "Theognis and Megara: A Poet's Vision of His City." In *Theognis of Megara: Poetry and the Polis,* edited by Thomas J. Figueira and Gregory Nagy, 22-81. Baltimore: Johns Hopkins Univ. Press, 1985.

Newiger, Hans-Joachim. *Metapher und Allegorie: Studien zu Aristophanes.* Zetemata, no. 16. Munich: C. H. Beck, 1957.

---. "Retraktionen zu Aristophanes' 'Frieden'." *Rheinisches Museum* 108 (1965): 242.

---. *Aristophanes und die alte Komödie.* Darmstadt: Wissenschaftliche Buchgesellschaft, 1975.

Newman, Rafaël. "Heine's Aristophanes: Compromise Formations and the Ambivalence of Carnival." *Comparative Literature* 49, no. 3 (summer 1997): 227-40.

Ober, Josiah. *Mass and Elite in Democratic Athens: Rhetoric, Ideology and the Power of the People.* Princeton: Princeton Univ. Press, 1989.

Onfray, Michel. *Cynismes: Portrait du philosophe en chien.* Paris: Grasset, 1990.

Ormand, Kirk. Review of *Sons of the Gods, Children of Earth: Ideology and Literary Form in Ancient Greece*, by Peter W. Rose. *Bryn Mawr Classical Review* 3, no. 6 (1992): 474-80.

Petersen, Leiva. *Zur Geschichte der Personifikation in griechischer Dichtung und bildender Kunst.* Würzburg-Aumühle: Konrad Triltsch, 1939.

Pettet, E.C. "*Timon of Athens:* the Disruption of Feudal Morality." *The Review of English Studies* 23 (1947): 321-336.

Pfeiffer, Rudolf. *History of Classical Scholarship from the Beginnings to the End of the Hellenistic Age.* Oxford: Oxford Univ. Press, 1968.

---. *History of Classical Scholarship from 1300 to 1850.* Oxford: Oxford Univ. Press, 1976.

Powell, Hugh, ed. *Andreas Gryphius' Herr Peter Squentz.* Bath: Leicester Univ. Press, 1957.

Quilligan, Maureen. *The Language of Allegory: Defining the Genre.* Ithaca: Cornell Univ. Press, 1979.

Reckford, Kenneth J. *Aristophanes' Old-and-New Comedy.* Chapel Hill: Univ. of North Carolina Press, 1987.

Reinhardt, Karl. *Vermächtnis der Antike.* Göttingen: Vandenhoeck & Ruprecht, 1966.

Reverdin, Olivier and Bernard Grange, eds. *Aristophane.* Entretiens sur l'antiquité classique, no. 38. Geneva: Fondation Hardt, 1993.

Richards, I. A. *The Philosophy of Rhetoric*. Reprint, Oxford: Oxford U. P., 1965.

Richardson, W. F. "Nummus in the Plays of Plautus." *Prudentia* 15 (1983): 27-34.

Richlin, Amy, ed. *Pornography and Representation in Greece and Rome*. New York: Oxford Univ. Press, 1992.

Robinson, Christopher. *Lucian and His Influence in Europe*. London: Duckworth, 1979.

Rose, Peter W. *Sons of the Gods, Children of Earth: : Ideology and Literary Form in Ancient Greece*. Ithaca: Cornell Univ. Press, 1992.

Rosivach, Vincent J. "Some Athenian Presuppositions About 'The Poor'." *Greece and Rome* 38, no. 2 (1991): 189-198.

Rösler, Wolfgang. "Michail Bachtin und die Karnevalskultur im antiken Griechenland." *Quaderni Urbinati di Cultura Classica* n.s. 23, no. 2 (1986): 25-44.

Schmidt, Oskar. *Metapher und Gleichnis in den Schriften Lukians*. Winterthur: Ziegler, 1897.

Schwartz, Murray M. and Coppélia Kahn, eds. *Representing Shakespeare*. Reprint, Baltimore: Johns Hopkins Univ. Press, 1982.

Scott, W. I. D. *Shakespeare's Melancholics*. London: Mills & Boon, 1962.

Seeck, Gustav Adolf. "Lukian und die griechische Tragödie." ." In *Theater und Gesellschaft im Imperium Romanum*, edited by Jürgen von Blänsdorf, 233-41. Tübingen: Francke, 1990.

Sfyroeras, Pavlos. *The Feast of Poetry: Sacrifice, Foundation, and Performance in Aristophanic Comedy*. Ph.D. diss., Princeton University, 1992. Abstract in *Dissertation Abstracts International* 53 (1992-93): 2357A.

---. "What Wealth has to do with Dionysus: From Economy to Poetics in Aristophanes' *Plutus*." *GRBS* 36, no. 3 (1995): 231-61.

Shapiro, H. A. *Personifications in Greek Art: The Representation of Abstract Concepts, 600-400 BC.* Zurich: Akanthus, 1993.

Shell, Marc. *The Economy of Literature.* Baltimore: Johns Hopkins Univ. Press, 1978.

Sissa, Giulia. *Le corps virginal: La virginité féminine en Grèce ancienne.* Paris: Librairie philosophique J. Vrin, 1982.

Slater, Niall W. "A Note on Plautus' *Trinummus* 705-707." *Classical World* 79 (1985): 33-34.

---. "The Dates of Plautus' *Curculio* and *Trinummus* Reconsidered." *American Journal of Philology* 108 (1987): 264-269.

Sommerstein, Alan H., et al., eds. *Tragedy, Comedy and the Polis: Papers from the Greek Drama Conference, Nottingham, 18-20 July 1990.* Bari: Levante Editori, 1993.

Spurgeon, Caroline F. E. *Shakespeare's Imagery and What It Tells Us.* Cambridge: Cambridge Univ. Press, 1958.

Stockert, Walter. *T. Maccius Plautus: Aulularia; Anmerkungen und Kommentar, Beilage Textedition.* Stuttgart: Teubner, 1983.

Süss, Wilhelm. "Scheinbare und wirkliche Inkongruenzen in den Dramen des Aristophanes." *Rheinisches Museum* 97 (1954): 115-159.

Taillardat, Jean. *Les images d'Aristophane: Études de langue et de style.* 2d ed. Paris: Les Belles Lettres, 1965.

Traversi, Derek. *An Approach to Shakespeare.* Vol. 2, *Troilus and Cressida to the Tempest.* London: Hollis & Carter, 1969.

Uhde-Bernays, Hermann. *Der Mannheimer Shakespeare. Ein Beitrag zur Geschichte der ersten deutschen Shakespeare-Übersetzungen.* Berlin: E. Felber, 1902.

Vernant, Jean-Pierre. *Mythe et pensée chez les Grecs: Études de psychologie historique.* Paris: François Maspero, 1965.

---. "Figuration et image." *Mètis* 5 (1990): 225-38.

--- and Pierre Vidal-Naquet. *Myth and Tragedy in Ancient Greece.* Translated by Janet Lloyd. New York: Zone Books, 1990.

Waltzing, J. P. *Les Trois Pièces d'Argent: Comédie de Plaute, imitée de Philémon. Traduction littérale publiée avec une introduction et des notes.* Paris, 1930.

Wheeler, Richard P. "'Since first we were dissevered': Trust and Autonomy in Shakespearean Tragedy and Romance." In *Representing Shakespeare,* edited by Murray M. Schwartz and Coppélia Kahn, 150-68. Reprint, Baltimore: Johns Hopkins Univ. Press, 1982.

Whitman, Cedric H. *Aristophanes and the Comic Hero.* Cambridge: Harvard Univ. Press, 1964.

Winkler, John J. and Froma I. Zeitlin. *Nothing to Do with Dionysus? Athenian Drama in Its Social Context.* Princeton: Princeton Univ. Press, 1990.

Woronoff, Michel, ed. *L'univers épique.* Rencontres avec l'antiquité classique, no. 2. Paris: Les Belles Lettres, 1992.

Wright, E. H. *The Authorship of "Timon of Athens."* New York: Columbia U. P., 1910.

Zagagi, Netta. "Amatory Gifts and Payments. A Note on munus, donum, data in Plautus." *Glotta* 65 (1987): 129-132.

Zeitlin, Froma I. "Travesties of Gender and Genre in Aristophanes' *Thesmophoriazousae.*" *Critical Inquiry* (winter 1981): 301-327. Reprinted in *Reflections of Women in Antiquity,* edited by Helene Foley, 169-217. London: Gordon & Breach, 1981.

---. "Playing the Other: Theater, Theatricality, and the Feminine in Greek Drama." In *Nothing to Do with Dionysus? Athenian Drama in Its Social Context,* edited by John J. Winkler and Froma I. Zeitlin, 63-96. Princeton: Princeton Univ. Press, 1990.

---. "Thebes: Theater of Self and Society in Athenian Drama." In *Nothing to Do with Dionysus? Athenian Drama in Its Social*

192 *The Visible God*

Context, edited by John J. Winkler and Froma I. Zeitlin, 130-67. Princeton: Princeton Univ. Press, 1990.

---. "The Artful Eye: Vision, Ecphrasis and Spectacle in Euripidean Theater." In *Art and Text in Ancient Greek Culture,* edited by Simon Goldhill and Robin Osborne, 138-96. Cambridge: Cambridge Univ. Press, 1994.

Zizek, Slavoj. *The Sublime Object of Ideology.* London: Verso, 1989.

---. *For They Know Not What They Do: Enjoyment as a Political Factor.* London: Verso, 1991.

Zweig, Bella. "The Mute Nude Female Characters in Aristophanes' Plays." In: Richlin (1992) 73-89.

Index

prosopopoeia, 82, 83, 86, 89,
93, 94, 100, 106n48
psychoanalytic criticism of
culture and ideology, 12, 30,
72, 100

recontainment, 11, 52, 147
reification, 28, 38, 51, 83, 89,
150, 165
Richards, I. A., 140n27
Robinson, Christopher, 137n3,
142n42
Rose, Peter W., 24, 29,
60n41&44
Rösler, Wolfgang, 20n55, 91,
108n64

Schmidt, Oskar, 140n28,
141n32, 142n42
Scipios, 75, 77, 83, 103n19,
104n28, 105n40, 110n77
Second Sophistic, 114,
137n3&4
Seeck, Gustav Adolf, 137n6
Sfyroeras, Pavlos, 57n24
Shakespeare: *A Midsummer
Night's Dream*, 167n9;
Hamlet, 168n13, 169n22;
King John, 169n18;
Merchant of Venice, 20n57,
162, 163; *Richard II*,
169n18; *Romeo and Juliet*,
169n18; *Timon of Athens*,
13, 101, 145, 147-49, 151,
156, 158, 161, 162, 166n6,
167n13, 168n15, 169n20,
171n36, 172n46, 173n57
Shell, Marc, 58n30
Solon, 138n11, 139n15
Sophocles: *Antigone*, 15, 73,
140n26, 172n45
Spurgeon, Caroline F. E.,
168n18
Steiger, Otto, 7, 12, 18n35
symbolic capital: Pierre
Bourdieu's notion of, 54n8

Theognis, 3, 14, 16, 17, 23, 27,
141

Theophrastus: *Historia
Plantarum*, 139
Timocreon, 3, 14
Treasure: or *Thesauros*. See
Philemon

use-value, 4, 33, 84, 166n6,
169n19

Vergil, 8
Vernant, Jean-Pierre, 9, 12,
17n20, 18n48, 59n33,
62n62, 138n6, 143n44
Vidal-Naquet, Pierre, 24
Voltaire (François-Marie
Arouet), 139n17

Waltzing, J. P., 97,
109n73&74, 111n82&84
wealth: as child (τόκος) or
interest, 4, 134; as daughter,
164; as gold, 32, 33, 44, 45,
61, 68, 76, 78, 81, 82, 84-
94, 96, 100, 106n40,
108n63, 114, 117, 118, 122,
123-30, 133-35, 143n45,
145-48, 150, 151, 156-61,
164, 165, 169n18, 172n42;
as land, 1-3, 6-8, 10-12, 23-
28, 36, 37, 41, 43, 44, 49,
58n30, 77-79, 92, 94, 95,
100, 101, 116, 117, 120,
136, 154, 156, 163; as object
of desire, 105n39, 124, 145;
as wife, 164; fetishized, 86,
89-91, 100
Wealth. *See* Ploutos
Wheeler, Richard P., 171n40
Whitman, Cedric H., 46, 54n4,
61n56, 62n58&59&61,
65n88, 66n90
Wilamowitz-Moellendorf, Ulrich
von, 109n70

Xenophon, 5, 15n13, 17n21;
Oeconomicus, 15n14, 56n15,
140n29